THE LEMURS' LEGACY

The Evolution of Power, Sex, and Love

Robert Jay Russell, Ph.D.

A Jeremy P. Tarcher/Putnam Book
published by
G. P. Putnam's Sons
New York

Contents

List of Figures & Photographs

FIGURES:

PHOTOGRAPHS:

Preface

This book explores the evolution of human behavior. Think of it as one long conversation about the evolution of the human psyche. Specifically, it's a conversation that reconstructs a dramatic, billion-year play of power, sex, and love. We begin our journey by addressing two basic questions: how the science of evolutionary psychology came to be (Chapter 2), and what is meant by "behavioral evolution" (Chapter 3). In Part II, The Animal Roots of Human Behavior, we follow the evolution of behavior from the origins of sex (Chapter 4) through an overview of the primate family tree (Chapter 5). Chapters 6 through 9 chart the course of human social evolution from ancestral insectivores of 70 million years ago, through lemurs and apes.

Chapters 10 and 11 in Part III, The Human Veneer, present the effect that language, a uniquely human adaptation, has had upon patterns of behavior that humans have inherited from their evolutionary past. The interplay of ancient behavioral imperatives and modern selection pressures is explored in Chapter 12 with behavioral topics that affect us all: war, civil unrest, child abuse, altruism, monogamy, changing gender roles, fatherhood, the population crisis, and AIDS.

Throughout our journey, we see that the behavioral legacies of our ancient ancestors weigh heavily in the behavior we exhibit today. How much of our behavior is immutably determined by the past? Does free will exist, or are the genders fated to replay ancient evolutionary dramas?

Chapter 13 entertains these questions and addresses the crucial issues of how much we can expect from psychotherapy or social engineering. The future of the new science of evolutionary psychology, dependent on the fate of endangered nonhuman primates in the wild, is considered in the epilogue.

This book, like all books and all conversations, is a personal synthesis. It has been decades in the making. Its direction was cast measurably by my jungle researches and library searches, and imperceptibly by millions of observed and often dimly registered social interactions. But the meat of this book—its argument—began as a conversation. It began in after-class discussions during my undergraduate years and progressed to graduate seminars at Duke University. Later, it was altered by questions from my students in California and critiques by my colleagues in Vienna. It was shaped by numerous conferences with scholars, and innumerable chats with friends. These conversations, one of science's greatest pleasures, should never end. Inevitably, they do. At some point, when the editor and publisher can no longer stand the author's delay, the book is finished, typeset, cast in ink, and bound in cardboard. The book becomes a frozen conversation, a one-way street between an author and a new, unseen audience.

I think words sprayed on paper are far too rigid. Words on paper— particularly old, polysyllabic scientific words on yellowing paper—are sometimes taken far too seriously. They become immutable gospel rather than a fluid, dynamic exchange between people. Understandably so, per- haps, because words on paper sound only in the reader's imagination. At best, they are heard as a monologue, the dialogue necessarily stilled. So much the pity, because the subject matter in this book—human power, sex, and love—is the stuff of truly great exchanges.

Someday, when most of us are linked by microprocessors, screens, and transmission wires, books such as this may be called up before you by pressing a few keys. If you find a paragraph confusing, an idea not credible, a reference missing, a thought worthy of expansion, you, the reader, will type a message that will speed to an electronic mailbox. I, the author, and many other readers will see your words and, if health and time allow, will type a quick reply. A grand conversation will grow. The book itself will evolve, shaped not just by the researches I have performed, the references I have read, the friends I have made, and the colleagues that I know, but by a whole planet of people with fresh ideas from pursuits in life unavailable to me or you. What a renaissance the future may hold.

For the present, though, you and I will have to make do with the technology of Gutenberg, not global net. I would suggest, then, that you imagine this book as a long conversation. Consider it, argue with it, think alternative thoughts. It is a book of science, and science, at its core, is a debate. To continue our debate, you may write to me in care of my publisher, Jeremy P. Tarcher.

Technically, *The Lemurs' Legacy* is a book of popular science, or "trade science" as it is termed in the publishing business. As such, it contains far less data than would be demanded of a scientific monograph. This is not because data are lacking, but because only an initiated few can adequately survey jargon-riddled prose punctuated by long, fine-print tables and probability statistics. To write a pop sci book, John Casti, a master popular science writer, employs what he calls the Three-*E*'s-Minus-One Rule: make a popular science book *e*ducational, *e*nlightening, and *e*ntertaining without making it *e*ncyclopedic.[1] Good advice. I have tried to follow it. I will have succeeded if, overall, you judge this book to be an enlightening, entertaining, educational conversation.

So much for the prologue. It is time for our conversation about power, sex, and love to begin . . .

Robert Jay Russell, Ph.D.
Van Nuys, California
September, 1992

Acknowledgments

Virtually every book has a place to acknowledge past conversations. It is a section to credit colleagues, exculpate them from blame, and to appreciate the friends and family who made the book possible. Clearly, such sections are necessarily incomplete. In my own case, acknowledgments could probably consume the lion's share of the printer's ink. So, I will be more brief than accurate here.

First and foremost, my career as a scientist—a necessary precursor to the book in hand—has been made possible through the support of family. My parents, J. Lewis and Roberta E. Russell, paid for a menagerie in my youth and often restocked my slim wallet to an extent far greater than most parents would suffer. Additionally, while I was conducting research in Madagascar, they provided logistical support that would have been the envy of a warrant officer in Operation Desert Storm.

In more recent times, my wife, Laurie Spalding Russell, has become my strength (and my editor of choice). Scientists always remain children, so their spouses necessarily become surrogate parents. I owe Laurie thanks and apologies simultaneously.

Friends have contributed both intellectually and spiritually to this book. Two compatriots included the late Jim Danilovitz and the late Jim Finale—I have greatly mourned the loss of their ideas and their camaraderie. But many dear friends remain to thank, including: Vince and Donna Civa, Robert Jones, Russell Kneeland, Stuart Levine, Kenneth Middleton, and Dick and Betsy Neill.

In the 1980s, I was welcomed into an institute of evolutionists. The group was originally called "WEEG," The Wednesday Evening Evolution Group, and was hosted, naturally enough, on Wednesday evenings by a young, up-and-coming professor of paleobiology, J. William Schopf. We were a diverse group, ranging from astronomers to zoologists, united by a passion to understand and debate evolution. At first, we numbered fewer than twenty souls. We took turns cooking dinner, sharing fried chicken, pizza, warm cola, and, I'll wager, some of the most intense, argumentative, stirring debates about evolution in the country. Everyone left their egos and academic rank at the door, rolled up their sleeves, and enjoyed one another's ideas. I will always be grateful for those early times of WEEG— evenings of spontaneous, selfless, unselfconscious collegiality. The institute still flourishes, albeit it is now an officially-endorsed, formal institute called CSEOL, the Center for the Study of Evolution and the Origin of Life, UCLA.

In Austria, through the great kindness of my good friend Dr. Rudi Rudelstorfer and his wife, Micaela, I was inducted into another institute, called IPOKRaTES (now with the Wissenschaftliche Landesakademie für Niederösterreich). It is unabashedly oriented to comradeship and joy in scientific research and teaching. In Vienna—at homes, conference centers, heurrigen, and beisels—I have made many friends and discussed many ideas in this book. I thank the director and founder of IPOKRaTES, Dr. Georg Simbruner, his wife Annette, and his good family. Georg's support and understanding has meant much to this work, as have the kindnesses extended by: Frau Gerda Jackson, Dr. Elfreide Katz, the Familie Rudolf Leyer, Herr Hans J. Prochaska, Dr. Beate and Michael Pietschnig, Lee Reichel and Peter Mikolasch, and Dr. Leonhard and Ursula Thun-Hohenstein.

Professors and professional colleagues have a profound impact on any scientist, and I have had my share of dynamic associates scattered throughout the globe. Many would agree with my analyses, some with little of it, but all have had an impact on my thinking. This is my chance to say thanks to a very few: Drs. Matt Cartmill, Lee Durrell, Kenneth Glander, Elliott Haimoff, Alison Jolly, Richard Kay, Peter H. Klopfer, Tom McIver, Jean-Jacques Petter, Elwyn L. Simons, Bob and Linda Sussman, Ian Tattersall, Ron and Meg Weigel, Marcus Young-Owl, and, lastly, the late Professor John Buettner-Janusch.[1]

This book would not be in your hands were it not for the professional book trade. My agent and dear friend, Sandra Watt, has been a constant joy; her knowledge, exuberance, and backing have been unstinting. Through her, I have been extremely fortunate to find a cautious, exacting editor, Daniel Malvin, and an enthusiastic, knowledgeable, and skillful publisher, Jeremy P. Tarcher. Katherine Pradt provided excellent copy editing. They have all provided just that essential touch of support at just that essential time.

Last, but hardly least, I thank a host of nonhumans from apes to zorillas. They've come from every corner of the planet. My beloved Malagasy Coton de Tulear dogs, especially Andy and Jael, provided love and trust at crucial moments. Without exception, the nonhuman creatures I've met have taught me much, and they have gladdened my life.

PART I

Psychology Evolving

CHAPTER 1

Revolutionary Ideas
for Troubled Times

Revolutionary, uplifting ideas sometimes rise from the moldering ashes of troubled times. The European civil upheavals of the 1830s and '40s led, perceptibly, to emancipation movements, the birth of socialism, and the triumph of modern science. Like the century before, the twentieth century has been fraught with social strife. Today, new social opportunities are barely perceptible, obscured by the dense smoke of old social orders in chaos. But opportunities for constructive change are developing. A new understanding of our behavior as individuals, as a society, and as a species is growing. We have begun to see much of our present behavior as a heritage of past behavioral patterns—legacies that reach backwards tens of millions of years. This new perspective—an important seed for our growth as individuals and as a society—is the subject of this book. This is an exciting time for those who want to achieve a better understanding of themselves and for those who want to change themselves or their society.

Fittingly, perhaps, I had scarcely finished writing the book's penultimate draft when violent, troubling times appeared disturbingly close at hand. Women clutched babies in the corners of darkened rooms; men raced through the night, throwing bottles filled with gasoline at silhouettes of looted buildings. Los Angeles was burning. Urban renewal, L.A. style, had erupted all around us. Telephoning me from his office on Wilshire Boulevard, my editor noted with characteristic dry wit, "It looks like the young males around here have far too much testosterone."

In truth, many predominantly male subgroups were in action that week. There were organized groups of criminals—the Crips and the Bloods, to name but two. There were organized groups of anti-criminals—the L.A.P.D., the Sheriff's Department, the National Guard, the U.S. Marine Corps, and others. Religious groups and other civilian agencies, elected, appointed, and self-appointed, sprang to the fore. The mayor, the governor, the president, presidential wanna-bes—titular heads of the most officially powerful male oligarchies in the drama—proclaimed their positions of strength and pointed fingers of blame in each other's direction. News organizations—from national television networks to the neighborhood weekly—jostled to fill newsprint and television screens, to figuratively thump their chests and announce their presence.

As the charcoaled bits of buildings settled in suburban backyard swimming pools, several truths were self-evident. Many male subgroups had redirected their aggressions outside their particular group's hierarchy, had asserted their presence, and had strengthened their dominance hierarchies. As the male subgroups—conquered and conquerors alike—proclaimed an uneasy peace, dazed women and children and a host of non-participants surveyed the ruins and decried the scorched resources and damaged social fabric surrounding them. It has always been so.

The spring 1992 riot in Los Angeles was ostensively triggered by a verdict in a jury trial. But, as days passed, other proximate causes were offered by nearly everyone who could gain access to a printing press or microphone. "Poverty and racism," said one. "Police brutality," cried another. "The riot was a manifestation of childhood traumas—a society in need of psychiatric healing," claimed a third. The United States' vice president blamed the riots on a general decline in morality, a lack of family values. So it went in Los Angeles. And so excuses for human behavior have gone worldwide since humanity first learned to make crude stick marks in clay. Everyone sought to explain that the riot had been an aberration; we humans are not like that *normally*. But, indeed, we are. Modern human behavior—from sublime acts of creation to sordid acts of destruction—is measurably a legacy of lemurs, of apes, of ancient humans. It is a legacy that we pass on to the next generation of our species. It is a legacy that we can modify to our advantage, but only if we understand it.

We humans, unlike the ancient lemurs and apes from which we descended, have evolved language—a complex form of animal communication that allows us to invent, then rationalize proximate motives for our behavior. Through language, we often obfuscate the ancient behavioral legacies that control us as surely as they controlled our unwitting ancestors, as surely as they will control our children. Some of those ancient, behavioral motives are the subject of this book—a book that presents human behavior in the light of a new paradigm, evolutionary psychology. It is a scientific paradigm that promises, given time and thought, to tell us much about ourselves as a species, and ourselves as individuals within our species.

Evolutionary psychology covers an enormous territory of information, ideas, and theories. No single book can bind this entire field. For that reason, I have chosen to concentrate on one of the most fascinating and timely aspects of investigation: how human societies are organized according to ancient gender differences in social behavior.

Mutual Corruption

Few of us can deny our captivation with gender. We all have opinions that govern our behavior toward members of the opposite sex. No one is gender-unconscious. Human gender is an endlessly fascinating story about power, sex, and love. "The two sexes," wrote Mary Wollstonecraft more than two centuries ago, "mutually corrupt and improve each other."[1.1] Men and women form societies, build cultures, and parent their future. Together, men and women have achieved unparalleled population densities; we have dominated the earth and struck off toward the stars. The human species is an unqualified biological success. Yet, for as long as humans have crafted words, the two genders have regarded one another with fear, suspicion, horror, admiration, awe, and sometimes, love. More often than not, it appears as if two alien humanoid species cohabit and mold our world. At times, the genders are combative, committing atrocities toward one another as horrendous as any seen in war. At other times, the sexes are in love, enmeshed in a sublime grip of caring, sharing, sexuality, and mutual satisfaction.

Men and women cannot survive apart, but often we have enormous difficulty living together. It is little consolation that throughout history, men and women have rarely agreed about how they should treat one another or how they should behave as a society. Psychiatrists' couches are filled with the flotsam of failed romances. The courts resound with gender battles continued from the workplace. Orphanages overflow with unwanted children. Widows and their children mourn their warrior husbands and fathers. Where the sexes meet, neglect, abuse, harassment, and unhappiness are relatively common.

As witnessed by our numbers and global range, the human species is a tremendous evolutionary success. Yet, our societies have not evolved neatly. At many times throughout the history of our species, we have actively sought to redefine and change our relationships. We are a species that constantly, continually attempts behavioral reform. Few of us today are content with some tense, unhappy status quo in our relationship with our mates, with colleagues of the opposite sex, or with our social order. Collectively and individually, most of us want to know why we behave the way we do. That knowledge, it is reasonable to hope, will allow us to argue how we should behave, and how we might behave differently.

Behavior Through a Naturalist's Looking Glass

How men and women build a society is a direct reflection of how men and women view their place in nature. Humans that perceive themselves as an integral part of nature are likely to find cooperative, workable solutions to social problems. Conversely, when we view ourselves as special and apart from the forces that shape the rest of nature, our societies can be set up to pillage individuals and the environment and to arbitrarily set the rules that govern social relationships. With an anti-natural world view, it is the unquestionable will of gods and the mandates of stern rulers or popular heroes, that proclaim truths and justify behavior.

Our understanding of our species and ourselves needn't be anthropocentric, arbitrary, or metaphysical. Science—humanity's most objective inquiry to date into the nature of things—offers a testable assessment of our place in nature. Scientists discovered humanity's physical place in the scheme of life more than a century ago. We are animals who have evolved from animals. That beautiful and powerful fact has yet to sink in fully to the public consciousness. As we enter the twenty-first century, we know that, like the shape of our skull or the pattern of teeth in our jaw, our behavior, too, has evolved. We can often trace and understand patterns of behavior between species with almost as much certainty as we can trace the evolution of their physical forms. Yet knowledge of the behavioral evolution of our species has yet to be widely exploited in our service.

The benefits of such knowledge are easy to envision. Tracing the roots of human behavior through time allows us to see the natural path of human actions. That, in turn, allows us to pose and answer questions of significance to us all. Is romantic love a recent, historical accident, or an adaptation, a product of millions of years of natural selection? What evolutionary baggage do we carry into the boardroom and the bedroom? How easy or difficult will it be to change the patterns of gender behavior we currently find limiting or objectionable? Is sexual or child abuse a product of a recently malformed mind or a few thousand years of mis-directed social pressures—or does such abusive behavior spring from biological roots, millions of years in the making? Can the genders coexist equally, peacefully, and profitably in the workplace? In the home? Can we create genuinely new forms of human interaction? How much of our behavior can we realistically change? What portion of our behavior is uniquely human? How do our societies channel, mold, amplify and distort the biological bases of human behavior? How do we, as individuals, fit into the larger social pattern of our species?

The answers to these questions (and to countless questions like them) will enable us to objectively, efficiently engineer our societies and our personal relationships. This capacity of ours to engineer social change is key. For even though a particular behavior is a natural product of millions of years of evolution, that fact alone does not mean we have to passively accept the behavior. "My evolutionary biology made me do it" may be an accurate explanation and worthwhile starting point for change, but it is *not* a justification for any behavior that a particular society (or individual) deems inappropriate.

We need working explanations, not excuses for unhappiness or what we define as social misconduct. We are, after all, the most curious and, in some ways, behaviorally dynamic creatures to yet evolve. Collectively and individually, we are the most persistent and capable behavioral modifiers on the planet. But how much of our behavior can we actually change? An evolutionary perspective is arguably the best tool yet developed to answer this question.

Curmudgeons in the Mist

Evolutionary psychology presents a new model of human behavior. Evolutionary psychology is a new paradigm, a new way of thinking about things, a coherent collection of ideas to ask questions about human behavior and seek answers for human problems. Other paradigms exist in psychology. Since the time of Freud, psychology has labored under a model for the roots—the prime motivations—of human behavior that emphasizes individual experiences over our biology. Freudian models stress the importance, indeed the omnipotence, of childhood experiences in the determination of our adult psyches. Evolutionary psychology does not deny personal experience, but rather places such experiences in the context of our biology. For an evolutionary psychologist, it is the evolutionary past, not the individual or cultural present, that largely determines the organization of our societies and the shape of our own, individual behavior. It is a difference in perspective that leads to a radical difference in the interpretations of our conduct.

Remarkably, an evolutionary perspective about human behavior is not especially new. In 1872, Charles Darwin offered the first outline of what we recognize today as evolutionary psychology in his book *Expression of the Emotions in Man and Animals.* Yet 120 years after Darwin's revelations, the fact that behavior evolves continues to be hotly disputed. Professional criticism has always been leveled against the techniques used to reconstruct the evolution of behavior. Such criticisms are the normal business of science and in no way denigrate the fact that human behavior has evolved (and continues to do so). Science at its best has always been an organized debate, a dialectic.

But a dialectic is often a power struggle between two or more opposing schools of thought. In this case, it is a collision of scholars with vested interests in maintaining the largely Freudian status quo on the one hand, and scholars bent on disrupting it on the other. Not surprisingly, then, a large industry of scholarship remains opposed in principle to the idea that human behavior evolved. The detractors of evolutionary psychology claim that humans, unlike every other creature known, dance to inner, wholly arbitrary puppeteers—puppeteers that can only be discerned, manipulated, and, if necessary, exorcised by a qualified professional. To these detractors, virtually all human behavior is unique—a recent, *de novo*

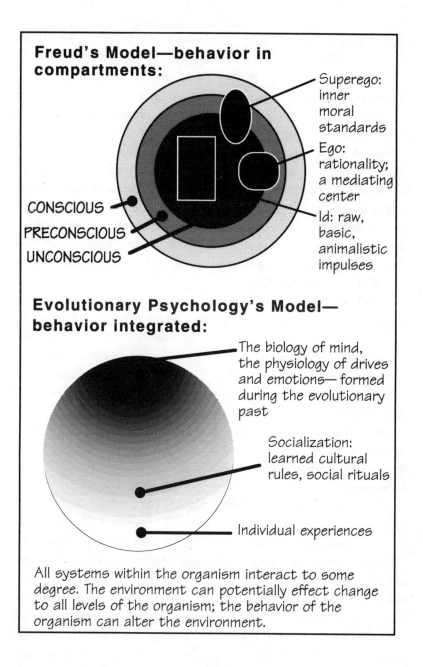

Freud's Model—behavior in compartments:

Superego: inner moral standards

Ego: rationality; a mediating center

Id: raw, basic, animalistic impulses

CONSCIOUS

PRECONSCIOUS

UNCONSCIOUS

Evolutionary Psychology's Model— behavior integrated:

The biology of mind, the physiology of drives and emotions— formed during the evolutionary past

Socialization: learned cultural rules, social rituals

Individual experiences

All systems within the organism interact to some degree. The environment can potentially effect change to all levels of the organism; the behavior of the organism can alter the environment.

creation of *Homo sapiens* or even a more recent, learned construction of some particular human culture or individual. Such anti-evolutionists find a home in many academic disciplines besides Freudian psychology including, most notably, cultural anthropology and, often, psychotherapy.

Evolutionary psychology is not a paradigm that arose as a politicized counter-argument to anti-evolutionists. Evolutionary psychology developed innocently enough as an attempt to reconstruct the evolution of human behavior largely by observing and comparing the behavior of chosen contemporary relatives—living, nonhuman primates such as lemurs and chimpanzees. Much criticism of evolutionary psychology has been leveled because many people find objectionable the fact that we share most of our genes and much of our behavior with apes. There remains a considerable residue of thought that holds that humans are somehow elevated creatures, unconstrained by most of their biology, far above related, contemporary species and just slightly below the angels on a fictive, ladderlike *Scala Naturæ*. [1,2]

Still other critics falsely disparage a biological explanation for human behavior as deterministic. Yet, determinism is not, on its face, a dirty word. After all, a psychologist who attributes an individual's behavior entirely to his or her childhood experiences is asserting a strong form of determinism. Similarly, biological determinism does not necessarily imply either gross simplicity or mindless reductionism. (The terms "simplistic" and "reductionistic" are two sobriquets for complex concepts which, for reasons unclear, arouse the hackles of some contemporary thinkers.) As an explanation for actions, biological determinism can be vastly more complex and more ornate and more satisfying than many current sociological or psychological explanations for human behavior. The crucial point for science is whether or not a given explanation is a testable statement—a statement that, given sufficient evidence, can be rejected. Many biological explanations of human behavior are indeed wholly and elegantly scientific.

During the twentieth century, science has built an impressive catalogue of information about the fossil primate ancestry of the human species, our anatomical and biochemical affinities with contemporary primates, and human and nonhuman primate behavior. The information is in place to build the syntheses, the explanatory theories, the grist for productive discussions. Unquestionably, we are at the dawn of a better, a more realistic understanding of ourselves as individuals, as a society, and as a species.

CHAPTER 2

The Monkeys
on Our Backs

Perhaps the greatest fault of psychology rests with the barren pedestal it has created for the human species. Most contemporary psychology estranges us from our primate kinship. Psychology, in its search for the origins of human behavior amongst shattered contemporary lives, deprives us of our rich past. If truths about human relationships are to be found at all, they will be mirrored largely in the eyes of our primate cousins and writ with the bones of our fossil ancestors.

To be sure, psychologists, influenced by Freud and his students, have provided some startling observations about human behavior. Their observations spawned scientific research in child socialization, addiction, child abuse, obsessive/compulsive behavior, belief systems, and the like. Yet, few of Freud's models or interpretations have survived modern science. For the present story of social relationships, one important Freudian contribution remains: humans are not aware of most of the motives that shape their behavior. Prophetically, Carl Gustav Jung, a student of Freud, stated one of evolutionary psychology's most enduring tasks:

> Man's task is to become conscious of the contents that press upward from [the unconscious]. . . . As far as we can discern, the sole purpose of human existence is to kindle a light in the darkness of mere being.[2.1]

11

Today, many professionals work with sensations, perceptions, emotions, and volitions—the primal "stuff" of human behavior and the traditional subjects of pre-Freudian psychology. They have rejected intestable, culturally biased, turn-of-the-century models and have turned to biology for their methods and philosophical underpinnings. With the advent of evolutionary psychology, history comes full circle and returns behavioral psychology to the realm of objective, biological science.

The Postwar Beginnings

The behavioral sciences grew well in the ashes of the Second World War. During the years following World War II, the behavioral sciences achieved unprecedented professional stature. Their scholarly organizations gained membership exponentially. Their research projects, buoyed by a windfall of postwar government funding, proliferated. The social sciences became so specialized and provincial that findings in one discipline were unknown and largely not interpretable in any of the others. Some (notably some fields of anthropology and psychology) turned visibly against science and embraced various and sundry metaphysical explanations. Our understandings of human behavior seemed destined to be scattered in three or more directions, forever confounded by the jargonized babel of competing academic disciplines. Fortunately, independent of the established social sciences, the seeds of a new science of human behavior had been growing for decades.

Primatology—the biological study of the human Order Primates—was launched as an academic discipline largely through the work of the famous, iconoclastic British intellectual, Sir Solly Zuckerman. In 1932, Zuckerman published his studies of captive and wild monkeys and apes in a pioneering book, *The Social Life of Monkeys and Apes*. [2.2] His seemingly overstated conclusions—that sex (gender) shaped primate societies—proved too difficult for most conservative, contemporary scholars to accept. The academe, then as now, tolerates change slowly and not well. Nevertheless, Zuckerman's work influenced many to study primates seriously.

Across the ocean, from his position in the Psychology Department at the University of Pennsylvania, Dr. Clarence Ray Carpenter pursued his pioneering studies of the behavior of wild primates from the 1930s through the 1950s. Carpenter claimed that he was studying the behavior of monkeys and apes "for their own right." His colleague, Wisconsin psychologist Harry Harlow, was less cautious. He studied the social behavior of Asiatic macaque monkeys to generate models of human behavior. Harlow did not attempt to impute evolutionary significance to his observations of mother-infant behavior or socialization. Instead, he used macaques as sophisticated models—behavioral laboratory rats—whose behavioral systems resembled our own. Harlow developed one of the world's premier primate research laboratories and conducted exquisite, experimental explorations of the mother-infant bond.

Soon, scholars from three different academic disciplines—anthropology, biology, and psychology—began to study primates. Some devoted their efforts to caged monkeys and apes, while others studied primates in their natural settings in tropical Africa, Asia, South America, Mexico, and Madagascar. Primatologists shared their information.

Usually, primatologists assiduously avoided mentioning any connection between their observations and observations of human behavior. Partly, they wanted to avoid the intellectually unpopular sin of anthropomorphism—making their nonhuman research subjects appear to be cute or brutish human parodies. Mostly, they wanted to avoid the polemics incurred whenever a biologist suggested that humans are animals, too, and can be best understood as such. Thus, preliminary primate studies concentrated on detailed descriptions of behavior called ethograms. Later, primatologists limited their investigations to tests of theories about ecology and the environment.

During the 1950s, Austrian ethologist Konrad Lorenz received worldwide fame through studies that extended Darwin's observations of the evolution of behavior. Lorenz and his contemporaries, Dutchman Niko Tinbergen and Austrian Karl von Frisch, propelled ethology into public view. Lorenz's first widely-read, English-translated account of animal behavior—*King Solomon's Ring: New Light on Animal Ways*—inspired many young people to become ethologists in the 1960s. [2,3]

Lorenz and his European colleagues had no inhibitions about comparing their observations of birds, bees, or mammals to human behavior. A world away in America, professional ethologists were not so bold. In fact, some Americans were openly hostile to European ethology, as an English ethologist wryly recounts:

Soon after the war, Tinbergen went to lecture in the United States. The negative response to Continental ethology convinced him that it was necessary to move to the English-speaking world, and he was attracted to Oxford . . .[2.4]

While American scholars initially rejected Continental ethology, an American playwright was extremely impressed by ethology in general and the work of Konrad Lorenz and South African paleontologist Raymond Dart in particular (Dart gained fame for his discovery of the first ape-man human ancestor, *Australopithecus*). In the early 1960s, Robert Ardrey passionately embraced the notion that human behavior was interpretable and understandable through an analysis of our history, our behavior, and the behavior of other animals.[2.5] Ardrey quickly became a self-taught scholar of the nature of human behavior; his popular books that followed sowed the seeds for modern evolutionary psychology.

Ardrey was not a member of academia's inner, professional circle, so he would write five well-referenced, evocative, best-selling books on the subject of human evolution without the fear of career damage from the round of professional reprisals that would inevitably follow. His best-known books, *African Genesis* (1961) and *The Territorial Imperative* (1966) portrayed humans as recently evolved, highly territorial, genetically-programmed killer apes.

Ardrey's early books, explanations for the seemingly unexplainable brutalities of war, captured the public's attention throughout much of the unpopular Vietnam war. For almost five years, Ardrey was the most read nonfiction author on American college campuses—a remarkable achievement since Ardrey's books were almost never assigned readings. Though Ardrey was vilified by most card-carrying academics, his books continued to gain popularity with the public. He published *The Social Contract* in 1970 and *The Hunting Hypothesis* in 1976.[2.6]

A few independent scholars built upon Ardrey's success with their own popular books that linked present-day human behavior to its nonhuman primate past. The public careers of Desmond Morris (*The Naked Ape,* 1967, and *The Human Zoo,* 1969) and Lionel Tiger (*Men in Groups,* 1969, and, with Robin Fox, *The Imperial Animal,* 1971) were launched.

With the end of the Vietnam war, the public's interest in biological explanations of human behavior flagged. Since there was never any support for biological interpretations of human social behavior amongst conservative, tenure-entrenched scholars, the once popular Lorenz-Ardrey synthesis faded from view. Indeed, it was driven into obscurity by critics like Harvard paleontologist Stephen Jay Gould. Gould—himself a well-known popularizer of evolution—disparagingly characterized Ardrey's work as "Pop Ethology." Gould called Konrad Lorenz a "godfather," Robert Ardrey a "dramatist," and Desmond Morris a "raconteur."[2.7]

Despite professional condemnations of "pop ethology," drawing comparisons between what monkeys and apes do and what humans do proved irresistible for some primatologists. Jane Goodall, a student of the late, unorthodox African paleontologist Louis S. B. Leakey,[2.8] wrote vivid accounts of the behavior of wild chimpanzees in the 1960s.[2.9] She was struck by the differences and similarities between chimpanzee and human social behavior. She even attempted to raise her first-born (a boy with the novel nickname "Grub") like chimpanzees raise their offspring. During the 1970s, other Leakey students studied other apes: Dian Fossey studied the gorillas of the Virunga Volcanos in Rwanda; Birute Galdikas studied the orangutans of Borneo.

Each of these women presented their work before a large, public audience via films produced by the National Geographic Society. Television films of simian mother-infant interactions, dominance struggles, problem solving, loyalties, alliances, affections, and even their moments of quiet contemplation, greatly enhanced the public's appreciation of the similarities between the great apes and humans.

Behavioral similarities between human and nonhuman primates were not lost on the current generation of scholars. Today, books that address human dominance, alliances, and language through observations of apes have become somewhat commonplace. Jane Goodall's *Through a Window: My Thirty Years with the Chimpanzees of Gombe* and Frans de Waal's *Chimpanzee Politics: Power and Sex Among Apes* and *Peacemaking among Primates* are acclaimed and representative of the current genre.[2.10]

Today, ethology and primatology are coming of age. This development is crucial for our new understanding of human relationships. As renowned British biologist P.P.G. Bateson proclaims:

> . . . terms such as "intention," "awareness," and "reasoning"
> are being used with increasing frequency in studies of animal

behavior, despite the well-known pitfalls of excessive anthropomorphism and teleological argument. It seems likely that . . .
ethology will expand and, as it does so, start contributing to the
study of the mind. [2.11]

Even now, one of the greatest blunders a scientist can commit is called
a "teleological argument." Teleology (from the Greek *telos,* end) is the use
of design, purpose, or utility to explain natural phenomena. Scientists'
anathema for the use of design arguments stems from the early battles
fought between biologists (who argued for natural selection) versus religionists (who argued that nature was God's plan or design). In fact,
evolutionists and religionists argue a similar point: natural traits and behavior are indeed largely telic (functional and for a purpose). The previously
contentious issue is what designed nature: mechanistic nature itself or a
god? God lost out in this debate decades ago.

Yet today, even though there is nothing fundamentally wrong with
saying, for example, that a bird's wing evolved *for* flight, an overly-sensitive
evolutionary biologist would recoil at the design or purpose implicit in that
statement. The continuing scholarly brouhaha over teleology is probably
overblown and atavistic. As the Medawars noted sarcastically: ". . . perhaps . . . [the] corruption of biology by teleology is not now so grave or
imminent a danger as it was once feared to be." [2.12]

Similarly, a few decades ago, a scholar's career could be seriously jeopar-
dized if colleagues stated that his or her work was "anthropomorphic."
Anthropomorphism—any characterization of non-human animal behavior
using terms that describe human behavior—is still considered an epithet
by many scholars. Nonetheless, contemporary primate studies have shown
that, if anything, much human behavior is "primatomorphic." Properly,
we now see a common behavioral ancestry reflected in the behavior of
humans and their closely related primate cousins. Today, most scholars
agree that humans are an evolved primate; that lemurs and chimpanzees
are related to humans by a common ancestry; and that nonhuman primates
share many physical and some behavioral traits with humans. The fear of
having one's work branded as anthropomorphic is giving way to a better
understanding of our species' evolutionary heritage.

The Rise (and Comeuppance) of Sociobiology

We have often seen that the products of technology can affect us directly. The products of scholarly debates are less obvious in their effects. During the 1970s, a synthesis of genetic and behavioral theory called Sociobiology (with a capital "S") made a significant impact on the direction of Western society—analogous to that made by Darwinian evolution more than a century before. A renowned Harvard entomologist, Edward O. Wilson, launched Sociobiology in 1975 with the widely reviewed book, *Sociobiology: The New Synthesis.* [2.13]

Quickly, two academic camps emerged in biology: traditional biologists versus sociobiologists. Their heated debates made (and continue to make) lively reading. [2.14] Wilson presented nothing really new in his authoritative book. He did, however, emphatically state that: "The pervasive role of natural selection in shaping all classes of traits in organisms can be fairly called the central dogma of evolutionary biology." [2.15] Relatively few biologists would agree with so strong a statement.

Even so, according to Wilson, every aspect of behavior had been shaped and formed by (Darwinian) natural selection. As such, he claimed, we could understand human behavior only as the uncompromising demands of our own genes. The media loved this image. *Time* magazine placed Sociobiology on its cover and ran long articles on the subject during the late 1970s. Professor Wilson's Sociobiological hypotheses were ascending.

In 1978 and again in 1981, Wilson wrote two books that placed all human behavior within the new synthesis of Sociobiology: *On Human Nature* and, as second author to mathematician Charles J. Lumsden, *Genes, Mind, and Culture: The Coevolutionary Process.* [2.16] Inspired by Wilson's success, other Sociobiologists pressed the issue of genes and behavior even farther. Richard Dawkins's *The Selfish Gene* proclaimed that humans are "throwaway survival machines for our immortal genes. Man is a gene machine: a robot vehicle, blindly programmed to preserve its selfish genes." [2.17]

Wilson predicted confidently that by the year 2000, all social sciences—including psychology—would be appropriated by biology. Predictably, most social scientists reacted uproariously to the suggestion that their specialized degrees and political positions would soon be worthless. Social scientists conducted symposia characterizing Wilson and his followers as "misguided" and "tyrannical."[2.18] But it was not the politics of the academe that ultimately softened Sociobiologists' claims. It was facts.

No matter how hard they tried, Sociobiologists could not account for all behavior using calculations of genetic success. According to science philosopher Philip Kitcher, attempts to prove the omnipotence of Sociobiological principles are, at best, logically tortured; at worst, fraudulent.[2.19] Nowadays, Sociobiologists are often mathematicians or population geneticists whose complex mathematical arguments for the pervasive role of natural selection are rarely tested by actual data.[2.20] In part, Sociobiology's dilemma rests with a central fact of biology, well known to Darwin, that natural selection is extremely difficult to test amongst the complexities of nature—the only place where nature actually does select.

The fact that natural selection is not all-pervasive in shaping an animal's form and behavior should have come as no modern surprise. Charles Darwin noted in 1859 that natural selection is "the main but not exclusive means of modification" of species.[2.21] Yet it remained for a new and extremely popular science—molecular biology—to expose Sociobiology's Achilles' heel. During the 1970s, molecular biologists demonstrated that at least some aspects of an animal's biochemistry—crucial parts of a molecule's form and function—were purely accidental and neutral with respect to natural selection. Some parts of an animal's form were hidden from natural selection; some structures were neither adapted nor maladapted to the Darwinian struggle for existence. In 1978, following the molecular biologists' lead, paleontologist Stephen Jay Gould and geneticist Richard C. Lewontin listed no less than six ways in which anatomical structures could evolve in species in the absence of natural selection.[2.22] Aside from anatomical structures, some parts of an animal's behavior can be hidden from the action of natural selection as well. Significant parts of human behavior may have little or nothing to do with natural selection. (Exactly which aspects of human relationships are governed by natural selection and which parts are the result of historic accidents is an ongoing inquiry.) So, Wilson's "Central Dogma of Biology," the all-pervasive role of natural selection, collapsed, and with it, many of Sociobiology's strongest statements disappeared as well.

Sociobiology is by no means a dead issue. In the 1990s, a less dogmatic version of Sociobiology achieved significant rehabilitation. Ernst Mayr, one of this century's most prominent evolutionists, now claims that Wilson only intended Sociobiology to mean "the systematic study of the biological basis of all social behavior." According to Mayr, it was "politically motivated opponents" of Wilson who disparaged Sociobiology as a strong form of genetic determinism. [2.23] While most scholars who followed the Sociobiology controversy from its beginnings would probably quarrel with Mayr's interpretation of Wilson's original intentions, a kinder and gentler form of Sociobiological analysis remains a useful tool to interpret human behavior. After all, as we shall see, natural selection formed and continues to form much human behavior.

Today, Sociobiologists are well-established in pockets throughout academia: at Harvard, Princeton, Cambridge, and Oxford, to name but a few locations. Some people still report that every human act—from painting a picture to selling real estate—is predestined in our genes. Unquestionably, Sociobiology has had a dramatic, if unappreciated, impact on society that continues even today. Sociobiology—at least the strong, original, Wilsonian version—heralded a new era of social Darwinism, a new age of Spencerian me-first, "Nature-Red-in-Tooth-and-Claw" thinking. [2.24] One of Darwinism's most eloquent early supporters was Alfred, Lord Tennyson. In an epic-length poem, Tennyson penned a line that has ever since been equated with the supposedly rapacious, unforgiving nature of a world crafted by evolution:

> *Who trusted God was loved indeed*
> *And love Creation's final law—*
> *Though Nature, red in tooth and claw*
> *With ravine, shrieked against his creed—*
> In Memoriam A. H. H., 56: 13–16

The early proclamations of Sociobiological theory were unflatteringly cynical toward gender relationships. One cover of *Time* magazine showed two lovers attempting an embrace. Strings were attached to their arms, bodies, and heads. Above, in the magazine's masthead, a double strand of DNA pulled the strings. Popular articles announced that science had discovered the double standard's genetic roots. [2.25] Many people, buoyed by Sociobiology's initial acclaim, equated genetic determinism with a personal justification for greed, sexism, and other self-serving, antisocial actions.

Simplistic, elegant Sociobiological cost versus benefit analysis was consciously adopted by business schools during the late 1970s and 1980s.[2.26] Business managers were quick to identify the biologist's equations of genetic success (gross number of offspring) with the unbridled success of a corporation (gross number of dollars). The rapacious American business climate of the 1980s—with its emphasis on the short-term gain and predatory leveraged buyouts—is, in tangible measure, a product of Sociobiological thought. Adherents applied a faulty logic: assuming that greed (or sexism) is natural, it must be good and it must be right. Of course, on close scrutiny, we can all agree that many things that are natural may not be judged either good or right. Few of us would maintain that just because incest, rape, cancer, heart disease, and AIDS are natural, they are good or right for us.

Sociobiology's original rigid, gene-determined view of power, sex, and love was extreme, but, as we will explore, not *entirely* incorrect. Ironically, Freudian theory and Sociobiological theory converged on one useful and critical observation: human behavior is guided by powerful forces of which most of us are blissfully unaware. For Freud, the unseen phantom was the unconscious mind. For Wilson, the unprovable drive was the mechanistic "will" of genes. Evolutionary psychology presents a different, more complicated, perhaps more realistic view.

The new paradigm of evolutionary psychology claims that human relationships have been shaped by hundreds of millions of prehuman social trials. This long social history has left the ghosts of conflicting goals in our mental machines. Today, these ghosts—or at least their shadows—appear in our behavior and in the behavior of our relatives clambering about in the branches of tropical trees. The legacies of ancient lemurs, apes, and prehumans largely formed the present human mind. The unconscious is a mental map whose roads were built through necessity and chance—through countless acts of natural selection and countless accidental incorporations. To an evolutionary psychologist, the mind is less a deep, unfathomable source of motivations and more a thick, multifaceted filter through which we view the world, process information in established ways, and project our actions.

Toward an Evolution-Based Psychology and Psychiatry

H. L. Mencken implored psychologists to "get together as the patholo-gists, physiologists and other scientists get together, pool their facts, scrap their theories, and so lay the foundations of a rational psychology[.]" [2.27] After more than sixty years, Mencken's called-for synthesis is near at hand. The new science of evolutionary psychology uses information about our fossil past, about human behavior and the behavior of our nonhuman primate relatives, and about how brains work to produce behavior. Then, for analysis, evolutionary psychology is a considered amalgam of modern evolutionary theory, cognitive science, and genetic, ecological, and behav-ioral information. In the end, evolutionary psychology is a reasoned, tempered look at primate and human sociobiology—a product of more than 100 years of thought and debate. It is a synthesis that admits natural selection, accidents, and non-Darwinian mechanisms for change. It is a science in an embryonic but useful stage.

At an ever-increasing rate, new scientific tools and exciting new informa-tion are available to evolutionary psychologists. We are, for example, on the verge of a comprehensive theory about how the brain and its attend-ant, emergent quality, the mind, works. We will soon exchange scientific metaphors for tangible, mechanistic explanations. Neuroscience—the original pursuit of the founders of psychology, the original profession of Sigmund Freud—has merged increasingly with computer science to give us a new discipline called cognitive science. [2.28]

While countless puzzles remain, the mind is no longer a black box. We know how nerves work, how minute chemical floods alter our thoughts and perceptions and how bundles of nerves act in concert. How hundreds of millions of nerves act together to produce our reality remains a mystery, but the dogged persistence of scientists will unravel this Gordian Knot, perhaps within our lifetime.

Legend has it that whoever could untie the Gordian Knot would rule the East. Alexander, not one for tedious puzzles, promptly cut the knot in two with his sword. It is rare that a scientific discovery leads to knowledge in so decisive or simple a manner. In practice, a scientist carefully con-structs a knot (hypothesis), then spends a lifetime attempting to untie it (testing the hypothesis). Nonetheless, science generations are passing by at an amazing clip nowadays. Even with dozens of holes in the present canvas of an overarching big picture, cognitive science offers us much in our quest to comprehend human social relationships. The new view of the mind is changing our erroneous past notions about separate realities (like the mind versus the body), free will, determinism, and chance. [2.29] Cognitive science, available to modern evolutionary psychologists, was not available to Freud. If it had been, Freud and his followers might have modeled human behavior in an entirely different way.

The new syntheses of evolutionary psychology is well and truly under way. As biologist Richard Alexander et al. stated in 1979:

> We may now ask whether or not anything useful is to be gained from considering humans in the general biological terms so far used to characterize other mammalian groups. We assume at the outset that humans possess no special features invalidating such a comparison. [2.30]

Productive comparisons and analyses now abound. Increasingly, biologists employ the term "evolutionary psychology" when discussing human behavior. [2.31] Martin Daly and Margo Wilson's popular psychology textbook *Sex, Evolution & Behavior* has promoted an evolutionary approach to human psychology since it first appeared in 1978. [2.32] In 1989, in a book entitled *Exiles From Eden: Psychotherapy from an Evolutionary Perspective,* Drs. Kalman Glantz and John K. Pearce argued that individual human problems can be best understood in the context of the comparative animal behavior. Although they used a few examples of primate behavior to redirect psychotherapy toward an evolutionary perspective, Glantz and Pearce attempted no systematic introduction to the evolution of human behavior. Significantly, though, Glantz and Pearce called for a new field of psychology—evolutionary psychotherapy—to reform psychotherapy and make it compatible "with what is known about the behavior of living things." [2.33]

Evolutionary explanations of human behavior are coming in fashion. Books for a wide audience, most written by biological anthropologists, promote the paradigm of evolutionary psychology by providing fresh examples and interpretations of behavioral evolution. [2.34] My work and that of many of my colleagues offers primate evolutionary models for the study of human psychological problems. A productive synthesis is forming bit by bit. There is already a critical history of the intellectual beginnings of evolutionary psychology, a certain indication that the paradigm is gathering attention.[2.35] *The Lemurs' Legacy* is an introduction to the paradigm from a naturalist's perspective—a sketch of what we know, don't know, and where future investigations of human behavior may lead us.

We have in place all the intellectual tools to achieve a fresh understanding—the first new representation of the psychology of human relationships in almost a century. Further, the new evolutionary model is accessible to all. In a tradition that hearkens back to Darwin, this synthesis is meant to be shared with a large public. Of course, some people, especially those not caught up in the drama of professional psychology, might argue that too much intellectualization spoils relationships; that science, in its reductionism, strips the mysteries from human behavior. To some extent, this is true. But, for each seemingly cold, mechanical explanation, poets will spin a hundred metaphors and soothing similes. Our new metaphors, unlike many of our old, will have the liberating ring of truth. Such is the close relationship between scientist and poet.

Bridges Between Science, Therapy, and Ethics

For any scientific paradigm to work, its hypotheses must initially be pursued without considerations of the consequences of its findings. One of the most laudable aspects of science is its amoral nature: science merely investigates what is, not what ought to be. In principle, moral considerations should play no role in an evolutionary analysis.[2.36] In practice, though, what a scientist chooses to investigate or ignore is often markedly influenced by the social prejudices—the political correctness—of the day.

"Ought" statements are the proper province of ethics, politics, or religion. Evolutionary psychology is a science. Psychiatry and clinical psychology—at least those major parts of the professions devoted to treating behavioral problems—can never, in a strict sense, be science. Prescribing a behavior is, by definition, telling someone what they ought to do. Therapy is ethics. This apparent semantic quibbling is by no means trivial. The distinction between science and ethics lies at the heart of the matter. It is the distinction between the science of psychology, which seeks to investigate behavior as objectively as is humanly possible, and the subjective, "applied science" of psychiatry.

In the past, psychiatry has often justified dispensing ethics through its mantle of science. I am not arguing here that contemporary psychiatry's brand of ethics is good, bad, or in some way flawed. I am arguing that when science and applied science coexist as one, then the boundaries between ethics (good, bad, or flawed) and objective knowledge is necessarily lost. For example, a psychiatric cure was considered evidence that the underlying assumptions about the nature of human behavior were correct. In this process, practitioners and patients often confused a value judgment or an ethical statement for an objective truth. Ideally, a future state of psychiatry will acknowledge that its prescriptions are, at least in part, based upon the prevailing, perhaps transient, mores of contemporary culture. In the future, psychiatry's paradigm—the method used to achieve its "truths"—may be grounded in the objective, amoral, ethically neutral science of evolutionary psychology.

This distinction between the results of psychology (knowledge) and the results of psychiatry (care-giving) enables us to distinguish objectively what our behavior is from subjectively what we would like it to be. Sustaining this distinction is essential if we are to effect any meaningful change in our evolutionary status quo. Pragmatically, only scientists can debate the psychology of human behavior in the realm of science. Yet everyone can—and perhaps everyone should—join the debate over what we would like our behavior to be. Properly, ethics are the dominion of everyone. At present, what human behavior should be is, in too many cases, the sole bailiwick of the therapist.

There is nothing amiss when a politician, a poet, a paperhanger, or a priest claims to know what gender relationships are all about. There probably is something wrong when a non-scientist claims to have discovered the scientific basis for behavior. This is not an elitist statement. It merely acknowledges, for example, that there can be five billion valid interpretations of love, but not all interpretations are scientific.

A broad, evolutionary perspective can help us all avoid the biases of ethnocentrism (culturally-centered bias) and anthropocentrism (human-centered bias). We can easily become myopic when we stare at human behavior in a mirror. Sigmund Freud made the mistake of ethnocentrism by concluding that the behavior of *Homo sapiens* could be understood from studies of behaviorally-troubled patients within his own society. We need to survey the range of human behavior from all cultures to avoid the mistakes made by the early proponents of psychoanalysis.

Even if we survey all contemporary human behavior, we can still suffer from anthropocentrism—the fallacy of thinking that all human behavior is uniquely human. Anthropocentrism obscures the root motivations, strengths, and weaknesses of contemporary human behavior.

For example, suppose we believe that the social bond between a mother and a daughter is merely a product of learning. An anthropologist might describe the bond as wholly cultural. What is learned can be modified significantly through further education. So, in principle, a woman suffering from the effects of a mother's maltreatment should be able to mitigate her problems through relatively straightforward therapy.

The picture changes significantly if we assume that the mother-daughter bond has a 54-million-year biological history. That history has shaped the female brain and most aspects of female behavior in a way far different from that of human males. A deleterious mother-daughter bond might have far more negative impact upon behavior than a deleterious mother-son bond, father-son bond, or father-daughter bond. With an understanding of the evolutionary roots of human behavior, we can attempt to deal with the multitude of problems potentially unique to a dysfunctional mother-daughter bond. These include deep-seated dominance, affectional, and sexual difficulties.

Evolutionary psychology is a powerful tool. It provides a reasonably reliable, expanding database to understand, build, and renew relationships. For example, to succeed, dissatisfied lovers must identify romantic images and explore ancient dominance and reproductive strategies that silently, predictably, inexorably guide their behavior as surely as a breeze pushes at the petals of a rose.

Evolutionary psychology calls first upon the individual to seek an understanding of the biosocial roots—the ultimate motivations—of his or her behavior. Through such understanding, a troubled individual can come to grips with a behavioral problem. Lady Macbeth's physician was perhaps the first to venture that an enlightened patient can best effect a cure . . .

MACBETH: How does your patient, Doctor?
DOCTOR: Not so sick, my lord,
   As she is troubled with thick-coming fancies
   That keep her from her rest.
MACBETH: Cure her of that!

Canst thou not minister to a mind diseased,
Pluck from the memory a rooted sorrow,
Rase out the written troubles of the brain,
And with some sweet oblivious antidote
Cleanse the stuffed bosom of that perilous stuff
Which weighs upon her heart?
DOCTOR: Therein the patient
Must minister to himself.
MACBETH: Throw physic to the dogs! I'll none of it.

Macbeth V, iii

Perhaps we needn't throw physic (psychiatry) to the dogs. For those who would seek therapy, evolutionary psychology might form the base for twenty-first century psychology and psychiatry. Evolutionary psychology (and the prevailing morality of the day) may be the paradigm that prescribes care—as surely and dramatically as the prevailing morality and Sigmund Freud's psychoanalytic approach guided our view of human behavior and caregiving in the twentieth century.

When can we expect that evolutionary psychology will set the new rules for clinical psychology and psychiatry? When will evolutionary concepts transform our world view and become the new vernacular, the common conception of human relationships? In some small, measured ways, evolutionary theory—a basis for medical training in biology, molecular biology, and anatomy in the United States—may have already influenced patient care. Even so, much of psychiatry remains shackled to a basic culture-bound model of human behavior expounded in the early years of this century. In science, a new world view overtakes an old more through accretion than revolution. "A scientific truth," lamented physicist Max Planck, "does not triumph by convincing its opponents and making them see the light, but rather because its opponents eventually die and a new generation grows up that is familiar with it."[2.37] Inevitably, inexorably, better scientific paradigms replace good old ones. A generation ago, only a handful of physicists understood quantum mechanics. Today, quantum mechanics are part of every physics student's tool kit.

Fortunately, time and the increasing intellectual and political clout of the life sciences is effecting a positive change in psychology. An exciting era of psychiatry and layperson understanding of relationships is coming. How humbling and wonderful is the view that the basic, warm, ennobling emotions that two people can share extend millions of years backward in time. The search to understand those years is an exhilarating voyage that we all can share.

While the reconstruction of the history of human evolutionary imperatives is inarguably scientific, it is also an interpretive art, not unlike the work of a detective in uncovering the history of a crime. That is, the experience and knowledge of the investigator must often be used to judge and balance the evidence. Even here, subjectivity is tempered by well-tested observations about how evolution works. The processes of evolution and the methods used to study evolution have been debated intensively for more than a century.[2,38] The time is opportune to apply our understanding of evolution to the complexities of human behavior.

CHAPTER 3

Behavioral Evolution

Evolution, biological and otherwise, may fairly be called the central theme of modern science. The universe has evolved and continues to evolve. Life originated from evolving chemicals; life evolved and continues to evolve. Evolution has shaped the heavens above us and the soil at our feet. Evolution has shaped our physical form, our perception of the world, and our behavior. The contention, then, that we can best understand human behavior through a study of its evolutionary legacy raises questions we must first answer. What is biological evolution? What is behavior? In what sense does a behavior evolve? How do minds evolve? How can we chart the evolution of behavior? How does the behavior of extinct ancestors affect our behavior? Does behavior progress through time to some better state?

What Is Evolution?

We are all part of a single, living, intrafertile population we call the species *Homo sapiens.* As individuals within this population, we grow, develop, change physically and mentally, and die—but we cannot evolve. Biological evolution is a dynamic of populations, not of individuals; it is measured as a proportion of changes between a parental population and its descendants. Only species evolve through time. Evolution occurs when a heritable part of a descendant population's behavior (or anatomy) differs from that of its ancestral population in a way that cannot be reversed.

Biological evolution is a concept often attributed to Charles Darwin. However, Darwin did not discover evolution. Instead, Darwin—together with an unsung contemporary, naturalist Alfred Russel Wallace—discovered one way in which evolution occurs.[3.1] They defined precisely and convincingly one of evolution's mechanisms—natural selection. An understanding of natural selection is essential for an understanding of the evolution of human behavior.

There are three unambiguous parts to the Darwin-Wallace theory. First, individuals within a species compete for limited resources. Second, all individuals show slight variations in their behavior. And third, those individuals whose behavior is better adapted to the task at hand will produce the most offspring—they are reproductively more successful than their peers, they are "more fit."

To win at natural selection, the *only* important tally is that of reproductive success. Whatever we do in the name of establishing, preserving, or breaking a relationship is neither right nor wrong, better or worse. It is either adaptive in that it leads to the production of more offspring (more fit) or it is maladaptive (less fit = less offspring). For example, romantic love—the courting, the posturing, the pledges, the gifts—is a complex pattern of human behavior that is subject to natural selection. Romantic love is the mental and behavioral foreplay that attempts to lead to successful reproduction, and reproduction is the *raison d'être* for romantic love.

There is even a special class of natural selection, first recognized by Darwin, called sexual selection.[3.2] Sexual selection is usually exerted by one gender on the other as a requisite for mating. Sexual selection resulted in the peacock's beautiful tail; hens preferred to mate with males who could display the most garish tail. Sexual selection can even run counter to natural selection. The peacock's clumsy tail puts the male at a distinct disadvantage when it comes to maneuvering away from predators in its woodland habitat. In the evolutionary game, mating success counts for more than a long life.

There are countless examples of how sexual selection has shaped the form and behavior of animals. Many of the effects of sexual selection are apparent even to the untrained. The flowing, colorful fins of male guppies, the coded blinking of fireflies on a summer's evening, the late-night song of a mockingbird are all examples of the products of sexual selection.

Humans are no less shaped by sexual selection. For example, men have preferred curvaceous, Rubenesque women since before the Paleolithic, 25,000 years ago, when obscenely rotund "Venus" statuary graced many of the world's stone altars. Large feminine breasts are particularly favored by most men—a fact not lost on the hundreds of thousands of American women who underwent breast augmentation surgery in recent years. [3.3] The preference for full-figured women expressed by many men is both an example of a sexual selective pressure and natural selection in action.

Today, by the age of eighteen, women, on average, have 15% more body fat than men. This process of selection for sexual dimorphism (literally, two differing forms between men and women) has far-reaching reproductive value. Women require an abundance of body fat to ovulate successfully. Thin women are often infertile. [3.4] Low body fat levels result in lower levels of the female reproductive hormone, estrogen, and consequentially, inadequate levels of hormones necessary for ovulation and implantation (i.e., follicle-stimulating and luteinizing hormones). Even a slight, 10%, loss of fat from dieting or exercise is sufficient to block fertility in women. Of course, the men who preferred rounded women did not comprehend fully the reproductive advantages of their choice, but folk literature abounds with the mythic (now scientific) belief that substantial women make productive, nutritive mothers.

Similarly, women have long valued older males who exhibit social and financial success over younger males with better physical appearance when they choose for mates. [3.5] This selective pressure has, in measurable ways, strongly influenced the behavior of men. The sexual selective power of women to influence men's behavior was recently suggested eloquently by rap music star Kool Moe Dee. "Ninety percent of the men who sell drugs," he suggested, "would stop selling drugs immediately if they couldn't get a woman because women didn't like men who sell drugs." [3.6] Implementation of Mr. Dee's observation might do more to alleviate the American drug problem than all the government's so-called "Drug Wars."

While natural and sexual selection are powerful, they are by no means the only mechanisms that have shaped human behavior. Since the 1960s, a new mechanism for evolution has been suggested. Biologists who have studied this new mechanism—called non-Darwinian evolution—suggest that some evolved behavior may have neither a positive nor negative impact on an individual's reproductive success. These sorts of behavior are neutral with respect to both natural and sexual selection. A commonplace example is snoring. Snoring neither increases nor decreases our potential reproductive success, but it often causes considerable social angst. In the same way, some aspects of power, sex, and love are probably neither adaptive nor maladaptive.

As we will explore, many aspects of behavior—such as male dominance in ape and human societies—appear to be the results of accidents, not the results of an evolutionary strategy or a selective design. Selection may play little or no governing role in the origin and/or persistence of many behavioral trends. Even maladaptive behaviors can survive in an individual as long as the bulk of one's behavior is adaptive. An abusive husband may succeed in fathering many offspring, particularly if he is a good provider. The persistence of this sort of deleterious behavior (in this case, spousal abuse) is appropriately termed "hitchhiking." Aspects of our behavior that once were highly adaptive may now be useless or maladaptive. They may be hitchhiking along with other adaptive behaviors that on balance assure survival and reproductive success.

There is evidence that selection, neutral evolution, and accidents have shaped the patterns of human relationships. This means that, at the outset, we cannot classify biologically our relationships or even our feelings about one another as adaptive, maladaptive, good, or bad. More importantly, not everything we do is nature's plan. Much of what we do, think, or feel may be best thought of as nature's ancient accidents.

Prisoners in Time Thinking about Behavior

Trying to define behavior adequately is almost as difficult as nailing jelly to a tree. When it comes to thinking about behavior, we are creatures trapped in and biased by a narrow time perspective. We perceive a part of anatomy—say a long bone like the femur—as a solid, tangible, immutable object. In contrast, we think of a behavior—say a sudden smile—as a mutable, ephemeral event. In fact, anatomy and behavior contain structured forms in time that share more similarities than differences. For example, they both display variations that depend upon inheritance and the environment. Ultimately, bones arise from genes acting within a fertilized egg; so does behavior. A femur may be thick or thin, bent or straight, depending upon genetics and the muscular forces that act upon it during life. Similarly, a smile may be broad or pursed, frozen or transient depending upon inherited perceptual abilities and the particular perceptions and emotions of the creature who is smiling.

Both bones and behavior can be described in detail, measured, quantified, and compared. [3.7] Details of the structure of bones differ between individuals in a species; so does the structure (the sequence of actions and inactions) of a behavioral act. Bones are structures that necessarily interconnect with other structures; similarly, no behavior exists in complete isolation from other behaviors. Just as for a bone's anatomy, the anatomy of behavior can be viewed on many levels. The more levels we view, the more complex the bone or the behavior appears. For example, swatting a fly may be little more than a reflex action; smiling at a prospective mate may elicit an ongoing, variable pattern of interactions, each of which may prove complex and variable in turn.

Time, more than anything else, appears to separate behavior from bones. A bone develops (grows) through time; so does a behavior. But a bone grows slowly. Behavior, at least most behavior, appears suddenly (to the human observer) and ends quickly (or so we perceive it). The human observer is thus a prisoner of his/her own narrow perception of time. We are most capable of describing the details of biological things that change slowly through time. With this time bias, we tend to dismiss things that change quickly as transient, ephemeral events. Somehow, behavior appears to be "less a structure," perhaps less real or important in evolutionary terms than body parts.

Since bones and behaviors are structures that exist in time, we can describe them and discuss them. We can form hypotheses about bones and behavior, and speculate intelligently about them. In this spirit, evolutionary psychology attempts to reconstruct the evolution of behavior. Here, we must deal with broad behavioral forms such as patterns of dominance and aggression, patterns of infant care, mating strategies, social organization, and the like. Evolutionary psychology traces these larger forms through time. It is a skill, sometimes inexact and not unlike tracing the history of entire bodies (rather than individual bone cells, muscle fibers, or arterioles). Details will always remain to be investigated, but bigger pictures emerge from this kind of analysis with satisfying, usable clarity.

Slaves of Static Terms

Behavior, far more than bones, is dynamic. A behavior may consist of a sequence of sounds, smells, and postures, each lasting seconds, minutes, hours, days, or years. Behavior is both action and inaction—every behavior has a form in space and is linked to a sequence of forms through time. Behavior is a tendency to act; there are many external and internal conditions which may affect behavior. Evolutionary biology uses more or less precise, static terms to describe the many dynamic elements of behavior.

At best, behavioral descriptions are only partially satisfying. A biologist describing behavior is not unlike a knowledgeable, relatively unbiased reviewer describing a movie. The movie always contains more action than words can convey, but with skill, the reviewer can convey the essential events. Further, as with any scientific term, behavioral definitions and descriptions are stripped of their emotive meaning. This does not make them "cold," it makes them understandable. Despite science's apparent descriptive shortcomings, science is the most reliable, repeatable process we have to review human behavior. It works remarkably well.

Evolutionary psychologists use many terms to describe relationships. These terms are easily defined, clearly related variables: reproductive strategy, mate selection, love, caring, dominance, courtship, romance, cultural rules, feelings, and so forth. One of Western societies' most prominent relationship terms, "romantic love," is a phrase that encompasses all the biological imperatives and cultural rules that enable successful sexual reproduction. It is rarely used in scientific analyses.

Romantic love is too cumbersome a concept to treat holistically and it must be rendered into parts for proper analysis. Few people can agree on the definitions of its parts. Some people argue that romantic love must be egalitarian; others support a less democratic view. For some people, romantic love is an intellectual exercise; for others, it is largely glandular. At present, the metaphor cannot sustain a definition that we can all agree upon, and it is therefore of little use to science (albeit some psychologists are working toward a useful definition).[3.8] Romantic love is a popular metaphor, or, as a psychologist might say, a gestalt. Much later, when we have achieved a better understanding of the elements within romantic love—of gender, mate selection, altruism, dominance posturing, and the like—we can reconstruct an emotive, perhaps universal metaphor for romantic love filled with all the poetry and wonder we desire. For the present, evolutionary psychology must stick with terms that have operational definitions—terms that are unequivocal. A few are presented below.

Sex is a word with many operational definitions. Two are used here: gender (male or female) and, in a narrow sense, sexual behavior. Sexual behavior is any behavior employed for copulation—foreplay and coitus. Yet monkeys, apes, and especially humans are unique amongst the mammals: much primate sexual behavior is not reproductive. Non-reproductive sexuality in our lineage serves as practice, as a dominance (status and power) display, and to reinforce social bonds.[3.9]

A reproductive strategy is the biologically-defined, optimal mode of reproduction; that is, the behavioral path that produces the most progeny. It can be in reference to the species as a whole or to a gender. The evolution of our species' reproductive strategy involved profound differences in the biological goals of men and women.

Mate selection is simply who chooses whom. The choice is, for humans, never simple and rarely obvious. Human mate selection is governed by both ancient biological imperatives and recent cultural rules.

Sexual love is a strong, affectionate bond between members of the same or different gender that leads to sexual behavior. Of course, not all love leads to sex. Nonsexual or platonic love is a strong, affectionate bond between members of the same or different gender. This bond can be as strong or stronger than a dominance bond (power alliance). It can even be applied to nonhuman animals and objects.

Caring is difficult to define. Lovers exhibit concern for one another, they care for one another's feelings, emotions, and physical well-being. In the popular view, such caring can involve altruism, a sacrifice of an individual's interests for the good of another. In contrast, some biologists have argued cogently that no animal cares for another at a real expense to itself. Sociobiologists believe strongly that no act of altruism is truly altruistic. They claim that every behavioral act is designed to maximize an individual's fitness. Sociobiologists note that all displays of caring are in fact conducted to enhance an animal's chances of successful reproduction. In other words, altruism is actually subtle self-interest. We examine this important romantic issue again later.

Dominance is a prime factor in all social relationships. Dominance is popularly considered power—the power of one individual relative to the lack of power (the submissiveness) of another. Dominance, therefore, requires a ranking of social members. There are at least two interactive dominance hierarchies within most primate social groups: a female hierarchy and a male hierarchy. Rank or status in a dominance hierarchy is determined through social interactions—who submits to whom. Initially and most importantly, an individual's position is determined by the rank of its mother.

Ranks within a hierarchy vary from the most dominant, the alpha animal, to the most submissive, the omega. Dominance ranking is really a study in shades of grey: most individuals are neither all-powerful nor all-unpowerful. There are usually legions in the middle, individuals who are submissive to the most dominant individuals, but who curry favor from them as well. These subdominant individuals (the highest-ranking of which are called beta animals) establish coalitions of supportive, high-ranking alpha and beta individuals. A clever beta animal will use politics— its support from an alpha animal, for example—to settle disputes with other beta animals. Ranks are, to a degree, changeable and dynamic; political maneuvering or an outright challenge may allow a beta animal to attain the rank of an alpha.

Courtship is the interplay of behaviors between partners that leads to sex. For most species, courtship is almost entirely a stereotypic ritual. There are elements of both ancient and modern rituals in human courtship as well. For many humans, romance is the human expression of courtship. It is governed by both biological and cultural inputs. The most important are mate selection, dominance, love, and cultural rules.

Cultural rules for behavior are learned values received from socialization. Some people have a greater effect on our socialization than others. Relative positions in a dominance hierarchy—power—plays a profound role in primate socialization. For humans, who we learn what from is often a function of where the teacher and the pupil are in the dominance hierarchy. As we shall see, there are major differences between the sexual and aggressive socialization of men and women. In the final analysis, all cultural values or rules either stand or fall according to the mechanisms of biological evolution. Those cultural values which decrease the chances of reproductive success may disappear as surely as the adherents to those values. Cultural values that cannot adapt to changing conditions may doom their adherents to extinction.

Last, but arguably the most important metaphor to us, are feelings. Feelings (or emotions) are complex processes. Feelings, such as anger or love, are initiated both externally and internally; they are both mental and visceral. So, for example, when we fall in love, we think about the object of our affections. Internally, our brain produces neurohormones, including L-Dopa and serotonin, that wash over receptors in our cortex—the rational, thinking part of our brain. The hypothalamus is bathed with the hormone luliberin, gearing up our sexual drive. The brain becomes sensitized. [3.10]

The expression "I'm getting high on love" is largely true. The biochemical tide heightens our awareness, but that awareness is distinctly colored—dopamine belongs to a class of drugs known as opiates. When in love, we often perceive events optimistically—"through rose-colored glasses." The brain's response to love affects other bodily functions as well, for example our heart rate and our digestion. Overall, we perceive a general body repercussion—a feeling—of our romantic thoughts.

Strong, positive feelings are important. They evolved to enhance our performance. When we are in love, we feel happy and can often accomplish our most creative acts—at least those creative acts that might potentially increase our success at mating. A successful relationship can help foster good health and creativity via the diffuse and powerful effects of neurohormones. In every culture, lovers are considered special. By and large, our fellow humans respond positively to us when we are in love. Conversely, a love affair gone wrong can produce feelings that lead to depression. Note, too, that the sorrow that follows rejection and the end of a love affair can also fuel creativity, albeit a Kafkaesque form of creativity. Human creativity seems most active at opposite points of love's pendulum swings.

Love's labors lost affect negatively our perceptions, our awareness, our responsiveness, our interactions with acquaintances, and even our physiology. Depression reduces the efficacy of the immune system response, exposing us to disease. It is more than merely pleasing to seek positive feelings like love in our lives; it is probably a biological necessity. [3.11]

Chaos and Uncertainty in Predicting Behavior

With so many variables involved in any behavior, predicting the outcome of a particular act is not merely difficult, it is impossible. If Shakespeare had left *Romeo and Juliet* unfinished, no scholar could confidently predict its tragic last act. The science of evolutionary psychology has real limits, similar to the limits experienced by physicists in the early decades of this century.

Uncertainty is not a comforting truth. In 1927, Werner Heisenberg shocked the academic community when he demonstrated that a physics experiment designed to discover the position of a particle, such as an electron, necessarily destroys our ability to simultaneously measure its momentum (and vice versa). Uncertainty, sometimes known as "Indeterminacy," also applies to measurements of energy and time as well as momentum and position. The particulars of Heisenberg's Theory are not important here. The fact that the Uncertainty Principle introduced the concept of uncertainty into science is crucial. Heisenberg demonstrated that we cannot know both the location and the speed of an electron. There are some things in the universe that are not merely difficult to know, they are *impossible* to know.

Physics recovered from the shock of uncertainty; in fact, uncertainty heralded a new era of ideas about the fundamental nature of particles and waves. Nonetheless, Heisenberg's observation introduced a note of pessimism into what was before an ever-optimistic outlook on the power of science to explain the world.

A world away and more than a quarter-century later, MIT meteorologist Edward Lorenz (no relation to animal behaviorist Konrad Lorenz) rediscovered a more profound version of uncertainty lurking within a computer program. Lorenz was searching for a mathematical model that could be used to predict long-term changes in weather. There were many variables involved in forecasting, but most were relatively well known. In principle, it should have been easy to plug numbers into a computer and predict when the next cold front would march across Iowa. It wasn't. The tiniest change in a variable—the mathematical equivalent of the flap of a butterfly's wings in Brazil—could completely alter the weather forecast a continent away. Lorenz's discovery, called "The Butterfly Effect," introduced a new, more pernicious form of scientific uncertainty. Tiny variations in complex systems, such as climates or even human romance, necessarily confound predictions. Like physics' Uncertainty Principle, Lorenz's Butterfly Effect spawned a productive new wave of research called, simply, "Chaos." Chaos Theory is actually a rejuvenation of an old field of mathematics called dynamics. [3.12]

For evolutionary psychologists, the mathematics of Chaos Theory demonstrates that no one can confidently predict the outcome of any individual human action. There are simply too many possible perturbations in too many complex variables like socialization, bonding, dominance struggles, and the like. Further, for the same reasons, everyone will likely experience some difficulty with any human relationship.

The course of a particular relationship is impossible to predict accurately. Nevertheless, we can increase the odds of having a satisfying and long-lasting relationship—sexual, romantic, business, or friendship—through knowledge about those variables. At present, a big picture is comprehensible, even if its individual mosaics are fuzzy. In the future, evolutionary psychology, like physics before it, will find that uncertainty can be a powerful investigatory tool. Behavioral scientists have only begun to explore uncertainty.

With definitions in mind, and with uncertainty the only certainty, we can begin to define behavioral evolution more realistically and precisely.

Genes and Behavioral Evolution

In the sense of sound scientific semantics, "behavior" cannot evolve. While the phrase "behavior evolves" is semantically incorrect, it is a necessary metaphor that replaces a cumbersome, semantically accurate expression. To wit: "The species that exhibited behavior 'X' was ancestral to the species that exhibited a homologous behavior 'X1'." It is far easier to bend semantics a smidgen and say: "Behavior X evolved into behavior X1."

Neither can a person "evolve." An individual can develop, it can grow, but the only living thing that evolves is a species. This is no game of wordsmanship. The fact is simple: a population of organisms—a species—evolves through a change in the frequency of its genes. We measure evolution by counting the species' genes twice: once in the past and again now.

It is not necessary to sample every gene in every individual—that is still an impossible task for us in most species. In practice we employ sophisticated, mathematical sampling techniques. More often than not, evolution is charted by taking measurements of gross physical features of a species (like bones or pelage color). Ostensibly, these features are chosen because we infer their relationship to the underlying genes that created them.[3.13]

We can get a feel for this using a fanciful, simplified example. Suppose the human species a generation ago contained two genes that controlled the length of all human ears. (Ear length and shape is indeed governed by genes, but these anatomical traits are actually governed by many genes operating in concert with the environment of the developing fetus. No need to fret this sort of complexity here.)

Half of humanity possessed the gene big "A" and had large ears; the other half possessed the gene little "a" and had tiny ears. A generation later, we again measured everyone's ears. Now, two-thirds of humanity had big ears (and thus harbored gene big "A"); only one-third of all humans had little ears (and thus harbored gene little "a"). *Voilà:* we'd proclaim that evolution had occurred. The frequency of gene big "A" increased from 50% to 67%; gene little "a" decreased from a frequency of 50% to a frequency of 33% in the human species.

If human relationships were formed by behaviors that we could identify directly with genes, then we could, for example, easily trace "Love Gene A," "Love Gene B," and so forth, through time. We could even imagine that a twenty-first century advice columnist would be a geneticist who could dispense simple, clear-cut advice: "Your problem, Ms. Megalopolis, is that your boyfriend has a recessive gene for love type 'B' . . ."

But—and this is crucial for our story—genes do not directly code for *any* behavior. Genes are portions of your hereditary molecule DNA that, through a series of neat, cellular gymnastics, manufacture proteins. Period. Proteins, under the partial direction of other proteins, link together to create larger structures like the tiny organelles within cells. Cells, under the partial direction of other proteins, form tissues. Tissues form organs. Organs form an organism such as you. And, at long last, you—interacting with the environment around you and within yourself—behave. Even so-called "[h]ereditary behaviour [*sic*]," states British biochemist Rupert Sheldrake, "is influenced by genes, but is neither 'genetic' nor 'genetically

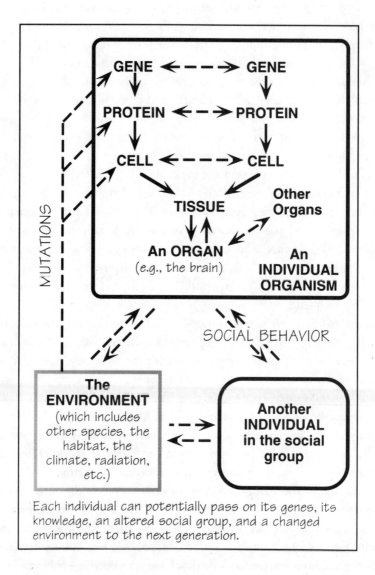

Each individual can potentially pass on its genes, its knowledge, an altered social group, and a changed environment to the next generation.

programmed' . . . the role of genes is inevitably overrated, and properties are projected onto them that go far beyond their known hereditary roles." [3.14]

The total biology of an organism determines its behavior. The structure of genes determines the primary structure of proteins which, in turn, build tissues, which build organs, which, together, build the structure of an organism. The organism interacts with itself, its environment and its fellow creatures—it behaves. The whole process appears complex because it *is* complex: there are many interacting variables. An individual, at the least, is an enormous complex of structures that act and interact. Individuals are really a consortium.

The dashed lines in Figure 2 indicate principal pathways of interactions that can affect materially either structure or behavior. Shown greatly simplified, the sum of this whole is deterministic and continually dynamic, but neither simplistic nor reductionistic. The environment, the interacting structures (from genes to organism), and organism's behavior change through time together, sometimes changing rapidly, sometimes slowly, and sometimes barely changing at all. Given changes that are inheritable, such as a change in the frequency of genes in the species, evolution occurs.

Although the genes themselves are many levels removed from your behavior, they are directly affected by your behavior. If you behave maladaptively and fail to reproduce successfully, your genes follow you to your grave and disappear from the playing field of life. On the other hand, if your genes have built a strong competitor in love and romance, you might reproduce exceedingly well. In the next generation, the genes that made you will increase in number (long after you are gone and perhaps forgotten).

The fate of genes depends upon the behavior of the creatures they construct. Through billions of years of evolution, genes have built us to exhibit successful behavior. Sets of genes that built unsuccessful competitors are as dead and gone as the unsuccessful creatures they constructed.

Behavior above the level of a simple reflex is governed by an enormous knot of nerves we call a brain. Genes are ultimately responsible for the brain's construction. The basic components of the brain are wired in place through the action of hundreds, perhaps thousands of genes. The limitations and possibilities of our behavior are to be found in that basic, gene-controlled blueprint. Yet, the brain is shaped—fine-tuned, if you will—by experience. It is a biochemical computer whose basic circuit boards are in place at our birth, but whose detailed wiring is revamped time and again by the experiences of our life.[3.15]

Perhaps the best example of how tightly or loosely genes control our behavior can be seen through a unique human behavioral trait, language. Although most creatures communicate with one another through vocalizations, only humans do so using language. Language is a specialized form of communication that, among other things, uses skills found in our ancestral species and adds one or two skills unique to our species. For example, some of our primate relatives utter unique sounds that stand for unique objects in their environment (words of a sort), but only we can string together and recombine sounds to form arbitrarily variable words and sentences. That vocal legerdemain is made possible by unique wiring in our brain—wiring that is laid down before birth by our genes.

Crucial differences between linguistic and non-linguistic communication were first pointed out by Hockett and Ascher almost thirty years ago.[3.16] Humans alone, they concluded, are capable of inventing an almost limitless number of unique words. We alone can agree on the meaning of an utterance (or a symbol); words are arbitrary, often symbolic, constructs. Our near relatives, the Great Apes (chimpanzees, gorillas, and orangutans), are capable of learning to use and even manipulate human language symbols. Yet, no animal save us invented and used naturally a primarily symbolic communicative system.

Experimental work continues to discover the limits of language learning by our near relatives. This work has a long and contentious history within primatology, dating to the captive chimpanzee studies performed by Russian Nadia Kohts in the 1920s. Today, apes communicate symbolically with computers and use sign language to communicate with people. Investigators have found that apes can interpret sentences with several phrases, use insults, lie, joke, and communicate new information. Interesting though these results are, they are not to be unexpected of animals that share more than nine-tenths of their genes with humans. The fact remains: under natural conditions, only humans create and habitually use language.

At birth, we humans and we alone are biologically predisposed to learn a language. But which one? Here, the postnatal environment—our culture—determines which language we will eventually speak. In turn, the language we learn will affect the circuits in our brain. How we think, what thoughts we can and will harbor, are constrained by our language and its effect of fine-tuning the circuitry of our brain. [3.17]

Both genes and the environment are responsible for our behavior. One does not exist without the other; they are inextricably intertwined. This fact allows us to ignore comfortably one of humankind's most ancient and troubling riddles: are we a product of nature (our genes) or of nurture (the environment)? The riddle has surfaced in many forms: "instinct versus learning," "inheritance versus environment," and "mind versus body." All these unresolved dichotomies, while sterling questions for cocktail party debates, are essentially moot. They are straw man arguments because the juxtapositions of words such as "nature versus nurture" implies a contrast of discrete, mutually exclusive categories which are neither discrete nor mutually exclusive. The total biology of an organism determines its behavior; genes are but one part of an organism's biology.

Behavior, then, can be productively thought of as a tendency to act that is shaped by genetically-programmed structures in the presence of particular external conditions. In our example, the ability to invent and learn language is a behavioral predisposition unique to our species. Linguistic behavior involves and requires both genetically-determined structures in the brain and social learning. It is pointless to argue whether biology (hard-and-fast neural wiring) or learning (in the human context, culture) is more important, since both are required and necessary for the expression of this behavior. Indeed, learning is nothing more than loading the brain with external information that the brain has been structured by evolution to seek and to accept. Ultimately, what we *can* learn is genetically determined; of that, what we *will* learn is environmentally defined.

The term instinct, as used in popular parlance, usually refers to a behavior strictly produced by the genes. We can see now that this concept is an incorrect holdover from the centuries-old nature versus nurture debate. Genes produce (code for) protein molecules—period. Proteins help build larger structures, such as organs, muscles, and bones. Larger structures, acting in concert and under the guidance of other, larger structures (nerve nets, brains), produce the actions we call behavior. *All* behavior is a product of genes only in this roundabout, ultimate sense.

The question of nature versus nurture, instinct versus learning, is largely an unproductive pursuit. All behavior is a product of both structural adaptations (anatomy, hence, nature) and learning (nurture). Nature and nurture, biology and culture, are inseparable, co-evolved components of every human behavior. The distinction blurs further when we examine the neural basis for behavior.

How Does a Mind Evolve?

At the core of understanding behavior is our rapidly-increasing understanding of the brain. The brain is our most important sex organ; it is the arbitrator of all disputes and the creator of all social relationships. It is at the heart of our romantic feelings and our concepts of love. Darwin determined that the mind was a product of the brain and the brain is a product of natural selection. The latest Darwinian thinking on the relationship of mind to brain is fascinating and instructive.

Nobel laureate Gerald Edelman proposed that the mind itself is the site of an ongoing struggle of natural selection.[3.18] Groups of nerve cells organize, correct, and adjust themselves as a result of interacting with the environment. Those clumps of cells that best serve the success of the whole organism survive, gain strength, and are passed on to the next generation. Memories that reside in these clumps of cells are continually reworked and recast. For Edelman, each of us harbors a struggle for the existence of brain cells with each thought that flashes between our ears.

MIT's Marvin Minsky views these clumps of nerve cells as unthinking, unintelligent units—a bunch of tiny machines that work together as a "society."[3.19] From this society's efforts, the emergent phenomenon of the mind produces what we recognize as intelligent behavior. Emergent properties, sometimes called epiphenomena (literally, "above that which is showing"), are constructions that are revealed only when we stand back and view a larger picture; the individual brush strokes tell us little about the picture. Emergent properties are like a "discovered check" in the game of chess. Their discovery is extremely satisfying to a scientist (it is claimed apocryphally, that, upon the revelation, the scientist exclaims "aha!"). The whole of the mind is necessarily greater than a mere sum of brain parts.

The brain's parts consist of anatomical structures—knots of nerve cells—that function biochemically. What you learn, what you perceive, what you ignore, what you know, what you feel, and how you behave is determined entirely within this structure of your brain. In turn, the structure of your brain, its basic architecture, has been determined by the course of millions of years of primate evolution.

The brain and its attendant mind is our own personal computer, designed and manufactured by millions of years of reproductive success and historical accidents. The brain is a patchwork of superimposed nerve cell clumps that have evolved at different times in our evolution and for different reasons. This fact was pointed out most eloquently by Paul D. MacLean of the National Institutes of Mental Health and James W. Papez. Their theory of brain evolution became known popularly as the Triune Brain.

The structure of our deep, inner brain first appeared more than 300 million years ago in primitive reptiles. Today, it governs vegetative functions like breathing and our immediate responses to pain. Later, when the

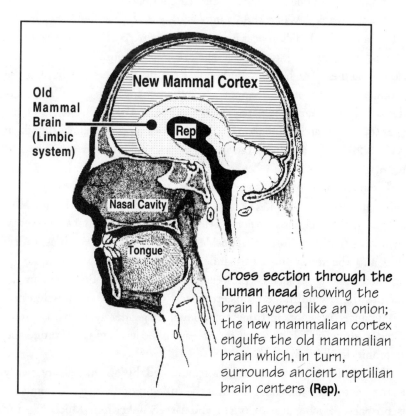

Old Mammal Brain (Limbic system)

New Mammal Cortex

Rep

Nasal Cavity

Tongue

Cross section through the human head showing the brain layered like an onion; the new mammalian cortex engulfs the old mammalian brain which, in turn, surrounds ancient reptilian brain centers **(Rep).**

first mammals appeared more than 200 million years ago, a layer of nerves capped this reptilian brain. Today, this cap (called the limbic system) lies in the middle of our own brain. It serves to relay messages from our senses, to process memories, and to initiate our emotions. Finally, about 65 million years ago, a new mammalian brain appeared wrapped around the old mammalian limbic system. This new cortex, as it is called, governs our higher thought processes, our ability to think and create metaphors and world views. The new cortex is a thinking cap of integrated nerve cells.

The human brain, clumped together like the layers of an onion through the fits and starts of major evolutionary change, isn't by any means a perfect or optimal design. Nonetheless, it works marvelously well. The brain, replete with its checkered, patched-together past, is the omnipotent controller of all human behavior. To paraphrase the allegorical words of psychologist Paul MacLean: when we fall in love, we are summoning a dinosaur (the reptilian brain), a shrew (the limbic system), and a primate (the new cortex). While the example presented here highlights major, crude, almost 100-million-year jumps in the brain's evolution, in reality the fits and starts of evolutionary change are much more subtle, and much closer together. The human mind could be productively thought of as the product of these major changes and other changes that we will chart through lemurs (approximately 54 million years Before Present), lemur-apes (approximately 24 million years B.P.), apes (approximately 20 million years B.P.), early hominids (approximately 4 million years B.P.), and so forth.

The many parts of our triune brain communicate well with one another, although conflicts can and do arise. Besides communicative wiring (called neurons), these clumps of nerve cells are awash in hormonal messages. Behaviors that were formerly considered strictly cultural (such as leadership and the quest for status and dominance) are now known to be organized and controlled by periodic floods of brain-produced chemicals, such as the sex hormone testosterone and the neurohormone serotonin. Dominance behavior, just one component of gender relations, is predicated in submissive individuals by increasing the levels of testosterone and serotonin in the brain.[3.20]

The particular dominance rituals exhibited by an animal are partly learned anew by each youngster, but the strength of the drive to dominate is probably biochemical in origin and largely inherited. Much like the imperative of dominance, gender differences in behavior originate in a biochemical computer shaped by literally tens of millions of years of selection and accidents.

As the many genes that control the primary circuitry of the brain change in frequency through time, the brain's structure evolves. Consequentially, the behavioral limitations and possibilities of the brain evolve. To understand present-day relationships, it is utterly essential to follow their long evolutionary history. Evolutionary psychology charts social evolution through millions of years of our history.

Charting Behavior through Time

Not long ago, the notion that we could describe the evolution of behavior was viewed with some scorn in both scholarly and public circles. The new synthesis of human social behavior is an historical reconstruction—an evolutionary story—and, as such, we can anticipate that it might be viewed with more skepticism than other tested hypotheses or accepted theories. No apologies are necessary:

> We are trained to think that "hard science" models of quantification, experimentation, and replication are inherently superior . . . so that any other set of techniques can only pale by comparison. But, historical science proceeds by reconstructing a set of contingent events, explaining in retrospect what could not have been predicted beforehand. If the evidence be sufficient, the explanation can be as rigorous and confident as anything done in the realm of experimental science. In any case, this is the way the world works; no apologies needed.
>
> STEPHEN JAY GOULD, 1991[3.21]

Evolutionary explanations about behavior are subject to tests of logic. They are extrapolations based upon two kinds of evidence: (1) a detailed evolutionary history (called a phylogeny—a tree of evolutionary relationships resembles, naturally enough, a branching tree), and (2) living models of extinct ancestral species. The living models are chosen because they represent a genetic continuum from an ancestral species and they are similar in both anatomical structure and habitat choice to the ancestral species. We are fortunate that the human order, the Order Primates, has a richly detailed fossil history and an abundance of living descendants worldwide.

One accepted method for determining the course of behavioral evolution was first described almost four decades ago by Nobel laureates Konrad Lorenz, Karl von Frisch, and Niko Tinbergen. It has proven invaluable. The aim of their technique is to identify behavioral homologies—patterns of behavior whose roots most likely date back to the behavior of an ancestral species.

Some scholars claim that behavioral analogies are unknowable because a given behavior might be the result of its inheritance or might have arisen *de novo* in a living species. Similarities of the behavior exhibited by the living species may be due to similar ecological pressures or similar genetic programming (*e.g.,* a shared instinct or taxis). At first glance, this would seem to present a serious stumbling block to interpreting behavioral evolution. After all, if the behavior in question is caused entirely by the environment, then it hardly reflects inherited patterns of action.

Stephen Jay Gould, a paleontologist, was fond of leveling this sort of criticism against what he viewed as "pop ethologists." Of course, an ethologist can level the same charge against paleontological explanations. That is, a particular fossil may have been genetically related to a particular living species or it may not. The argumentation on both sides of the debate is sophisticated (at least it employs sophisticated polysyllabic rhetoric), but unproductive.

Fossils exhibit no behavior whatsoever, so the identification of homologies requires cautious and clever detective work. First, a credible evolutionary history of ancestral fossils and living, descendant species is presented. Ideally, two sorts of evidence are used to reconstruct this evolutionary history. The best evidence is obtained by comparing details of the anatomy: the bones of the fossils and the bones of living specimens. Another line of evidence is obtained by comparing the many soft parts (organs, tissues) of the anatomy of living species with each other. Yet another line of evidence can be obtained by comparing the anatomy of some of the molecules (most often blood protein molecules such as hemoglobin or albumin) of the living species.

For three decades, a debate has raged within biology over the value of molecular data versus traditional anatomical and fossil bone data for the reconstruction of human evolutionary history. [3.22] The essence of the debate hinges on three endlessly arguable points. First, we can't tell for certain whether one set of fossil bones represents an ancestral type of any other set of fossil bones. Yet, if we accept one species as ancestral and another species as descendant, then, through dating the geological strata in which they were found, we can tell almost exactly how long it's been since the two species separated. Second, we can tell exactly how similar or different one molecule is in one species compared to the same molecule in another species, but this does not tell us how long it has been since they shared a common ancestor. Third, molecules may be similar to one another but unrelated genetically (this is called convergent evolution), and bones or soft tissues of different species may be similar to one another due to convergent evolution.

In short, both lines of anatomical evidence share similar faults. Nonetheless, taken together, the different lines of evidence tally a powerful, independent argument for evolutionary relationships. In all cases, the final evolutionary tree is always an hypothesis—a best guess—and a judgment call on the part of the scientist. In the best case, a tree of evolutionary relationships can then be drawn that accounts for the best fit of these several lines of evidence.

Once we have presented our best guess about the evolution of a lineage of animals (such as our lineage, the Order Primates), we can study the behavior of the living species in detail. In a hypothetical case diagrammed in Figure 4, the evolutionary history of three living species has been determined from the fossil record. The three living species, "A," "B," and "C," have been studied and their behaviors, which we will call numbers "1," "2," "3," and "4," described.

To make these numbers more real, you can think of behavior number 1 as "grasping," behavior number 2 as "balancing an object in the hand," behavior number 3 as "swinging the object at the end of the hand," and behavior number 4 as "hitting another object with the object being swung by the hand." [3.23] These behaviors form component parts of a pattern of behavior. Species "A" exhibits only components "1" and "2" while Species "C" shows an elaborate pattern of behavior which includes all the component parts:

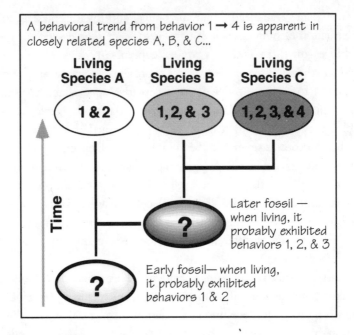

A behavioral trend from behavior 1 → 4 is apparent in closely related species A, B, & C...

Living Species A   **Living Species B**   **Living Species C**

1 & 2   1, 2, & 3   1, 2, 3, & 4

Time

? Later fossil — when living, it probably exhibited behaviors 1, 2, & 3

? Early fossil— when living, it probably exhibited behaviors 1 & 2

We can now infer the probable behavior of the ancestral species. The early fossil, ancestral to all three living species, probably exhibited behaviors "1" and "2": it could grasp an object and balance it in its hand. Its extinct descendant, the later fossil, inherited not only behaviors "1" and "2," but also acquired behavior "3": it could grasp, balance, and swing an object. Living species "C" has a recently evolved behavior, number "4." We say that behavior "1" → "4" represents an evolutionary trend. Species "C" can grasp, balance, and swing an object at yet another object. Species "C" can play baseball.

The behaviors at each point along the path of this trend were adaptive. The ancestral species were not trying to play baseball. Each was presumably quite successful without playing the game. But Species C *can* play baseball—and that behavioral ability represents what is called an emergent property of the trend.

Of course, the behavior of extinct ancestors can never be proven beyond a doubt. But science does not work by proving anything. Instead, all science is based upon testing statements logically. Scientific statements are called hypotheses. Hence science is hypothetico-deductive—we deduce theories from the tests of statements about the world. The first rule of a theorization is that the explanation presented must be the simplest one consistent with the facts at hand—in this case, consistent with both the fossil record and with the behavior of living species.

Our Evolutionary Past Determines Our Present

We know that what happened in the past in the evolution of a lineage can profoundly affect what will happen in the future. Traits acquired in the past may have a profound impact upon the possible range of traits seen today. This non-independence of traits is a great aid in the reconstruction of the history of behavior. For example, assume that ancestral species "A" acquires a particular adaptation out of a nearly infinite range of possible adaptations. For the sake of argument, we'll call this behavioral adaptation number "45."

If the behavioral adaptation, "Behavior 45," acquired by ancestral species "A" had no effect on the possible behavioral adaptations of its descendant species "B" and "C," then the reconstruction of the evolution of behavior would prove difficult or impossible. Each descendant species would merely choose its behavior from an almost infinite range of possibilities. The course of behavioral evolution would be a nearly indecipherable, random walk through time:

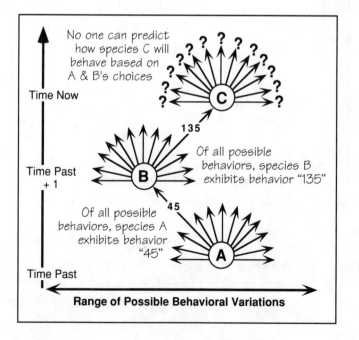

In this example, the behavioral choices made by species "A" had no impact on the behavioral choices open to species "B." The choice of behavior "135" by ancestral species can tell us nothing about what behavior its descendant, species "C," will display, and so forth.

Fortunately, for most behavioral (and physiological and anatomical) traits, descendant species "B" and "C" will not have a nearly infinite range of possible adaptive choices open to them. The choice of adaptation number "45" by Species "A" will limit, in predictable ways, the evolutionary choices available to its descendants. Technically, we do not predict the course of past evolutionary change. A better word might be "postdict," a term proposed by Stephen Jay Gould which means that an evolutionary history is *a posteriori* deduced. Hindsight is the only vision in paleontology:

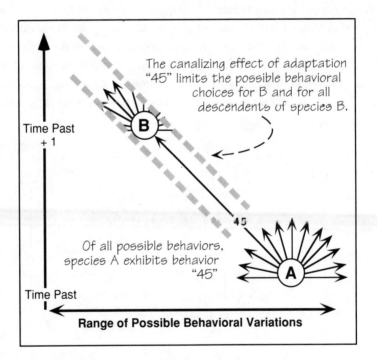

The canalizing effect of adaptation "45" limits the possible behavioral choices for B and for all descendents of species B.

Time Past + 1

Of all possible behaviors, species A exhibits behavior "45"

Time Past

Range of Possible Behavioral Variations

Here, the adaptation of "Behavior 45" by ancestral species "A" limits—*canalizes*—the range of possible behavioral adaptations for its descendant species, "B." Canalization is the observation that each change that occurs to a species tends to narrow (or, less often, enhance) the choices and opportunities available to its descendants. The art or detective work of reconstructing the evolution of behavior largely depends upon correctly identifying which adaptations canalize behavior and the exact nature of the limitations imposed.

An example serves to further illustrate this point. Two hundred million years ago, the placental mammals (from which we are descended) were locked into a particular, specialized reproductive adaptation that involved a suite of anatomical, physiological, and behavioral adaptations. Among these adaptations were the development of an embryo within the body of its mother and the post-birth feeding of the infant by the mother's mammillary glands. As a consequence of this initial adaptation, the first bonding and socialization of a placental mammal infant is necessarily limited to its mother. Giving birth to an infant and maternal nursing canalizes—requires—that the infant's first exposure to the behavior of its species must be provided by the mother.

In contrast, birds adapted (actually, continued the adaptations of their dinosaur antecedents) egg-laying and two-parent investment in fledgling care. In the eyes of the fledgling bird, the first sight of a member of its species need not be the sight of its mother. For birds, the first bonding experience and subsequent infant socialization can be via either the mother, the father, or, commonly, both the mother and father. Birds and placental mammals (like us) begin their lives with an altogether different perspective.

Now we can better appreciate why tracing the evolutionary history of social relationships is crucial: what happened in our evolutionary past has constrained and predestined, in measurable ways, what our behavior is today. Behavior does not rise anew in each of us or, for that matter, in our species. The shape of contemporary human relationships has a history. Gender differences in aggression and social bonding have a history. What we do today is contingent in large measure on what our lineage did in the evolutionary past.[3.24] These old natural histories can hang like a flock of albatrosses around the necks of those who are ignorant of the past. Conversely, those who understand our evolutionary history can strengthen present weaknesses and take advantage of its past strengths.

Does Human Behavior Naturally Progress?

Just prior to Darwin's revelations about the nature of evolutionary change, the sciences grappled with a notion of progress called progressionism. Life on earth, it was believed, changed through time; as world conditions changed, a new round of creation would bring forth ever more perfect species. Life could be arranged on a *Scala Naturæ*—a ladderlike "scale of being," from pond scum at the base to man, just below the angels, at its pinnacle. Darwinian evolution, itself, was a concept that caught fire in the industrial Victorian Age—an age infected with an unabashed, nearly religious belief in the inevitability of progress. So perhaps it is inevitable that today, many people believe that evolution is some sort of progressive drive that creates ever more perfect, complex, well-adapted beings.

Nothing could be farther from reality.

Evolution creates change. Sometimes, species evolve from fairly simple forms to forms that display more complexity. Sometimes, species evolve from intricate forms to forms that display great simplicity. Sometimes, species just change. Consider, for example, that most multicelled animal parasites are little more than digestive and reproductive tracts attached to a mouth. These modern parasites evolved from more mobile, sensate, complex organisms.

If we survey a single, evolving lineage through time, we often see a trend. Antlers may appear larger in later forms than they did in their antecedents; a complex reproductive organ may appear simpler in descendants than in ancestors, etc. A trend is merely a direction that we perceive in hindsight. It is not a progression from something imperfect to something more perfect. Evolution isn't progress, it's history.

The direction we see in evolutionary history—the trend—is often caused by canalization. For instance, canalization often creates an extremely good fit between the shape of a bird's bill and the qualities of a bird's food. Yet, canalization does not insure survival. Often, canalization dooms an animal to extinction. When a particularly specialized bird's food source declines, so too does the bird's only chance for survival.

There is a humbling lesson here. Humans are not the end product, the high point, the perfection of some evolutionary plan or goal. Humans, like earthworms, robins, and everything else alive today, are merely one more generation of life form undergoing change through time.

Humankind's capacity to form social relationships is not necessarily greater or lesser than any other social creature's capacity. Our relationships are not necessarily more complex or less complex, kinder or gentler, kinkier or more conservative, better or worse, than the social interactions of other animals. We can say that our behavior is different in some ways from that of other animals, but we can find no perfection in our behavior and we should ascribe no inadequacy to theirs.

Most importantly, evolution offers us no assurances that today's gender relationships will be progressively more egalitarian or more satisfying in the future. Progress is strictly a human construction. If we want to progress from some allegedly lesser condition to some hoped-for better state, then we must thoughtfully engineer the change. Evolution has bequeathed us an awesome power to change our behavior, but only if we understand its animal roots.

PART II

The Animal Roots of Human Behavior

CHAPTER 4

Inequality in the Puddle
Where Sex Was Born

Tom is a handsome young man. He has been happily married to Leigh for almost four years. She is an easygoing, attractive, passionate, and faithful wife. They have a one-year-old son, and they have good relations with both sets of in-laws. They are prosperous and enjoy each other's company. Tom truly loves Leigh. Yet, Tom has had two extramarital affairs since their marriage began.

After his last affair, he promised a sobbing, confused Leigh that he'd join her in counseling. The counselor classified Tom's problem as Don Juanism, male hypersexuality attributable to a poor self-image. Tom, successful in his career and satisfied with his occasional trysts, was not impressed. Neither the therapist's label nor the discussions that followed appreciably affected Tom's behavior. Last week, secretly as always, Tom began to court yet another girlfriend.

Tom, like most men, is romantically attracted to more than one woman. Recent American surveys have shown that men have, on average, more than two sex partners after marriage. Tom and many other men are unknowingly fostering an ancient reproductive strategy, one that began in a puddle about one billion years ago. Tom is dancing to the ghosts of very ancient ancestors.

The Legacy of Sex

We begin our exploration of gender relations at a time long before we—or for that matter, sex—appeared on the earth. Although here I offer a straightforward, simplistic account of the origin and evolution of sex, the subject is actually complex. There are literally dozens of kinds of reproduction which are neither asexual nor fully sexual. The precise evolutionary route our ancestors took remains conjectural until the vertebrates—creatures with backbones—evolved. Even then, vertebrates display a remarkable range of reproductive capabilities. Some fish and reptiles are hermaphroditic (both genders alternate in the same individual); some reptiles and amphibians are capable of virgin birth (parthenogenesis). The subject is fascinating, though maybe difficult for the non-professional to decipher: most discussions of the issues are rife with tongue-twisting jargon.[4.1]

Caveats notwithstanding, the root of sex is the union of two unique individuals to produce yet a third. Surprisingly, most organisms that share the earth with us do not reproduce sexually. At life's origin, better than 3.5 billion years ago, a single-celled creature merely duplicated the genetic material within its cell, then the cell divided in two.[4.2] This method of reproducing a new generation was wildly successful, and we can see it today as the fast, efficient, asexual method of reproduction practiced by countless billions of bacteria, algae, and other single-celled inhabitants of seas, the atmosphere, ponds, and even our bodies. Barring the accident of mutation, each new cell reproduced asexually is a perfect clone of its parent. The abilities and limitations of the parent cell are continued in the new cell, and in the new cell's progeny, and so forth.

Asexually reproducing organisms are, in a sense, immortal. The parent cell's genetic material continues through time and the parent cell need never die. A parent cell merely divides in two periodically, filling the puddle with identical copies of itself. Barring the infrequent mutation of the genetic material itself, the species of clones will be frozen, invariant, duplicates through time: they cannot adapt easily to new environments.

About 900 million years ago, a mutation in a puddle-dwelling population of single-celled creatures introduced a radical new method of producing offspring. Instead of merely dividing in two, two different, individual cells joined briefly to share their genetic material before dividing. Any accidental, mutational differences between the two cells were now shared, and the new individuals they produced were a unique combination of genetic traits. This halfway measure between asexual and sexual reproduction soon gave rise to full-blown, sexual reproduction.

Mating and a Little Death

The sharing of genetic material gave rise to the production of germ cells of genetic material. Each parent cell produced a germ cell—a small cell containing half its own genetic material. The male germ cell is the sperm; the female's is the egg. These tiny packets were expelled from one parent to unite with a packet from the other parent. The united germ cells formed a single cell containing the genetic instructions from both parents for forming a completely new, unique individual.

After the germ cells combined, the parental cells were no longer necessary. They could then wear out and die. *Bona fide* sexual reproduction begat both aging and death—the end of immortality, the primal exit from the Garden of Eden.

Perhaps it is of some comfort to know that the adaptation that ushered the inevitability of death into the world endowed life with tremendous advantages. Sexual reproduction and its novel product—new generations of unique individuals—proved highly successful. This genetic variety was indeed the spice of life, because now, an entire species was composed of unique individuals. These individuals differed from one another in their abilities and their faults. Individual variation enabled species to survive almost any environmental catastrophe, and to colonize new puddles, new habitats.

The new populations in different puddles soon differed in characteristics as a group from the characteristics of their ancestors. The colonizers were subject to different selective pressures in life. For example, a puddle in a shadow differs in conditions of temperature and illumination from a puddle in the sun. Different sorts of individuals would survive in each puddle—new species evolved quickly.

The success of sexual reproduction is unequivocal. Complex, multicellular organisms may not have been possible without sexual reproduction. Sexual reproduction allows bits and pieces of genetic material to recombine in ways that cloning can not. Sexually reproducing organisms are constructed of shuffled modules of information. New arrangements of genetic modules can quickly produce new and complex structures—new species. [4.3] Insects, fish, reptiles, amphibians, birds, mammals, and most plants reproduce sexually. We share the planet with many complex, adaptable, gender-conscious, and mortal species who, like us, owe much of their form and behavior to sex.

The Sexes Were Not Created Equal

At first, there were no sexes *per se*. Cells that joined to share genetic material were nearly identical. Some could be distinguished only by the presence or absence of a particular gene. But, as multicelled organisms evolved, the product of mating (a single cell) required time and nutrients to develop into a many-celled adult. Gender evolved. One gender, the male, provided only a rudimentary gamete—a germ cell that contained half its creator's genetic complement. The other gender, the female, produced a gamete that contained not only half its genetic complement, but also an environment for the fertilized egg to grow—to divide into the many cells that would form an adult. Its gamete was necessarily larger, contained nutrients, and required more energy to produce. From that day forth, the females would bear the greatest energetic and temporal burden of reproduction.

Differences in the production of germ cells necessitated differences in the anatomy of males and females. This difference is called sexual dimorphism, literally "two forms of sexes." At first, these differences in form were small. But soon, different lineages of animals (and plants) specialized not only in the production of germ cells, but in reproduction tasks as well. In many lineages, females—who produced the large, relatively immobile germ egg—held the egg for fertilization. It was the task of the male to seek out this egg and fertilize it. After fertilization, the female held onto the fertilized egg as it became a developing embryo. Pregnancy and parenting had evolved, and the only pregnant parent was the female.

Fast forwarding through more than a billion years of evolution, we can profitably see the development of sexual dimorphism in a typical mammalian species—us. At conception and for the first seven weeks of our lives, male and female embryos are indistinguishable physically. Scientists call those first seven weeks of our embryonic lives the period of sexual undifferentiation. By the seventh week after conception, the first signs of sexual dimorphism appear.

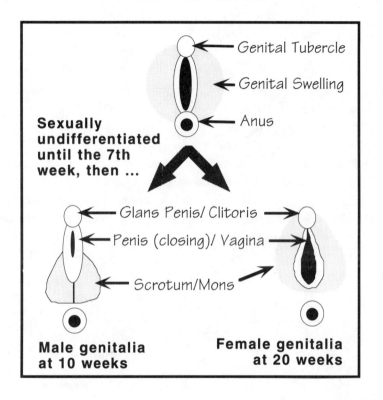

If the embryo will develop into a boy, the genital swelling enlarges, becoming a scrotal sack. Eventually the sack will receive the testes, the organs of sperm production that sink like two pearls from a position within the body. Tiny sperm with their high metabolic rate do not survive well at the normal human body temperature of 37°C. Their manufacture and storage in a sack outside the body allows the male greater fertility.

For a female embryo, there is no obvious change: the genital swelling persists (eventually it will become the region known as the pubic mons). Unlike the male, the female retains her egg-producing organs, the ovaries, fixed within her body.

By the tenth week after conception, a male penis is visible. The slit on its bottom surface closes slowly. At the tip of the penis, the genital tubercle becomes the sensitive glans penis—a direct homologue of the female's clitoris. In the female, the border of the primitive slit does not close over, nor does the region elongate into a penis. Instead, the slit remains open as the vagina; the lips bordering the vagina become the vulva.

From identical beginnings, males and females become different creatures. The crafters of these gross physical changes are minute chemicals known as hormones. For this task, the genes that predestine our gender build a remarkably simple and related set of hormones known as steroids. [4.4] One small detail must be mentioned here: not all steroids are hormones and not all hormones are steroids.

Steroidal androgens are responsible for maleness and steroidal estrogens for femaleness. Both androgens and estrogens start out in each of us as the chemical compound cholesterol. Our sex-determining genes instruct the chemical pathway to produce one or another hormone in abundance at precisely the right time in our development. In each of us, four hormones associated with gender differences develop from the precursor chemical, cholesterol.

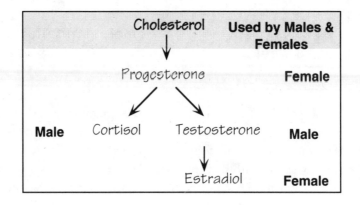

An increase in the production of embryonic testosterone during the seventh week after conception builds a boy. If no testosterone is present, the embryo will become a girl. Testosterone is performing an organizing function here, persuading cells to organize—to group together and grow into one form or another. Later, this same hormone performs an activating function, empowering the previously organized tissues into performing. Between the ages of 13 and 14 years, a spurt in the production of testosterone activates puberty in males. An elevation in the quantity of the estrogen estradiol at about 11 or 12 years initiates puberty in girls.

The profound differences between a man and a woman are initiated by molecules that differ only by a few atoms. Overall, they are remarkably similar chemicals: the chemical composition of testosterone is 19 carbon atoms, 28 hydrogen atoms, and two oxygen atoms; estradiol lacks only one carbon and three hydrogen atoms. "It is," as Oxford biochemist Peter W. Atkins says, "extraordinary what difference an extra —CH₃ group and a slight rearrangement of a ring of atoms can make":[4.5]

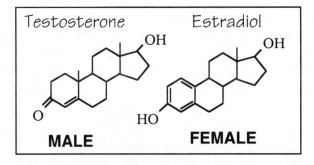

The bodily differences between a man and a woman exceed primary characters, like the penis versus the clitoris, and the commonly observed secondary sexual characteristics of body fat, musculature, and facial hair. Men and women age differently and suffer gender-specific or gender-enhanced diseases. Both our forms and our physiologies differ. As adults, men and women appear so different that if a hypothetical Martian biologist were to visit Earth, it might conclude erroneously that men and women were two different species—unless, of course, the Martian observed our prodigious and oft-practiced mating capability.

Androgens and estrogens have effects on us far beyond their primary role in creating the bodily sexual features of infants and pubescents. The sex hormones are the most important chemical in our romantic lives because they provoke, in a nearly direct fashion, differences in the behavior and goals of men and women. The influence of testosterone on the fetal brain leads to measurable differences in the brain's structure and function between men and women.

Men and women show structural differences in the parts of the brain that govern emotions and the relay of information within the brain. Technically, we have found significant sexual dimorphism in the corpus callosum (a band of neurons that shuttles information between the left brain and the right), the nucleus of the pre-optic area, and the hypothalamus (crucial regions for emotion and visceral reactions like temperature regulation). Even the structure of certain neurons differs between the sexes, although we do not know what that bodes for behavioral differences yet. [4.6]

Men and women have measurable differences in the size and configuration of their new cortex—the large thinking cap that so distinguishes humans from most other animals. These cerebral hemispheres—which together resemble a gigantic, fleshy-grey walnut—differ both in absolute size and in lateralization (the difference in size and function of the right and left hemispheres). [4.7] Men have an enlarged right hemisphere which governs spatial, three-dimensional thinking and the understanding of facial expressions. In women, the left hemisphere that governs language skills is nearly equal in size with their right hemisphere.

Men and women think with different brains that are internally influenced by different chemicals. For example, a flood of testosterone leads to male-male aggression; an absence of this tidal flow allows cooperative play in girls. Studies of childhood gender differences in behavior are subject to many observational criticisms and are admittedly controversial. [4.8] Nonetheless, many studies have reached conclusions similar to the pioneering study offered by social psychologists Eleanor E. Maccoby and Carol N. Jacklin: [4.9]

- Boys are more aggressive than girls.
- Boys have greater mathematical abilities than girls.
- Girls have greater verbal ability than boys.
- Boys have better visual-spatial abilities than girls.

Neurologist Doreen Kimura states that ". . . the effects of sex hormones on brain organization occur so early in life that from the start the environment is acting upon differently wired brains in girls and boys." She notes that the gender differences in behavior lie in "patterns of ability." Girls are not smarter nor dumber than boys, just different in predictable ways.[4.10]

The current tally of gender differences is not all-inclusive. The more that scientists learn about the biology of gender, the more they discover about biologically-based behavior differences. For example, one day hormone-induced behavioral differences may help explain broad, global gender differences in adult careers, perceptions, and lifestyles.[4.11] Most of these gender behavioral differences may be ascribed to the action of a single gender-specifying hormone, male testosterone.

Testosterone produces an increase in aggression overall. This, in turn, may lead to selection favoring brain structures (wiring) that enhance rapid, three-dimensional target analysis, *i.e.,* "If I attack him there, where and when will I have to duck?" Women, not influenced by testosterone, perform better than men on problem-solving tasks that require precision matching and fine motor skills—tasks important to a patient and persistent ancestral primate mother's ability to pick nutritive food for its family. It is reasonable to suggest that many other adaptive gender differences in behavior may follow the initial effect of differences in gender-producing, gender-sustaining hormones.

Yet merely stating that girls, in general, have a greater verbal ability than boys does not mean that some boys will not have consummate verbal skills—especially in our society, where verbal aggression has been developed into a fine art. Conversely, some girls become mathematicians like Lady Lovelace[4.12] or aggressive leaders like Margaret Thatcher.

Girls are not unaggressive. Under particular cultural conditions, girls will engage in violent behavior and acts of covert aggression. According to anthropologist Carol Lauer, Israeli girls average fewer fights than Israeli boys, but they initiate fights more frequently than do American boys. Lauer attributes the heightened aggression of Israelis of both sexes to the consequences of living in a constant state of preparation for war. Anthropologist Laura L. Cummings found that in adolescent, working-class gangs in Chihuahua, Mexico, female gang members often fight female gang members from neighboring gangs and join male gang members in their fights.

In Finland, women have long held positions of power and influence within society. They use physical or verbal aggression less frequently then Finnish boys. Yet, according to anthropologist Kaj Björkqvist, if gossiping, breaking confidences, writing nasty notes about others, and manipulating others to do one's dirty work count as aggressive acts, then Finnish teenage girls are as aggressive overall as their male counterparts. Human aggression takes many forms. [4.13] Hormones create a mental bias, not a mental strait-jacket. Hormones initiate gender differences, with a cascading effect that touches each of us personally from our cradle to our grave.

"We Know What We Are, But Know Not What We May Be": Gender Ambiguity [4.14]

Sex hormones bias our embryonic form to become masculine or feminine. The presence of androgens biases the brain toward masculine patterns of thought; in their absence, the brain is biased toward feminine patterns of thought. Yet, it is too strong a statement that genetically-induced hor-mones absolutely and unequivocally determine our gender.

Our different primary sex organs start out with the exact same anatomi-cal features. There is a fundamental structural kinship between the sexes. If this seems difficult to fathom, consider the male nipple. Functionally, it is of little use in men (although it can be an erogenous zone). The nipple shows our embryonic kinship. It also shows that evolution does not elimi-nate so-called "useless" structures if such elimination would cost more than would be gained by simply ignoring the structure. The male nipple is neutral in respect to natural selection: it causes neither reproductive advantage nor reproductive disadvantage.

The hormones that make us men or women share a common assembly line. Both male hormones and female hormones are present in each of us. Under normal circumstances, a man produces more androgens than a woman and a man has androgen receptors in appropriate target organs (for example, in the brain, in the gonads, and the adrenal gland). Similarly, under normal circumstances, a woman produces more estrogens than a man and a woman has estrogen/progesterone receptors in appropriate target organs. Nevertheless, none of us are, strictly speaking, one hundred percent male or one hundred percent female. From conception onwards, each individual's gender is a strong probability, not an absolute certainty.

Disturbances in the production and availability of hormones may ac-count for much human behavior, especially behavior sometimes termed aberrant. A detailed account of such errors in metabolism is beyond the scope of this book. Suffice it to note, however, that an androgen that isn't present (or isn't properly received by a cell receptor) at a crucial time in development may lead to feminization of both form and behavior in a man. [4.15]

Neuroresearcher Simon LeVay of the Salk Institute has recently shown that a minuscule region of the brain that seems to control much human sexual activity is twice as large in heterosexual males as in homosexual males. [4.16] Similarly, this brain region is twice as large in heterosexual males as in heterosexual females. This possible structural cause for male sexual orientation may well have its origins in the quantity of testosterone present in the brain at a crucial stage of fetal development. Conversely, an abundance of an androgen at the wrong time and place can produce a masculinized woman. Recent heritability studies by psychologists Richard C. Pillard and J. Michael Bailey suggest that several genes may influence sexual orientation in women; the identity of those genes and their effect on the brain remain unknown. [4.17]

To make matters more complex, the flow of sex hormones is not constant throughout our adult lives. Human males tend to produce a high level of testosterone from puberty to almost sixty years of age; human females show a steady decline of estradiol after age thirty. [4.18] Perhaps the best known examples to date of normal swings in sex hormone balance that produce dramatic swings in behavior are the dreaded Premenstrual Syndrome (PMS) and menopause. What effect the diminution of testosterone has on the aging male is unknown, but a yet uncharacterized behavioral shift similar to menopause is likely.

It is possible (though not tested) that subtle, sub-optimal deviations in the production of and/or sensitivity to sex hormones may affect us all at one time or another. We may all endure small, barely perceptible behavioral swings like a sandstone beach that gradually changes from the waves gently lapping its shore.

With such biological ambiguity built into our gender, it is not surprising that many of us experience some difficulty in gender identity at one time or another. Our new brain cortex—enormous for an animal our size—introduces additional ambiguities. To some extent, each of us can learn to identify with our opposite gender; we can act out or temporarily assume the role of our opposite sex. Humans are not necessarily locked into a single gender role.

Finally, culture—a society's collective social experience—can create, favor, or castigate gender-specific behavior. For example, in most Latin American societies, the machismo ethic rules nearly absolute. Yet in trendy parts of other societies, androgyny (the unisex or generic person style) is in vogue. Many Western entertainment icons exhibit public sexual ambivalence: Liberace, David Bowie, Boy George, George Michael, Michael Jackson, Prince, Grace Jones, k. d. lang, and Madonna, to name but a few.

> At the Century's beginning, Virginia Woolf believed that everyone is partly male and partly female. She saw the mind as a taxi that could be boarded by a man or a woman, with the male brain predominating in men and the female in women. [4.19]

For most of us, that taxi travels a direction due opposite that of our mates (most of the time). The route we all must travel is not without curves and bumps.

Competitors in Love

Sexual reproduction carries many problems unknown to the earliest, asexual life-forms. The most obvious and persistently vexing problem is getting two individuals to join to share genetic material—two individuals who, moments before sexual union, may have been competing with each other for food or other resources essential to their own survival.

The problems of courtship and mating have been solved many different ways by the hundreds of thousands of species that reproduce sexually. For our species, the most sought-after form of courtship and mating ritual is called romantic love. It is a courtship still attached but far removed in time from the puddle where sexual reproduction was born.

At the outset of sexual reproduction, it was clear that each gender had to conquer different limitations to maximize their own reproduction. Each gender evolved its own reproductive strategy. The male need only produce minute sperm cells, each designed like a biotic, target-seeking missile. The female must produce a larger, nutrient-rich, more energetically-costly egg. A male could produce millions of sperm at roughly the same energy cost at which a female could produce a single egg. A human female can produce no more than a few dozen offspring; a man can potentially place his genes in thousands of progeny.

According to the tenets of natural selection theory, each individual will strive to achieve its maximum fitness, that is, its highest possible reproductive rate. For males, the optimal reproductive strategy is to contribute its abundant, easily-produced sperm to as many eggs as possible. For females, limited in the number of eggs they can produce, the best reproductive strategy is to insure the survival of their fertilized eggs. The gender reproductive game is decidedly unbalanced.

Simply put, the Darwinian game for males is to fertilize as many females as possible. The game for females is to insure the quality and survival of their precious embryos. There is little doubt that this basic, ancient calculus governs much of human romance. [4.20] In part, it accounts for the importance of male hypersexuality and sexual aggressiveness—in one subtle form or another, universal human behavioral traits.

Unbalanced reproductive strategies also account for differences in the way men and women fall in love. In a crude sense, men are predators, seeking to fertilize any and every egg possible. Men must gain access to as many females as possible. Men must pursue their "prey." Men must fall in love easily, often, and with conviction—with sufficient drive to pursue the object of their affections. That pursuit can be rigorous indeed. Potentially each male in a society must compete with every other male to impregnate a female. In a hypothetical social group of just three males and three females, a male who chooses to impregnate all three females must win their affections and block access to the females by the rival males.

Women, though, are by no means passive prey. Their optimal reproductive strategy is to chose the best possible male to contribute his genes to her egg. After all, unlike the male, the female's reproductive capabilities are limited. The female must secure its genes in the best possible package for the future. In most cases, it is the female who chooses the male. Females can aggressively pursue males and often do. Mate selection need not be passive, although females rarely rape males. Ultimately, it is the female who either permits copulation or protests it.

Mate selection, in fact, plays the greatest role in shaping romantic love. Females seek stability in romance and a high-quality partner for love. In many species, a single female cannot care for her growing offspring alone.

In these species, a female seeks a mate who will remain with her to care for the offspring. In such cases, the males of these species sacrifice quantity of impregnations to assure the survival of their genes.

The Puffery of the Sexes

Mate selection forces males to display their wares such that females can choose an appropriate mate. But what are these appropriate wares? How do females decide what is appropriate? How do males know what to display? Do the males display their best attributes only before, not necessarily after mating? How much of this is a conscious, planned, premeditated activity? How predetermined is the game of love?

Males, of course, also choose the females that they will pursue. What actually governs their choice? If natural selection governs our behavior, shouldn't all men behave like Tom, the adulterer whose story began this chapter? As one journalist put it crudely: shouldn't a male "try to make it with anything that moves"? Why is it that some men form long-lasting, truly monogamous bonds? Do human females value their offspring more than their mate? Are men inherently romanticists and women essentially pragmatists?

These and other questions can be addressed only by a journey through our primate evolutionary past. A journey that reveals how natural selection and the vagaries of historical accidents have shaped the primitive reproductive strategies of the ancient puddle to conform to the complex societies of today. In the next chapter, we continue to trace the evolution of gender relationships with living mammals that serve as models for our behavioral evolution.

CHAPTER 5

Fossil Ancestors
and Living Models

The shallow seas of a billion years ago set the stage for many of the gender imbalances that perplex us today. For sexually reproducing species like us, the female must bear the primary burden of carrying a fertilized egg to term, giving birth, and nurturing the infant. Her potential reproductive capacity over her lifetime is distinctly limited relative to the male of the species. Every male can potentially impregnate many females, with little concern about the huge costs of reproduction that follow copulation.

While this unbalanced reproductive theme underscores almost all human gender relationships, it is by no means the entire symphony. The particular elements of human power, sex, and love that consistently harness our attention—romance, aggression, war, child rearing, fatherhood, monogamy, physical and sexual abuse (to name but a few)—developed full force only during the past sixty million years, the period of time that our order, the Order Primates, has evolved.

The Order Primates spans seven geological epochs in Earth history, from the Paleocene through the most recent division, the Holocene. Fortunately, we have a rich fossil history to chart the course of our evolution from primitive insectivorous mammals, through ancient lemurs (the first primates), extinct apes, and ape-men to modern humans.

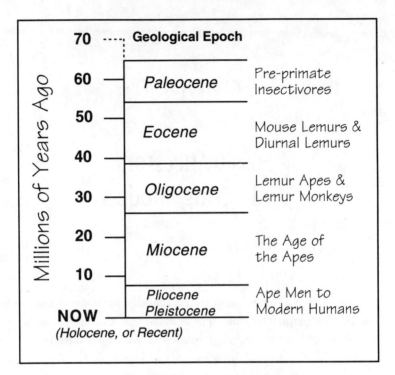

We also have a rich resource in the living relatives of the ancestral insectivores, lemurs, and apes. Some of these descendants can serve as models to help reconstruct the evolution of their extinct ancestor's behavior.

Snuffling in the Leaf Litter Where Our Ancestors Were Born

Seventy million years ago, before our ancient primate ancestors evolved, the earth was strangely different from the earth we see today. The last of the ruling reptiles, the magnificent dinosaurs, still filled the earth's habitats with their enormous presence. Their disappearance, over approximately a seven-million-year period at the end of the Cretaceous Period and the beginning of the Paleocene Epoch (66.5 million years B.P.), marks one of science's greatest mysteries.

Climates on the partially co-joined continents of the northern hemisphere were mild, not unlike the southern United States today. No present-day mammalian families had yet evolved, but many extinct mammalian groups predominated. Sheep-like grazing animals called condylarths roamed the fields. Five-foot-long (1.5-meter), small-brained creodonts, armed with a formidable battery of pointed teeth, were the predators of the age. The first true carnivore, the eight-inch-long (20-centimeter) *Miacus,* preyed upon bird's eggs and fruit—its descendants, the familiar dogs, cats, hyenas, seals, and bears of today, would not appear for more than a dozen million years. Ancestral marsupials were commonplace in this semi-tropical land. Multituberculates, curious rodent-like creatures with cheek teeth that resembled razor blades, filled many ecological niches. Everywhere, the high-pitched shrieks of primitive, insectivorous mammals gradually replaced the thunderous bellows of dinosaurs.

Some extinct insectivores, technically known by the tongue-bruising appellation "lepticid insectivores," led to many groups of contemporary mammals. Therein lies a problem: at this early time in mammalian evolution, the ancestors of rodents, hoofed mammals, bats, hedgehogs, and primates looked very much alike. The seventy-million-year-old fossil *Purgatorius* is a good candidate to represent the primitive insectivorous line that led to us. It weighed no more than three-quarters of an ounce (20 grams). Yet, we are not certain of *Purgatorius*'s evolutionary progeny. In most cases, only seemingly trivial differences in the pattern of bumps on the teeth separate the many fossil mammalian groups. Exactly which insectivore gave rise to which modern mammal group may never be deciphered to everyone's satisfaction.

No matter here. We can draw worthwhile inferences about the lifestyle of our primitive preprimate ancestor from comparisons with many modern, tiny mammals that must face similar challenges for food, thermoregulation, survival, and reproduction. The behavioral models here are drawn from studies of generalized, contemporary insectivores—species that belong to the Order Insectivora.

Today, the Order Insectivora is an enormous classificatory catchall.[5.1] Taxonomists—those biologists who attempt to reconstruct the evolutionary history of life—create a few classificatory boxes into which they can place troublesome fossil remains that don't seem to fit into other, pure classificatory boxes. The Order Insectivora is commonly called a wastebasket taxon because at least some species placed in it are there only because no one knows where else to put them. The Order Primates, in contrast, is a more or less pure, easily explained box.

The Order Insectivora contains familiar creatures like garden variety shrews, hedgehogs, and moles, as well as genuine evolutionary oddballs like the bizarre Caribbean solenodons and the diverse Malagasy tenrecs. Both these latter families of insectivores have retained many primitive, unspecialized features of anatomy and behavior. They are very useful for our reconstructions of behavior. Unfortunately, the solenodons have been seldom studied and are nearly extinct. The tenrecs are also threatened with extinction, but, fortunately, we have more information about them. [5.2] Isolated early on Madagascar, without competing mammal groups that evolved later elsewhere, tenrecs evolved into many convergent species that resemble shrews, moles, rodents, hedgehogs, and even otters.

Perhaps the best models for the behavior of the tiny, ancient insectivores can be found in our own backyards: shrews. [5.3] There are at least 246 species of living shrews distributed throughout North America, Central America, Europe, Africa, Asia, and northern South America. Where present, they are ubiquitous, with population densities exceeding thirteen per acre (more than five per hectare). Commonly, house cats bring shrews back to their owners, but, most often, shrews are mistaken for mice— although they clearly lack the buck-tooth incisors that characterize rodents.

We are not limited to insectivores when we choose models for ancient insectivores. We can glean much useful information from studies of tiny mammals not directly related to modern shrews and primates. Some of the tiny marsupials of Australia can offer instructive insights into the long-lost world of sixty-plus million years ago. The many striking behavioral and ecological similarities between these marsupials and placental mammals of similar size and habitats unmistakably point to the canalizing effect of natural selection. Much of their behavioral repertoire is convergent with unrelated placental insectivores. All tiny, terrestrial (ground-level-living) mammals can respond in only a few, limited ways to the uncompromising natural demands of temperature, vapor pressure (humidity), energetics (the high energy requirements of their small bodies), predation, and reproduction.

Further, their absolutely small brain mass affords the small mammal little chance to reason or devise options; their behavior, therefore, tends to be highly stereotypic. Scholars have argued for decades that intelligence—the ability to reason, to solve novel problems via analysis and planning—is a function of brain size and body size. We usually compare species' intellectual potential by standardizing their brain sizes—by dividing their brain mass by their body mass. That means that a tiny shrew, with its tiny brain, may have computing power equivalent to the enormous brain of a heavy dolphin. There is wisdom in this approach. A dolphin's brain must control far more tissue (muscles, organs, skin, etc.) than a shrew's brain.

Yet, our burgeoning knowledge about information theory and computer processing suggests that the bigger the processor and memory chips, the greater the computer's processing capability. The bigger the brain, the more potentially powerful it will be. As they say in automobile racing, there's no substitute for cubic inches. The emergent property of the primate brain that we call the human mind is probably a result of brain size crossing a threshold of absolute, not relative, size.

In a crude sense, then, all tiny-brained insectivores are miniature robots—furry microbots, if you will—programmed by both the on/off demands of their internal metabolism and by genetically-timed, environmentally influenced cycles of reproductive hormones. A small mammal's life consists of one reaction after another.

Unlike smaller mammals, larger mammals have many behavioral and physiological options available to them by the dint of their greater mass and larger brains. Selection of a proper model ancestor amongst the larger mammals requires somewhat greater care.

Climbing the Branches of the Tree Where Humanity Was Born

We humans are but one of about 150 species of primates alive today.[5.4] All living primate species can be pictured as the growing end buds on the branches of a vast tree. The tree is more than fifty-eight million years high. Scientists—paleontologists, zoologists, and physical anthropologists— have attempted to reconstruct the tree as best they can. The shape of some of the branches are difficult to discern; a consensus about exactly how the tree looks may never be possible. Even so, as we approach the twenty-first

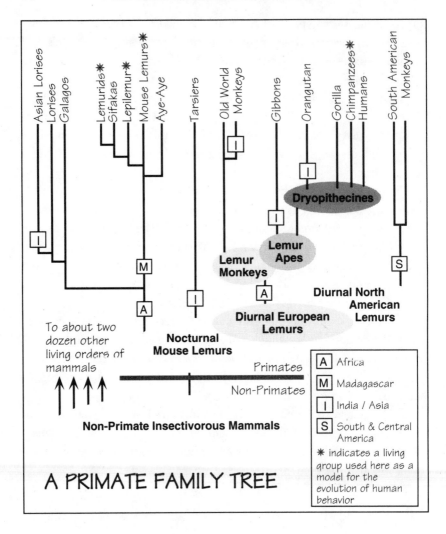

A PRIMATE FAMILY TREE

century, we can draw our ancestral tree in considerable, satisfying detail. We know that all living species are related to one another through extinct, common ancestors—the many forks in the evolutionary tree.

The modern Order Primates is divided into two suborders: the Prosimii (the prosimians, sometimes classified as strepsirhines) and the Suborder Anthropoidea (sometimes classified as haplorhines). Along with monkeys and apes, we belong to the Anthropoidea. All the anthropoids, though, are descended from certain extinct prosimians.

These first prosimians were the size of a field mouse. They possessed grasping hands and feet, and their fingers were tipped with nails and backed by finger pads that bore distinctive fingerprints, much like our own. Their face was far from rodent-like: their snouts were small, and their eyes faced forward, also much like our own.

Fossils of the first prosimians are rare. Tiny bones of bush-living mammals rarely survive long enough to fossilize under rain forest conditions. Among the earliest specimens known is *Shoshonius cooperi.* Skulls of this tiny, fifty-million-year-old primate were excavated from 1984 to 1987 in Wyoming and described in the British journal *Nature* in January, 1991, by paleontologists K. Christopher Beard and Leonard Krishtalka of the Carnegie Museum, Pittsburgh, and Richard K. Stucky of the Denver Museum of Natural History. [5.5]

Our earliest primate ancestors resembled closely these modern prosimians: an 800-gram (28-ounce) *Lepilemur* from Madagascar [A., in the sketch below], and [B.] a 100-gram (3.5-ounce) Dwarf Galago, popularly called a "bush baby," from Africa. Both are active only at night.

Mouse lemurs, today found only on the Island of Madagascar, are the best living representatives of these extinct, ancestral prosimians. They serve us here as models of the first, unequivocal primates. Mouse lemur behavior has been studied independently on Madagascar by British primatologist Dr. Robert D. Martin (now at the University of Zürich) and myself.

Mouse lemurs are members of a prosimian Family called the "Cheirogaleidae" (mouse lemurs, dwarf lemurs, and fork-marked lemurs). The Latin species name for the grey mouse lemur is *Microcebus murinus,* which means "little monkey mouse"; the other species, the brown mouse lemur, *Microcebus rufus,* translates as "little reddish monkey." These *nomina* are misleading: prosimian mouse lemurs are quite distinct from anthropoid monkeys and apes. Today, there are more than 32 living species of prosimians; 21 live exclusively on Madagascar.[5,6] Madagascar is a wondrous refugium—a place where living fossils cling to survival, isolated from competition from other species that followed them. Unfortunately, human migration during the last fifteen hundred years has caused the extinction of many lemurs. Even so, a classification of living and extinct Malagasy prosimians reveals living groups especially useful for the reconstruction of behavioral evolution (shown in boldface):

Class Mammalia (Mammals, in contrast to birds, insects, reptiles, etc.)
   Subclass Eutheria (placental mammals, in contrast to those who lay eggs or
       nurture their embryos in pouches like kangaroos)
    Order Primates (prosimians, monkeys, apes, and humans)
      Suborder Prosimii (the prosimians, sometimes called strepsirhines)
       Infraorder Lemuriformes (the lemurs)
          Family Adapidae (extinct, early diurnal lemurs including the North
              American *Notharctus* and the European *Adapis;* these lemurs
              were ancestral to all later lemurs, monkeys, apes, and humans.
              They disappeared millions of years ago; none of their fossils has
              yet been found on Madagascar.)
          Family **Cheirogaleidae** (the tiny, nocturnal, Malagasy mouse lemurs;
              about six species remain alive today)
          Family **Lepilemuridae** (a model we will use for mother-daughter
              learning; two species and numerous subspecies remain alive
              today on Madagascar)

Family **Lemuridae** (the larger, diurnal, Malagasy "true" lemurs like
   the brown lemur and the ring-tailed lemur; about eight species
   remain alive today)

Family **Indriidae** (medium-sized to large monkey-like lemurs that
   appear somewhat convergent with gibbons; at least one recently
   extinct genus)

Family **Daubentoniidae** (the aberrant Aye-Aye, a nocturnal lemur
   that seeks bark-boring beetles much like woodpeckers do elsewhere)

Family **Megaladapidae** (recently extinct, large lemurs that appeared
   convergent in form with the Australian Koala)

Family **Archaeolemuridae** (recently extinct, monkey-like lemurs)

Family **Paleopropithecidae** (recently extinct, monkey-like lemurs)

Following the extinct, mouse-like lemurs, we reach a point almost
halfway along the climb toward today. We find a large branch containing
a new, larger form of lemur—the extinct, day-active lemurs in the Family
Adapidae ("adapids"). These larger variants of the original mouse lemur
theme were about the size of a house cat. About forty-five million years ago
during the Eocene Epoch, they cavorted in a vast forest that spread across
what would later become North America and Europe.

The first day-active (diurnal) lemurs walked the branches on all fours.
They had a fox-like face and a large bushy, raccoon-like tail that served for
balance like the tail of a kite when they leapt between trees. Their fossils,
some nearly complete, are well known. Many specimens are known, including *Adapis* from European geological deposits and *Notharctus* from
North American deposits. They are classified in the extinct lemur Family
Adapidae; were they alive today, they'd appear strikingly similar to modern diurnal lemurs from the Family Lemuridae ("lemurids").[5,7]

Excellent living models of adapids—the lemurids—live today only on
the Island of Madagascar. *Lemur catta,* the ring-tailed lemur, is an appropriate choice for a model and has been well-studied. The first diurnal
lemur field studies were performed by Professor Jean-Jacques Petter and
his colleagues from France's Museum of Natural History. But Princeton
University's Professor Alison Jolly is the acknowledged pioneer of long-
term diurnal lemur social studies. Her work with the ring-tailed lemur and

a larger, monkey-like lemur, the Sifaka (*Propithecus* in the Family Indriidae), began in Berenty, Madagascar, in the 1960s.

Dr. Jolly first discovered female dominance in lemurs—an observation
that upset the male-centric interpretations of primate behavior that came
before. Her first field study, *Lemur Behavior: A Madagascar Field Study*,
published in 1966 by the University of Chicago Press, ranks as a classic of
the genre. The "lemur biologists" who followed Dr. Jolly, like Dr. Alison
Richard of Yale University, Professor Robert W. Sussman of Washington
University, St. Louis, Dr. Ian Tattersall of the American Museum of
Natural History, New York, Dr. Pat Wright of Duke University, and
British primatologist Jonathan Pollock, have contributed much information about a few other species of diurnal lemurs as well.

Many branches of primates diverged from the extinct diurnal lemurs. At
the present time, the shape of these branching forks is poorly known. We
do know that about 34 million years ago, the world's geography and
climate changed drastically. Cold, seasonal weather spread across the
northern hemisphere as the conjoined continents of North America and
Europe wrenched free from one another. The Atlantic Ocean formed fully,
isolating the lemurs of North America from those of Europe and Asia. The
northern subtropical and tropical forests vanished and were replaced by
temperate forests, rich in pine trees. A few fortunate lemurs escaped a
chilling extinction by migrating south to the few remaining areas of tropical
and subtropical vegetation. Some lemurs escaped from North America to
South America; others fled Europe for Africa. Many lemur populations
changed dramatically in their new, southern habitats.

Darwin used the term "connecting link" to describe fossils that present
an array of ancestral and descendant features. Such connecting links,
large-brained lemur-monkeys like *Dolichocebus,* appeared in South American jungles following the great northern chill. Eventually, these monkey-
like lemurs would produce the New World monkeys and marmosets of
today. A few mouse lemur–like prosimians escaped from Europe to the
jungles that cloaked Northern Africa about 34 million years ago. One
population of mouse lemur–like prosimians led to today's African bush
babies (galagos) and African and Asian lorises. Others led to Old World
monkeys and apes. In turn, proto-humans arose from the apes.

Another population of Northern African mouse lemurs would be carried to Madagascar. There, in isolation, they produced the rich variety of

modern lemurs that survive exclusively on that island: *Lepilemur,* the curious Aye-Aye *(Daubentonia),* the Sifakas *(Propithecus, Avahi,* and *Indri),* the modern mouse lemurs, the diurnal brown and ring-tailed lemurs, and families of recently extinct, giant and monkey-like lemurs. As noted, at least three groups of these primitive Malagasy survivors—the mouse lemurs, *Lepilemur,* and the diurnal brown and ring-tailed lemurs—are especially valuable for the reconstruction of our own social history. They are, for the purpose of evolutionary psychology, living fossils.

Lemur-Monkeys and Lemur-Apes

Two transitional lemur groups appeared in Africa more than 30 million years ago. Transitional lemur-monkeys and transitional lemur-apes roamed the vast, tropical jungles of Northern Africa. These primates proved highly successful, and very different from their ancestral lemurs. For one thing, they were all diurnal and highly social. For another, they had a larger brain—a far more intricate social computer. Transitional lemur-monkeys like *Apidium* and *Parapithecus* thrived. Much later, their familiar Old World monkey descendants (like the rhesus monkey and the baboon) populated the contemporary forests of Africa and southern Asia.

For our story of the evolution of human psychology, the modern monkeys of South America and the Old World must be considered distant cousins. Our ancestors were never monkeys. They were transitional lemur-apes. Remains of these medium-sized, interesting creatures named the Egyptian Ape, *Aegyptopithecus,* were unearthed in the Fayum badlands of Egypt in 1906. They remained unappreciated until Elwyn L. Simons, now of Duke University, articulated their importance more than five decades later.[5.8]

The fossil *Aegyptopithecus* is a true connecting link between extinct diurnal lemurs of the Family Adapidae and apes. Its skeleton is a patchwork of features reminiscent of ancient lemurs and prescient of modern apes. Unfortunately, nothing exactly like it remains alive today. So, here our story—and our choice of living models—must leap-frog to the immediate descendants of *Aegyptopithecus,* the first apes of 24 million years ago, the dryopithecines. The fabulously successful dryopithecines were the immediate ancestors of modern orangutans, gorillas, chimpanzees, and through yet other proto-human connecting links, to us.

Parting Company With the Apes

The African dryopithecine most likely ancestral to modern gorillas was probably similar to *Dryopithecus major,* an enormous specimen whose importance was recognized in the 1950s by famed paleontologist Louis S. B. Leakey and anatomist W. E. Le Gros Clark. Humans and chimpanzees probably share a common ancestor in *Dryopithecus africanus.* This species is also called "Proconsul" after a chimpanzee popular in the London Zoo during the 1930s. Proconsul is exactly what we'd expect for such a generalized ancestor—not exactly a chimpanzee and not quite an ape-man.[5.9]

According to a consensus established by the paleontological evidence, *bona fide* and distinct ancestors of gorillas, and common ancestors of chimpanzees and humans, are found more than 16 million years ago in African geological deposits. Yet anthropologists who study only molecular evidence of living chimpanzees, gorillas, and humans conclude otherwise. According to their interpretation of the structural differences between the molecules of apes and humans, we shared a common ancestry with the chimpanzee not more than four million years ago. The argument, while interesting, is not especially cogent to the problem of reconstructing our behavioral history. If paleontologists are correct, human behavioral history has been separate from that of the apes for at least 16 million years. If molecular anthropologists are correct, human behavior and chimpanzee behavior were one and the same less than four million years ago. In either case, ideal models of our common ancestor live today in the forests of Africa—the chimpanzees.

Two species of chimpanzee remain alive. The larger common chimpanzee, *Pan troglodytes,* has been studied almost continuously in the wild by Dr. Jane Goodall and her students since 1960. The smaller pygmy chimpanzee, *Pan paniscus,* has been much less intensively observed in the wild. Both chimpanzees share many features of their behavior, although some authorities claim that pygmy chimpanzees are far more like humans, both physically and behaviorally.

Ecce Homo

Darwin argued that the classificatory system—the ranking of species according to their similarities—should reflect our view of their evolutionary relationships. Almost all contemporary classifiers agree on this point. The hierarchies we create reflect a shorthand ladder of relationships. The most distantly related are those species like earthworms and dogs who belong only to the same kingdom (in this case, the Animal Kingdom). At the other end of the ladder are those closely related groups who belong to the same species like mastiff dogs and Chihuahuas. Each species, alive or extinct, has a unique address on the classificatory scheme. For us:

Superkingdom Eukaryota (large, nucleated cells; not bacteria)
   Kingdom Animalia (animals, not plants)
      Phylum Chordata (animals with a hollow nerve tube like a "spinal cord")
         Subphylum Vertebrata (animals with backbones)
            Class Mammalia (mammals, not birds or reptiles, etc.)
               Subclass Eutheria (mammals whose embryos develop with a placenta)
                  Order Primates (not dogs, or cats, or shrews, or rodents, etc.)
                     Suborder Anthropoidea ("higher," haplorine primates, not prosimians)
                        Superfamily Cercopithecoidea (Old World Monkeys, apes, humans)
                           Family Hominidae (humans, not apes)
                             Genus *Homo* (3 species, only one alive today)
                                Species *Homo sapiens* (modern humans)

Like every species, the human species is unique. Even so, we share more similarities with our contemporary ape relatives than differences. Since Darwin's sobering revelation that our form and behavior was derived largely from past animal forms and their behavior, many people have chosen to deny this fact. Indeed, it is an extreme irony of evolution that the only creatures capable of uncovering their own evolutionary history choose so often to cover it up. Even our scientific classificatory scheme is not immune to this sort of prejudice. In essence, the classification of humans versus nonhumans is a cover-up of sorts.

Anthropologists have distinguished humans from ape ancestors and living ape cousins by placing us in a unique family group, the Hominidae. Contemporary humans are the only living members of this family. At a point considerably up the ladder, we parted ancestry with apes. Yet humans are not very distinct anatomically from dryopithecines or modern chimpanzees. Biologists routinely include animals far more diverse than humans and chimps within the same family (and sometimes, within the same genus). Biochemically, we are barely a separate species from chimpanzees. Human DNA is more than 98% identical to the DNA of modern chimpanzees.[5.10] Note that biochemical differences are, in fact, microanatomical differences; the structure of a biochemical is merely another, tinier aspect of an organism's anatomy. There are far fewer gross anatomical differences between humans and chimpanzees than there are between different breeds of domestic dogs—and *all* domestic dogs from mastiff to Chihuahua are classified as members of the same species, *Canis familiaris.*

It is prejudice—not the even-handed application of the principles of animal classification—that separates humans from contemporary chimpanzees by so great a classificatory distance. A hypothetical, objective Martian biologist would probably consider humans, chimpanzees, gorillas, orangutans, and the extinct dryopithecines members of the same family: the Pongidae, the Great Apes. For all practical purposes, humans are—as UCLA naturalist Jared Diamond said in a moment of only slight hyperbole—the third (species of) chimpanzee. Even so, prejudicial classificatory schemes are part of the unique behavioral fabric of humans. Prejudice—at least arbitrary, ritualized, socially-inspired prejudice—is a human prerogative.

The prejudice to distance ourselves from other animals is reflected in our unending quest to define what is uniquely human. To be fair, modern *Homo sapiens* are distinctly different from apes on two counts. We have an enormous brain—far larger than the brains of extinct or living apes. And modern *Homo sapiens* have a unique form of communication, language. But these traits—one anatomical (brain size), the other behavioral (language)—appeared only recently. They are not even part of the scientific definition of the human family. The first humans, in fact, had an ape-sized brain and in all probability an apelike behavioral repertoire (although we have no living models of this transition between apes and modern humans). The first humans walked using their two hind legs. They were walking apes that would otherwise prove barely distinguishable from their ape ancestors, the dryopithecines.

In fact, the fossils of early members of the human family are distinguished from apes in few ways other than their bipedal stance and concomitant changes in pelvic and hind limb anatomy. In addition to postural changes, early hominids (members of the human family) can be distinguished from apes by considering additional changes in dentition; for example, hominids have small canine teeth relative to apes. The basic point remains: fossil humans are distinct from fossil apes because they walked upright and apes didn't.

Ape Men to Modern Humans

A gap, indeed a chasm, follows the dryopithecine ape fossils of twenty million years ago. The next unequivocal human ancestor appears in the fossil record of south and east Africa at about four million years B.P. The first human, *Australopithecus,* was little more than a bipedally-erect ape. Its head was similar to that of an ape, and its brain was ape-sized. Its stance and its dentition show clearly that it was our ancestor, a connecting link between apes and humans.

We have many fossil specimens of several species of australopithecines. For three million years, they were very successful walking about the savannahs of African Pliocene. Nonetheless, nothing quite like them survives today. The same holds true for their descendant, *Homo erectus.* Our larger-brained ancestor from about two million years B.P. until about 50,000 years ago was even more successful than its australopithecine forebearers.

The remains of *Homo erectus* are found in Africa, southern Europe, China, and southeast Asia—a range greatly expanded from that of its ancestral australopithecines. Erectus are associated with evidence of the use of fire and with Acheulean hand axes, large stone tools probably used to prepare hides and render carcasses. While undoubtedly successful, *Homo erectus* became extinct; replaced by its descendants, *Homo sapiens,* who now populate the globe in numbers exceeding those of any primate that ever lived.

Lacking living models, the behavior of australopithecines and *Homo erectus* must be inferred from the crude artifacts they left behind and from their skeletons which, for example, tell much about what they ate, how long they lived, and even what sounds they probably uttered. Further inference can be gained from comparing chimpanzee behavior (what came before) to that of humans (what followed).

Our own species' behavior is the best studied of any living primate. Throughout recorded history, humans have been obsessively curious about themselves. Without doubt, the human model is the most detailed behavioral model of all, replete with a range of individual and cultural variations on the theme of power, sex, and love unequalled by any species of life. Our understanding of this wealth of contemporary human behavior is made measurably clearer by charting its evolutionary course, beginning with tiny, preprimate mammals—the shrews—that darted about the forest floor many millions of years ago.

CHAPTER 6

The Loves of a Shrew

We are kneeling in the primal, subtropical forests of Montana, in the hazy morning twilight of a day seventy million years in the human past. Huge leaves of magnolias, hickories, and oaks blanket the forest floor. A tiny, small-eyed creature snuffles beneath them. She is smaller than a pocket lighter. Her actions are frenzied as she pokes her pointed, pink-tipped snout quickly under one leaf, then jerks her head back to explore the next. Her dense, sleek, short-cropped grey fur ripples with the constant activity of her tiny muscles. She pauses for a split second, then her forelegs become a blur as she paws rapidly in the moist, blackish soil. Her minuscule fingers, tipped with minuscule claws, uncover a fat, glistening white beetle grub almost as large as she. She pierces its body with the razor-like points of her teeth. Within seconds, she devours the hapless larva with rapid, scissor-like movements of her widely-hinged, smileless mouth. Pausing only long enough to draw her forelegs over the battery of long, stiff whiskers that sprout from her muzzle, she begins her frantic search for food anew. She is insatiably hungry.

The sleek, silverish mammal is an ancient relative of ours, a shrew-like creature that we now call a "primitive insectivore" after, appropriately enough, her principal diet (although many primitive insectivores probably included a fair amount of fallen fruit in their diet).[6.1]

She was an opportunist who scrounged the forest floor for any package of edible energy that her sensitive nose or vibrissae (facial whiskers) could uncover. Her appearance and her lifestyle, far removed from our own, begins the second pertinent act in the long play of human relationships.

Who she was, exactly, we cannot say. Most probably, she was a creature much like *Purgatorius* whose fossilized remains were unearthed in the Purgatory Hills of Eastern Montana in 1965. [6.2] She probably weighed no more than three-quarters of an ounce—so small that she lived in constant fear of being eaten or stepped on by the ruling reptiles that dramatically inhabited her realm.

Our heroine continues her urgent quest for food. Her tiny body burns a prodigious amount of fuel. Her gut will empty completely in only three hours; starvation would follow less than two hours later. This ravenous quest for food energy is a pressure that we humans might find difficult to comprehend. This is because the metabolic rate of a tiny mammal—relative to its size—is far greater than our own. The relationship between body size and metabolism is well known. For a given body weight (measured in grams, approximately ⅟₂₈ of an ounce), the minimum level of metabolism, expressed in kilocalories of energy needed each day, is easy to reckon:

$$\text{Basal Metabolic Rate} = (\text{Body Weight})^{0.75}$$

This basic formula tells us that for every gram more body weight, an animal will increase its metabolism by less than one kilocalorie. The larger the animal, the higher its metabolism will be absolutely, but the lower its metabolism will be relative to mass. That is, the number of kilocalories necessary to sustain each gram of its large body mass will be less than that needed to sustain a smaller mammal.

This truism is not really as paradoxical as it seems. A train hauling one hundred boxcars from New York to Los Angeles will burn absolutely more fuel than a loaded 747 making the same trip. Yet, relative to the weight each carrier hauls—the pounds per gallon ratio—the smaller 747 burns much more fuel. Our ancestral insectivore was a 747 relative to our train-like energy requirements. Small is fast, but large is efficient—two principles of energetics that have driven mammalian evolution since its beginnings.

So, our tiny, insectivorous heroine must forage nearly round the clock. Her present search for energy draws to an abrupt halt as the ground virtually leaps upwards beneath her. Not more than a yard from her, a trash-can-sized leg stomps the leaf-litter with the sound of a jackhammer pounding away in a bowl of corn flakes. A startled bull three-horned dinosaur, *Triceratops,* beckons its herd from the clearing as a rumbling, guttural growl of a *Tyrannosaurus,* the terrible thunder lizard, echoes off the mossy trunks of giant sequoia trees. Herons nearby take flight to join a circling pterodactyl.

Our diminutive ancestor pauses only long enough to choose another, less busy path through the fallen leaves. These immense denizens of her world will pay her no attention, although smaller dinosaurs are a constant threat. [6.3] There are dinosaurs here which probably dined on tiny mammals like her. For example, *Ornithomimus,* the swift "bird imitator," reached twelve feet in length and preyed upon mammals, small birds, and eggs with its ostrich-like head and sharp, toothless beak. A close relative, the six-foot-long *Saurornithoides,* had large eyes adapted to hunting at night. Both these bipedal running dinosaurs were relatives of *Tyrannosaurus.* For reasons detailed above, their smaller body size would have required them to seek food often, so our ancestors' world was a frightening one indeed.

Every so often, in passing, our insectivorian ancestor touches her genital area to a twig and deposits a barely perceptible drop of urine. The spot will quickly dry, but trace amounts of the byproducts of her cast-off estrogen will scent the area for perhaps a day or more. The perfume will instantly identify her as a female coming into estrus—sexual heat. Although she and the other members of her species are solitary loners, the whiff of her hormones in the leaf litter will attract males from nearby.

To these primitive insectivores, the start of sexual activity ignites as quickly as a thrown switch. The switches are all olfactory. Their brains were overwhelmingly geared to unthinkingly respond to odors. Relative to our brain, these insectivores probably devoted one thousand times more space to olfactory processing centers than do we. And, to make them more adept at instant, unequivocal responses to sexual stimuli (and to other smelly things like food), their new cortex—their thinking caps—occupied less than 15% of their total brain. For comparison, the human new cortex accounts for 80% of our total brain size.

No endocasts (fossil remains of brains) remain for primitive, ancestral insectivores like *Purgatorius,* so I used comparable living mammals' brain dimensions—the brains of shrews like *Sorex araneus.* [6.4] Shrews and our earliest ancestors shared a "similar morphological grade," a phrase which translates that they closely resemble one another in size and proportions. My estimates here are merely "ball park"; good enough to illustrate the point.

It should also be noted that brain size also refers to both brain volume and brain mass. The volume and mass of biological tissues are, for all practical purposes, nearly equivalent: the major component of tissues is water (one cubic centimeter or milliliter of water has a mass of one gram). We are all still swimming about internally in the puddle-where-sex-was-born, even though we're conveniently wrapped up in skin.

Later that afternoon, our ancestral shrew's first suitor arrives in the tunnel through the leaves that demarcates her territory. Normally, she would fight fiercely any member of her species that dared this incursion. But this afternoon, her aggressive, defensive behavior is clouded by her internal hormones. She finds the odd-smelling intruder strangely attractive. Nonetheless, they greet one another with open mouths armed with pointed teeth and a cacophony of threatening, high-pitched squeaks.

Ever cautious, the male approaches, withdraws an inch, then approaches again. This approach-withdraw behavior characterizes the ambivalence with which they both greet the sex act. They are compelled by hormones to mate, but they are cautioned by experience (and other hormones) to regard all strangers as interlopers and stealers of food, and, in the beady little eyes of our heroine, an interloper may even be an eater-of-babies.

The male persists with his advance an indication that he is a confident but not overly aggressive male. Within minutes, the male lunges forward. Their noses touch. It is a good sign. She could have bitten his nose savagely, inflicting a wound that could prove ultimately fatal to an animal so dependent on its sense of smell. Encouraged, the male circles her and sniffs her anus, then noses her side, her ear, the nape of her neck. She is placated. With his nose touching her crown, he mounts her from behind, thrusting rapidly and with extraordinary speed. It is over within ten seconds. He uncouples from her and, a second later, he scurries down the tunnel of leaves and twigs and disappears.

She may or may not see him again. Not all modern shrews copulate and conceive on the first attempt. A mating pair of North American short-tailed shrews may remain together for a day, copulating twenty or more times. [6.5] The important detail for our story is that long-term male-female bonds did not exist at this stage of preprimate evolution, nor do they exist in modern shrews.

There are seven other females who live within the same acre of woodland. Her suitor has left her to find another female in estrus; he'll have a choice if he can bully, bluff, and fight his way past an inevitable gauntlet of competing, sexually aroused males.

Meanwhile, her desire to mate wanes within hours of her brief coupling. She will now fight off other suitors, or run away from them. In less than three weeks, she gives birth to a litter of eight, squirming, pink pups. They are altricial—which means, essentially, born defenseless. But they grow quickly; within a week, they are following her like a miniature train as she digs up grubs and munches the odd fallen fruit and flower blossom.

She never explicitly shows her offspring anything about the world they will enter. Instead, they learn by observing her actions for a few weeks, then experiencing life on their own. Like her, most of their behavior will be governed by built-in, inherited chemical cycles and by nearly automatic, "hard-wired" reactions to the scents, the sounds, and, to a lesser extent, the sights that confront them.

Within two weeks, her milk glands run dry. The juvenile males, responding to the stirrings of testosterone within them, wander far away. In their wanderings, many will fall victim to a predator's skills. The juvenile females must be forcibly evicted—a harsh, always traumatic weaning. They scatter, then demarcate and settle into close-by, solitary territories on the forest floor. The young females, closer to home, expose themselves to fewer predators and inherit a more proven resource base than their far-ranging brothers.

Like the rest of her life, our heroine's romance and child-rearing activities pass quickly—less than two months from conception until the empty nest. The cycle will begin anew within days. In a good year, she'll produce six or seven litters this way. If she avoids the jaws and the feet of dinosaurs, her life will run its course and end without notice in about two years.

If she is an heroically successful mother, she will produce nearly 100 children. Only about one or two will survive to reproductive adulthood. The world of our ancestors of seventy million years ago was unforgiving. Yet she and her kind were fabulously successful. They endured for millions of years after the last dinosaurs mysteriously became extinct. More important for our story, these primitive insectivorous mammals gave rise to many of the modern mammals we see today, including bats, rats, hedgehogs, our next model ancestor, the mouse lemur of Madagascar, and ultimately, to us.

Think Small

Our shrew-like ancestor of seventy million years ago was distinctly unlike us. Her world, though graced with some of the same plants and animals that populate our towns, was almost unimaginably different. The selective forces that shaped her form and behavior were, for the most part, dissimilar from the forces that shaped us. Yet, this world and this creature set the stage and, to a measurable extent, canalized the route for our own gender relationships.

Many of the differences we see are a matter of scale. She and most of the other mammals that scurried beneath the feet of dinosaurs were tiny. The ruling reptiles inhabited and dominated most of the ecological niches that today are filled with furry beasts. As we noted, her small size relegated her to an unending search for energy. Small mammals require far more energy per ounce of body weight than larger mammals like us.

Furthermore, small mammals have far more surface area per ounce of their body size than do larger mammals. Accordingly, a small mammal will gain or lose heat from this relatively enormous surface many times faster than a larger mammal. This relationship between surface and mass (weight) and heat exchange is intuitively obvious to anyone who cools their martini or soft drink using ice cubes. Suppose you were at a party and wanted a cold drink quickly. The host said you could have two ice cubes, or he'd/she'd be happy to grind up the two ice cubes in a blender. Which would you prefer? Intuitively, you recognize that two crushed ice cubes will cool faster (they'll gain heat from the drink quicker) than two uncrushed ice cubes. Similarly, if you want to "nurse" a drink for a long time, you'd probably order the uncrushed cubes. They'll cool the drink less quickly, but on the other hand, they won't melt and dilute your drink as quickly as the crushed cubes will. Ice cubes gain heat more slowly than their crushed counterparts. Even though both the cubes and the crushed ice your host offered were exactly the same mass, the crushed ice has a far greater surface area than it had as a cube.

The heat gain or loss for a small versus a large mammal works just like the example of crushed versus cubed ice. Surface area is a function of mass (body weight). The greater the relative surface area, the faster the gain or loss of body heat. [6.6] What would be a cool breeze to us, felt like an arctic blast to our tiny ancestors. So, they had to continually seek optimal microclimates amongst the not-too-hot and not-too-cool leaf litter of the forest floor. There were insects and some fruit in the branches of nearby bushes and trees, but this world above the forest floor was too hot during the day and filled with munching dinosaurs and birds anyway. She stayed low and specialized in her own uncrowded, stable universe.

Our tiny, primitive ancestor was driven by its high metabolic rate, buffeted harshly by slight changes in temperature and humidity, and eyed hungrily by animals too small to offer us even modest threat. Their lives passed by at breakneck, unexamined speed. Their sexual affairs, too, seem painted on an alien's canvas.

A Life and Love Unlike Our Own

For the female insectivore, love was a thoughtless, steroidal urging from within her body. Her first concession to the internal demands of courtship was to mark—to establish a pattern of odorous urine spots within her territory. Odors that serve as communicative signals are called "pheromones." Her pheromonal perfume was actually a waste product of her changing internal chemistry. Discarded droplets, the broken parts of the steroids coursing within her, were a clear signal to any male whose olfactory brain decoded it: this female is filled with the chemicals that presage ovulation.

Understandably, we find it difficult to relate to creatures so driven by minute changes in temperature, constant hunger, and unthinking chemicals that stimulate their brains and act as perfume in their urine. Yet, smugness is uncalled for here. Our temperature regulation and hunger requirements differ only in scale from these miniature mammals.

Most of us subject our bodies to a galaxy of perfumes, colognes, aftershave lotions, mouthwashes, deodorant roll-ons, and scented douches. While our romantic impulses are by no means triggered and governed by olfaction like the courtship of shrews, our sense of smell is an important component of human sexuality.

Bottled odorants are clearly artificial pheromones, but humans, like ancient shrews, secrete waste products formed from the breakdown of sex steroids. Both human men and women show elevated levels of 17-Oxy(keto)steroid in their urine corresponding to internal levels of sex hormones. Whether these or other chemicals secreted in our urine or sweat may serve as subtle pheromones is largely unexamined.

In any event, chemically, the female insectivore is signaling that she is or will soon be sexually receptive. In turn, the male shrew did not respond with reasoned interest. His brain, like hers, was hard-wired to respond quickly to the female reproductive chemicals detected by his prodigious nose. The perception of her steroids set loose a hormonal cycle within him. Testosterone production increased, and his testes began to make sperm. The tide of testosterone instigated even more chemical changes; his aggression and energy level increased. His newfound energy sent him off in search of more and fresher feminine scents. Courtship, such as it was, was launched.

From launching to zero-hour copulation, courtship was a brief ritual that momentarily overcame both partners' justifiable reluctance to yield their individual space to another member of the same species. We find no sign of caring, bonding, or a purely social exchange here.

The logic of the puddle-where-sex-was-born prevailed in these insectivores. Males were driven to mate frequently with as many females as could be found and approached. Their chase was unremittent. Males will risk life and limb and will fight other males in their mating quest. For some contemporary small, primitive mammals, the mating chase is invariably fatal. Male *Antechinus,* a mouselike Australian marsupial, are born in spring. They mate with such frenzied abandon that no male remains alive by October. [6,7] They die because they give up the search for food in a hectic quest for multiple mates; most males succumb to stress-related disorders, disease, and ulcers of the stomach and intestines.

Pregnant female *Antechinus* survive until the next year to give birth to the next generation of males and females. The unequal toll of mating and inevitable lethal risks taken by the wandering, solitary males affects populations of other small mammals as well. For our primitive ancestors, an equal number of male and female babies were born, but adult males were far less common than females.

From our towering perspective above the forest floor, we perceive that survival is decidedly balanced in favor of the females. In adulthood, the sex ratio—the number of females to the number of males—is skewed in the females' favor. Such is the force of selection. Males are good for only one thing: providing sperm to eggs. Males are expendable sperm banks. It does not take an equal number of males and females to accomplish fertilization and infant rearing; a few males and many females will do handily. In fact, the fewer males, the better. Resources that females could use are not wasted on adult males who can neither birth nor care for offspring. The excess males, some of whom fall prey to predators, provide in their passing a measure of passive protection for females: they help satiate predators. Natural selection is often a harsh judge of gender's worth.

Motherhood Machines

Pregnant females are nature's most essential creatures and female primitive insectivores were infant-producing machines par excellence. They had to be. Their small size placed them at the top of many other animals' grocery lists. Their reproductive strategy—the production of many offspring, few of which survive—is technically known as r-selection. It is in marked contrast to the overall human reproductive strategy of K-selection, the production of few offspring, most of whom survive.

Neither reproductive strategy is especially better or worse than the other on the face of it. With r-selection, much life material and energy is wasted as infants and young disappear down the mouths of predators. With K-selection, an inordinate amount of energy is expended to assure the survival of a few offspring. Each strategy works best under particular ecological conditions. r-selection is characteristic of a species that can rapidly increase its population size to accommodate large fluctuations in its environment. K-selected species produce superior competitors in stable, predictable environments.

Motherhood is the oldest mammalian profession, although its finer, refined trappings are minimally displayed by our ancestors of seventy million years ago. Only the essentials were provided the young: milk, warmth, protection from predators, and a brief social period when a pup could explore the world and imitate some of its mother's limited behavioral repertoire. A brief period of social learning was all that was necessary.

The small brains of these insectivores could accept only a limited amount of information anyway. Adulthood guidance was provided by internal chemistry, brain circuitry, and by a limited amount of trial-and-error learning. The crucial aspects of life—instantaneous responses to olfactory clues in the environment—were genetically programmed before their birth. The behavior of adult ancestral insectivores was most likely routine and stereotypical. So, while insectivores explore their habitat continually in search of food, they are nevertheless incurious. This seeming contradiction of terms is justified: an insectivore's explorations are nothing more than an imperative to follow particular scents until satiation. Scents that are not pre-programmed are avoided without examination.

These ancient relatives of ours were solitary. Bonds between adults lasted only a day or two at most. Courtship, driven by hormones and pheromones, lasted hours; copulation, seconds. Even the mother-infant bond lasted only a few weeks. The roots of human love spring from these ancient insectivores, yet the roots are so deep and so unlike the rest of the trunk that we scarcely notice that we inhabit the same tree. For our story, the love life of the ancient insectivores was most important for what it would soon become.

The Ascent of Shrews

While the dinosaurs stalked the earth, mammals were limited to fringe habitats, those niches that dinosaurs were poorly equipped to exploit: tiny places, like leaf litter (the provenance of primitive shrews, marsupials and rodents); dark, aerial places, like the night air where bats glided and flapped; and so forth. In a flash of geological time, within a period of 3–7 million years, the dinosaurs became extinct. Their relatively sudden, unexplained exit from the pageant of life left innumerable places in the ecosystem untapped. The voids were quickly filled with mammals of nearly modern appearance.

The shrews, of course, remained. Many insectivore species changed relatively little in the sixty-odd million years that followed. They were the well-adapted, specialized, minuscule champions of the dank between browning leaves and rotting logs. Yet, the world above their heads offered a wealth of energy packages just a few feet beyond their grasp.

There were bushes, festooned with flowers abuzz with insects. The flowers transformed into berries—balls of sugar that surrounded a core of fat and protein. A veritable arboreal feast existed for any small animal capable of negotiating a maze of thin branches. Insectivores, with their clumsy, claw-tipped paws, were poorly equipped to grasp the fine branches of this new supermarket. Further, their sensitive noses were of little or no use in tracking fast-moving, winged insects that frequented the flowers.

The insectivore's tiny eyes, placed on either side of its broad, long snout, impeded its visual capabilities. Animals whose eyes are located laterally (on the side of their heads) do not perceive depth in three dimensions. Three-dimensional depth perception—stereoscopic vision—requires frontally-directed eyes whose field of vision overlaps. To demonstrate this, cover one eye, then take a walk in a room you are not familiar with. Even though your brain allows you to roughly estimate some distances via perspective (close objects, you've learned, appear bigger than distant ones), you'll probably misjudge distances between objects in the room. One-eyed, you see the world in flat, two-dimensional perspective. Now imagine how terrifying it would be to leap between the branches of a tree with only two-dimensional perspective. Insectivores could not see stereoscopically in 3-D—a perilous disadvantage in negotiating the complex, three-dimensional, arboreal world of a bush. Judging distances accurately is a prime requisite for hopping from branch to branch.

The world of the bush required adaptations beyond those held by the ancient insectivores. New mammals evolved. The process was neither sudden nor simple. At first, perhaps, a few shrews were born with more flexible fingers and shorter claws on their paws. In the terrestrial world, these poor mutant infants would have difficulty digging up beetle grubs. But in the new world above their heads, they could awkwardly grasp a branch and climb up to a wealth of nearly untapped resources.

Instead of a disadvantage, the mutant's grasping paws and fingernail-like claws proved an enormous selective advantage. Their offspring, bearing their parents' genes for their own mutated paws, thrived. The mutation became the commonplace. And so it went: mutation, natural selection, mutation, natural selection, and on and on for millions of years.

We even have a living model for a transitional stage of evolution between a ground-living insectivore and an arboreal mammal: the tree shrews of Asia. Tree shrews, at one time considered to be primates, are now given their own order (the Order Scandentia), a move that reflects scholarly confusion about precisely where they fit.

Tree shrews are fascinating, extremely active creatures that eat fruit, hunt fast-moving prey, and scamper like squirrels from the forest floor to the tops of trees. Yet, their claw-tipped paws are poorly adapted to negotiate the fine branches of bushes. They are more likely tangential to our story of primate evolution. Our ancestors did not (at first) run to the tree tops; they mastered the bush.

By about fifty-four million years ago, the descendants of the ancient insectivores were very un-insectivore, un-tree-shrew–like creatures. The human order, the Order Primates, appeared clambering and hopping about the bushes of what would eventually become North America, Europe, and Asia. With them, the evolutionary story of human social relationships was off the ground.

CHAPTER 7

Mouse Lemur
Mother Love

Late at night, on the tropical Indian Ocean island of Madagascar, a tiny, mouse-like creature stealthily hops along a branch. She is cold. Her dense, chestnut-brown fur coat glistens with dew in the moonlight. She pauses to lick her fingernails, then she scans the thick, fragrant night air with her enormous, flexible ears. There, just before her, a loud, droning buzz. Her eyes fix on a hovering object, silhouetted in the petals of a large blossom. She draws closer to it, snaking her body silently along the branch. Suddenly, she lunges from behind the flower, grabbing wildly with extended arms and outstretched hands. It is over in a heartbeat. Only a dust of wing scales and dislodged pink petals momentarily hang, then flutter downward in the night air. The mouse lemur huntress scurries away, clenching a lifeless giant moth in her delicate hand.

These tiny, exquisite mammals have changed little in more than 50 million years. Mouse lemurs are prosimians, the most primitive living representatives of the origin of the human order, the Order Primates. Their story offers a glimpse at the beginnings of human social behavior, and the tangled roots of human power, sex, and love.

Mouse lemurs are markedly different from the insectivores that came before them. Instead of paws tipped with claws, prosimians have hands whose wide fingers are backed by a supporting nail (a broad, much-modified claw). Each finger pad contains ridges and valleys of sensitive skin—branch-gripping, traction-enhancing fingerprints like our own.

101

The early prosimians' eyes were enormous and directed forward; the visual fields of each eye overlapped, providing excellent, three-dimensional, stereoscopic vision. Their snouts were greatly reduced in size, indicating that the sense of smell was less well-developed than in the ancestral, ground-living insectivores. These early prosimians relied on vision and an acute sense of hearing to negotiate the fine branches of their arboreal world and to find fast-moving, buzzing insect prey. The first prosimians of fifty million years ago resembled contemporary mouse lemurs in these and many other anatomical features as well.

Mouse lemur on a branch.

A Fair Weather Kind of Love

Mouse lemurs, like their ancestral insectivores, are tiny: an adult weighs 35 grams, barely more than an ounce. Yet, unlike their ground-dwelling ancestors, mouse lemurs are subject to the harsh microclimate changes of the bush. Changes of only a few degrees temperature from inside a bush to its leafy outside are significant to so small a mammal. Above all, mouse lemurs must avoid the radiation of sunlight that their ancestors could ignore in the constant, dank blanket of the leaf-littered forest floor. Mouse lemurs can be active only at night. During the day, they hide in tree hollows or nests that they construct. Also, because they are so small and their bush habitat fails to buffer the extremes of temperature and humidity of the larger climate, they must avoid the thermal stress of cool tropical winters. Mouse lemurs hibernate for brief periods. [7.1]

Not only do mouse lemurs hibernate, they also lower their body temperatures during the day to conserve energy—a pattern of physiology and behavior similar to that of bats and some Australian marsupials. Hibernation and daily torpor both reduce energy requirements and reduce metabolic wear and tear on body parts. This reduction in mechanical stress may account, in part, for the extraordinary longevity of mouse lemurs (and many bats and marsupials). These tiny mammals live longer than fifteen years; a comparably-sized rodent lives about a seventh as long.

For the smallest members of the human order, mating must be timed precisely to avoid giving birth to infants during the coolest part of the year. Pink, bean-sized mouse lemur infants could not survive if born during the cooler portions of the year.

Precise timing of the mating act is therefore crucial. Accordingly, both male and female mouse lemurs are capable of mating at only one brief estrus window during the year. For most of the year, the testicles of the males are shrunken and retracted into the abdominal cavity. The vaginas of females are covered completely by fast-growing connective tissue—a foolproof, scar-tissue chastity belt.

Several weeks before mating takes place, mouse lemurs are flooded by hormones that prepare them for their precise mating date. Females begin to wander away from the other females in their group. Their vaginas swell open. Like their ancestors, the ancient insectivores, female mouse lemurs begin to mark their private territories with hormone-laced urine that proves an attractive perfume—a pheromone—to nearby males.

Mouse lemurs have a more acute olfactory system than ours. They have a pair of special organs in their snout known as the Jacobson's Organ. These tubular pouches of scent receptors (similar to those found in some fish, amphibians, and reptiles) are probably attuned precisely to the changing urinary chemistry of nearby females and males. In any case—and not unexpectedly—the human nose cannot perceive any changes in the odor of mouse lemur urine.

When not in estrus, both male and female mouse lemurs continue to urine-mark their territories, albeit at a reduced rate. They mark via a specialized form of marking called urine washing. They urinate while drawing a hand and a foot across their genitals, then they rub their hand and foot vigorously along a branch. When not dousing the bushes with sexual pheromones, mouse lemur marking probably serves as an announcement to would-be intruders: "This bush belongs to me—stay out."

The odors of a female coming into estrus (sexual heat) time a remarkable change in the behavior and physiology of nearby males. Normally placid, docile, solitary males become aggressive. Under the influence of internal testosterone, their testes descend into scrotal sacs and sperm production begins. Suddenly, they become more active and seek contact with other mouse lemurs. These hormone-flooded "Mr. Hydes" become combative toward other males and even aggressive toward females. The personality transformation of sexually quiescent males into mating male mouse lemurs is as dramatic and sudden as that of Jekyll into Hyde.

This testosterone cycle in males is partly driven internally by an annual biological clock. That is, it will occur in an unchanging laboratory environment and in the absence of any females. The urine marks of females seem to entrain—to synchronize—the male's internal biological clock. Similarly, the female's ovulatory cycle is driven by an internal, annual biological clock. These internal clocks, called circannual rhythms, assure that the mating timetable will not be fooled by any transient changes in the weather like a warm day in winter or a cold summer day. Such a mating miscue would prove disastrous for these tiny mammals. In the past, mouse lemurs with unreliable circannual clocks probably produced offspring at the wrong time of the year—and therefore left no descendants. Unreproduced unreliable clocks disappeared quickly. That's natural selection.

Mating is accomplished when a male invades the territory of a female and chases her. The mating act is a form of slightly subdued aggression; both male and female approach one another with a series of displays of threat and appeasement. Within days after mating, the males, hormones on the wane, return to a solitary, submissive lifestyle in their territories at the periphery of female ranges. Testosterone reduced, they remain docile, mild-mannered "Dr. Jekylls" for the remainder of the year.[7.2]

First Considerations of Mouse Lemur Motherhood

The mature and successful female mouse lemur usually bears three young each year. This is a large number for a primate, but in marked contrast to the litters of eight to ten produced every other month by the ancestral shrews. There were several reasons for the dramatic reduction in the number of progeny. First, mouse lemurs are committed to an arboreal life. The mother builds an arboreal maternity nest, but a nest to contain more than three wiggly tots is probably beyond her engineering skills. Secondly, as we will see, a mouse lemur mother must transport her nearly helpless infants frequently; three infants tax her taxiing skills to the limit.

Most importantly, mouse lemur infants are born with an enormous brain for an animal their size. Three infants strain the capacity of both the mouse lemur womb and birth canal. The struggle to birth three infants can take longer than three hours. In contrast, a litter of eight shrews takes less than an hour to deliver.

Mouse lemurs share with us and all other primates a singular characteristic: all primates have much larger brains than we'd expect for an animal their size. As yet, we do not know why this is so. Unlike the smell-oriented brain of ancestral insectivores, the primate brain is dominated by large areas devoted to vision and even larger regions known as associational areas. Associational areas of the brain are not specifically tied to a single perception (like touch, taste, smell, sight, sound). They probably function to associate, compare, catalogue, and remember perceptions. At least some of these associational areas process social information.

It is likely that the complexities of primate social life, especially primate sex and power relationships, have selected for a phenomenally large social computer. The primate brain and its associational areas have continued to increase in size from lemurs to apes to us, far outstripping their humble origins in ancestral shrews. Beginning with the first primates, long-term social commitments—mating bonds and alliances—distinguish our lineage from those of the insectivores that came before.

Child Care, Mouse Lemur Style

Each adult female has a large, individual foraging territory of bushes within the center of a forest. When not giving birth and raising toddlers, females who hold adjacent territories usually commune with each other and sleep together during the day. Sleeping groups of up to seventeen females are not uncommon. These communal daytime sleeping groups were probably the first primate social group. They formed not from some spirit of camaraderie, but because a ball of tiny animals bound together at rest effectively exhibits the surface area of a much larger mammal. Since heat is gained or lost through the surface area, these communal sleeping balls save each participant many kilocalories of energy otherwise wasted on thermoregulation each year.

Less than two months after mating and before a mouse lemur gives birth, a pregnant female severs her social ties with nearby females and strikes off on her own. She will raise her offspring apart from her colleagues. Mothers probably raise their infants in isolation because the other female mouse lemurs, especially those not pumped full of maternal hormones, would probably mistake tiny pink offspring for edible prey objects.

Alone in her range, the pregnant female constructs a substantial nest. It is not unlike a medium-sized bird's nest, save its top is covered with leaves and it contains a small opening on the side. She gives birth to triplets in this temporary shelter. The infants are helpless at birth. In fact, the infants' heads are so enormous that for several days, they cannot raise them. The newborn's enormous cranium acts like a fisherman's sinker. An unattended infant flails its arms and legs, but can only manage to rotate its body in a circle around its unmoving head.

For these first few days, the mother mouse lemur remains with her helpless infants, licking their fur and allowing them to suckle. At night, she leaves the nest to feed, but returns to them at hour intervals to warm them, nurse them, and groom them.

Within a week, the infants can support their weight unsteadily and can grip their mother's fur firmly in their fists. At this juncture in their development, the mother mouse lemur begins a complicated nocturnal ritual called "infant parking." As she exits the nest to forage, she carries a single infant in her mouth. She travels some distance from the maternity nest, then deposits her charge on the branch of a bush. She returns to the nest, grabs another infant, and deposits it on the branch of another bush. She repeats the process once again until all three infants are clinging to branches in separate bushes. The infants cling motionless and in silence, like so many furry Christmas tree ornaments.

Infant parking serves to protect the infants from predators who might otherwise find an aging, smelly maternity nest filled with three bite-sized mouse lemur babies an easy meal. Mouse lemurs, infants and adults alike, are relatively easy prey for almost every vertebrate predator in the Malagasy forest. During the day, a small, blue-jay-sized shrike (a native bird of prey, *Vanga curvirostris*) can easily tear apart a nest and eat a mother and her triplets. The Malagasy day abounds with larger raptors—one, the Madagascar Harrier Hawk, *Gymnogenys radiatus,* has even evolved special hind limbs that allow it to cling to tree trunks and tear apart tree hollows where many mouse lemurs hibernate or sleep away the daytime heat. At night, jungle "cats" (primitive, genet-like carnivores called viverrids), arboreal boa constrictors, and owls pose a threat to mouse lemur survival. While mouse lemurs are small enough to be on nearly every predator's shopping list, mouse lemurs have always been relatively uncommon; no predator has evolved specifically to eat just them. That fact—and a stealthy lifestyle—is their only means to avoid predation.

Infant parking minimizes loss; one infant may be eaten at night, but the dispersal of the others assures that one or two will probably survive. The infants are not abandoned at night. The mother returns to each one in turn every hour or so throughout the night. She plucks them one at a time, then transports them to yet another branch on another bush within her territory. At the new location, an infant becomes animated. The mother and infant play together, then settle down for a few minutes as the baby nurses and the mother rests. Quickly, before the infant can detect her stirrings and protest, the mother will push it off her nipple and leap away. The infant's response to this sudden abandonment is to freeze motionless on the branch. It will not budge a muscle until its mother returns. As morning approaches, the mother will gather each infant one at a time and return them to the nest, where they can rest, play, nurse and be groomed continuously throughout the day.

Gradually, as the infants mature, infant parking takes on an important role far beyond predator avoidance. Whereas young infants freeze in position on a branch for an hour or more, older infants are explorative. When dropped off by their mother, they will clamber about on the branch. As curiosity overcomes fear, they explore nearby branches until soon, they've investigated the entire bush before their mother returns. Along the way, they'll nibble a flower or fruit, chase an insect, eat a spider, and sample a drop of sap. Throughout the night, as their mother deposits them on one different bush after another, they repeat their tentative explorations.

Invariably, a mother mouse lemur places her infants on bushes from which she feeds. Other bushes within her range that contain toxic leaves or inedible fruit are avoided. Learning what foods are edible is arguably the most important lesson any lemur infant can learn. The leaves and fruit of the earth are, more often than not, rife with toxins.

Bruce Ames, professor of biochemistry and molecular biology at the University of California, Berkeley, notes that:

> Plants couldn't survive if they weren't filled with toxic chemicals. They don't have immune systems, teeth, claws, and they can't run away. So throughout evolution they've been making newer and nastier pesticides. They're better chemists than Dow or Monsanto. They've been at it a very long time. [7.3]

More than 10,000 natural plant poisons have been identified worldwide so far. Plants manufacture toxic lipids, toxic dyes, and cyanide—to name but a few surprises in this toxic smorgasbord. Plant eaters, biochemist Lena B. Brattsten says, "expose themselves to the hazard of being poisoned with every meal." [7.4]

In a truly passive fashion—a combination of parental discretion and infant curiosity—each infant learns what to eat; it avoids novel bushes. Like the ancestral insectivore mother before, at no point does a mother mouse lemur explicitly train or teach her progeny what to eat or even how to behave. Nonetheless, the social context of a mouse lemur mother parking her infants in her territory—a form of passive learning—is absolutely essential for the survival of the young. Learning what to ingest and what to avoid is something of a lost skill with human primates. Humans seem particularly attracted to forbidden fruit. Many enjoy and become addicted to toxic plant chemicals like nicotine, caffeine, and opiates. Most other mammals assiduously avoid such poisons.

I learned the irreplaceable importance of a mouse lemur mother when I attempted to rescue three dozen motherless infant mouse lemurs in Madagascar. I had no difficulty supplying the infants with a suitable milk formula. They grew up quickly and were in good health. Yet, when I attempted to reintroduce the juveniles to their natural habitat, disaster struck. The eager juveniles ran wildly throughout the bushes, expending so much energy that they soon collapsed and had to be rescued again. The infants had no concept of a normal activity pattern or an exploitable range size. Their substitute mother (me) had not taught them energy conservation via infant parking.

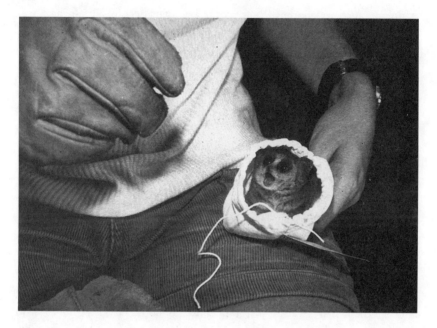

Adult mouse lemur in a transport sack.

In subsequent release attempts, I saw that the juveniles had no idea what to eat. Worse, they had no idea what a predator was; some were eagerly dispatched by a nearby flock of owls. Those that could be recaptured had to remain forever in captivity. The importance of passive learning at the hands of a natural mother was indelibly inscribed in my memory.

Such infant learning experience is best considered selective serendipity. It is the result of countless trial-and-error child-rearing practices culled by natural selection. For example, mothers who placed their infants on bushes that contained toxic fruit left no offspring to carry on their genes (or repeat their infant parking mistakes).

As we will see, for many primates and humans, learning social graces and romantic desires is primarily a passive learning experience—selective serendipity. Yet, learning about social relationships is no less important to us than learning what to eat.

Mama's Girls and Macho Boys

As infants mature, gender differences in behavior become apparent. Juvenile females are far less explorative than their brothers. Male infants soon explore not only the bush that mother deposited them in, but nearby bushes as well. In less than two months, the infants are juveniles, half the size of adults. Juvenile females remain with their mother, but juvenile males wander off, never to return. Occasionally, juvenile males will join together in wandering bands of two or three. Most of these juvenile males, awash in androgynous hormones, young and inexperienced, will take risks and fall prey to predators. For example, it is not unusual to find a small group of curious young males playing a game of tag and chicken with the business end of a resting boa constrictor. Females, in contrast, never engage in such potentially fatal displays of bravura and curiosity.

The loose-knit band of rambunctious juvenile males does not last for long. The gang soon disperses and each remaining young male travels far through the forest. Some will even descend to the ground and scamper across open fields to seek other patches of forests. As yearlings—young adults—their male wanderlust tapers to an end. The few males who remain alive establish a large, individual, solitary territory at the periphery of the territories of females. There, a male must learn the ropes of avoiding predators and finding food and shelter by himself. Except for a brief, annual search for sex, an adult male spends his life alone. In fact, he will avoid contact with females and will remain submissive to them except for the short mating season.

Growing up is a markedly different experience for the juvenile females. They follow their mother throughout her territory, and they learn about their world by watching their experienced mother avoid predators, find food, and construct shelter. In a few months, when they are half-grown, they and their mother return to the communal sleeping hollow—a hole in a centrally-located tree—and join the other females in the neighborhood for their daytime rest. Mothers, daughters, and neighboring females remain in contact throughout their lives. Eventually, the juvenile females

Lepilemur mother and daughter in a tree.

inherit the established, proven territory of their mother either because she dies, or because she establishes a new territory adjacent to her old one.

Daughters inherit much more than mere territory from their mother. Unlike the independent, solitary sons, daughters become a virtual behavioral clone of their mother. A measure of how precisely information is transmitted passively from mother to daughter can be seen in the study of another prosimian, *Lepilemur,* a prosimian closely related to the mouse lemur. *Lepilemur* has no adequate English name, although it has been called "the weasel lemur" and the "sportive lemur." In Madagascar, it is known as the "Songika," the animal that lives in the "Sony" (pronounced "SUE-knee") tree.

Lepilemur mothers and daughters share the same 1,600 square meter territory (about 0.4 acre), but they forage independently at night. Even though a mother and her daughter go to different places in their combined range at different times of the night, cumulative maps of their independent use of this space show an incredible, almost exact similarity.

The usage maps shown here are computer-drawn and based on my long-term field study of these animals in Madagascar. Technically, the distortion of each grid on the map represents a four-month average of the distance traveled by each animal through each grid. Both maps were standardized (that is, the greatest distortions for each map were set equal to "1") so that they can be compared properly. The use of the space traveled by a mother and daughter *Lepilemur* is shown as peaks (high usage) and valleys (low usage): [7.5]

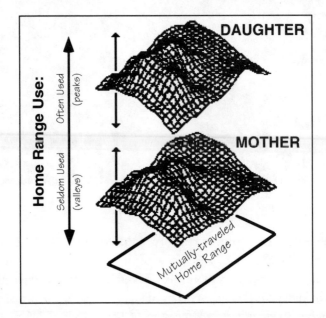

Note that the usage maps are nearly identical, although each animal travels this mutual range area independent of the other. In essence, mothers unwittingly program their daughters' future travel plans and activity.

The Neighborhood of Females

Unlike the solitary males, the social females establish strong bonds between the mothers and daughters in particular and the neighborhood females in general. Seven to twenty females form the neighborhood of females, the protected core of the original primate social group. Their territories—established, explored and proven for generations—assure them an abundance of food and shelter. Their social bonds, especially the enduring mother-daughter bond, provides lifelong warmth, stimulation, grooming, shared experiences, and a measure of protection from predators. Mouse lemur social organization consists of many mother-daughter social groups, surrounded by a few solitary males.

The earliest pattern of primate social organization, shown below, probably consisted of the ranges of solitary, submissive males surrounding territories of dominant mothers and daughters. Juvenile males left their mother's range, but a daughter remained with her mother and eventually inherited her mother's territory as well as social relationships with a neighborhood of females. This pattern of social organization is known as the mouse lemur pattern:

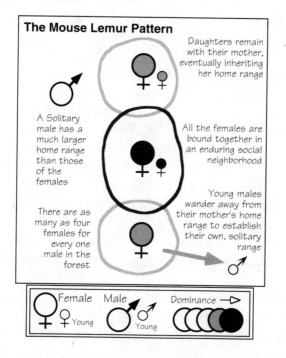

The Mouse Lemur Pattern

Daughters remain with their mother, eventually inheriting her home range

A Solitary male has a much larger home range than those of the females

All the females are bound together in an enduring social neighborhood

Young males wander away from their mother's home range to establish their own, solitary range

There are as many as four females for every one male in the forest

Female Male Dominance ▷
Young Young

Males inhabit the unproven, untested, fringe areas of the forest. They are not social and therefore cannot benefit from mutually-found resources. Their nightly wanderings encompass an area of about 3,000 square meters (the size of a football field), nearly twice as large as that of the females. A predator can eat a male and no other mouse lemur is the wiser. In contrast, females utter alarm calls, warning their female colleagues of the presence of a predator in the neighborhood. Many eyes, many ears, and collective experiences are a prime survival advantage for the neighborhood of females.

The male's independent struggles for survival, coupled with their macho inquisitiveness as juveniles, greatly reduces the number of adult males. The ratio of adult females to adult males in this sort of social condition may easily exceed four females for every one male. Yet, this gender imbalance is no detriment to the species.

For the survival of the species, a male is required only once each year, and then, only for a few days. During this brief mating season, a single male can impregnate many females. A mouse lemur male, like the male of most other mammalian species, can be sexually re-aroused quickly by a novel female soon after intercourse. This phenomenon is known as the "Coolidge Effect"—named after an amusing, perhaps apocryphal anecdote from the life of the late president and his wife:

> President and Mrs. Coolidge, visiting a government farm, were taken around on separate tours. At the chicken pens Mrs. Coolidge paused to inquire of the overseer whether the rooster copulated more than once a day. "Dozens of times," said the man. "Tell that to the president," requested Mrs. Coolidge. The president came past the pens and was told about the rooster. "Same hen every time?" he asked. "Oh, no, a different one each time." Coolidge nodded. "Tell that to Mrs. Coolidge," he said. [7.6]

The Coolidge Effect characterizes the male sexual response in virtually all mammalian species. Anthropologist Donald Symons explains that for humans,

> . . . it is adaptive for a man to experience lust for [a woman] without respect to her physical attractiveness or other personal

attributes; that is, it is adaptive for males to be able to be "blinded" by lust. For men, celibacy of relatively brief duration appears to be a powerful aphrodisiac which profoundly affects [their] perception of female beauty. . . . It is not to a woman's reproductive advantage to copulate with most men even if there is little effort or risk. . . . Hence, it would be generally maladaptive for women to be "blinded by lust" and it would certainly be maladaptive for women to lust for men without regard to their attractiveness . . . [7.7]

In the primitive primate social system, the base of our own social system, the best evolutionary strategy for a male is to impregnate as many females as possible, then retire innocuously to his solitary range and await other mating opportunities the next year. Mouse lemur males dance to the tune of the Coolidge Effect, precisely choreographed by their own testosterone, once each year. For mouse lemurs and for most of our distant ancestors, there was no need to form and reinforce long-lasting bonds between the sexes.

For a female mouse lemur, on the other hand, the optimal reproductive strategy is to choose the most mature, most experienced male to father offspring. An experienced, elder male—one that has survived in a large, nearby territory—stands the best chance of providing her offspring with the genes that will aid them in their own struggles for survival. After mating, the fate of the male is of no consequence to her or her offspring. The mother devotes her efforts to insuring the survival and success of her female juveniles.

The close, long-lasting, consonant, caring, touching, mother-daughter bond exhibits many qualities we humans call love. The mother-daughter bond is humanity's earliest and most enduring social bond. The matrilineage—the social neighborhood of females—is the extension of the mother-daughter bond that serves as the cornerstone of primate social organization.

The mother-daughter bond is a special, almost unavoidable alliance that surfaces time and again to influence and often to determine the course of modern human relationships. From a time fifty million years in the human past until today, mothers in particular and the matrilineage in general have been the primary source of a daughter's concept of mate selection, love, and romance. As we will see, sons build their understanding of gender relations elsewhere and in far different ways.

Falstaffian Males and a Key to Companionship

Strictly speaking, romance, the human courtship ritual that emphasizes (or at least promises) long-lasting care, awaited the evolution of close, consonant, sexual male-female bonds not seen in mouse lemurs or our earliest prosimian ancestors. Such bonds are always established between relative strangers who are pubescents or adults. In comparison to the mother-daughter bond, a male-female bond is difficult to establish and is usually a tenuous association at best.

Even among mouse lemurs, though, not all males are permanently excluded from the neighborhood of females. A very few males—about one male for every ten or more females—have been found sleeping in tree hollows with the females during the day. [7,8] These males are not only tolerated, they are also groomed—the social equivalent of a human, nonsexual backrub. Why are some males tolerated, and others spend their lives alone?

Tolerated males share several important characteristics. They are almost always old. They are usually fat. They are docile and nonaggressive. My measurements of mouse lemurs in Madagascar indicates that these males may weigh 50% more than the females and they may be more than ten years old. Mouse lemurs can live to the age of fifteen or so in the wild.

They are, in brief, the grandfatherly Sir John Falstaffs of the forest. Falstaff was a fat, witty, ribald, politically astute character in Shakespeare's *Henry IV* and *The Merry Wives of Windsor*. Falstaff befriended the powerful, offering jest in lieu of heroics or aggression. It is unknown whether Falstaffian mouse lemur males actually mate with the females in their neighborhood, but it is likely that they do. In any case, it is clear that they benefit greatly from their sociability.

The social success of mellow mouse lemur Falstaffs indicates that mouse lemur females prefer to associate with older, nonaggressive males. Selection of a male companion by a female is not based upon macho bravura or aggressive demands on the part of the male. A female's preference for a mellow male companion is characteristic of almost all primates studied so far. A low level of male aggression appears crucial to sustaining a male-female bond.

The Legacy of Mouse Lemur Love

The human concept of love was some distance away at this early stage of our evolution. Nevertheless, the female preference for nonaggressive males was born in the jungles of North America, Europe, and Asia more than fifty million years ago. It, too, is a recurrent theme in the evolution of romantic love. In this first primate society, gender differences in aggression and inquisitiveness are apparent. Fifty million years ago, males were surplus, asocial, docile, and, except for a once-each-year aggressive act of insemination, irrelevant.

The behavior of our most ancient primate ancestors defined the ground plan for primate societies that followed. Their descendants built new social orders upon the mouse lemur plan. The most obvious legacy of the ancient mouse lemurs is the profound mother-daughter bond. Female primates—from modern mouse lemurs to humans—obtain their most enduring images of love and romance from their mothers. Equally important, the matrilineage—the neighborhood of females—defined the first society of primates. It remains with us today as the stable base of primate social groups, including to a measurable extent our own. Females attain their self-image and their preferences primarily from within the matrilineage. Males go elsewhere.

Social bonds are an almost mechanical, dependent fit of behavior and underlying emotions—an interplay of actions and reactions that accommodate two individuals. Establishing an enduring social bond requires that each individual attains a working knowledge about the behavior of the other. In this regard, the mother-daughter bond has many things going for it. First, it is formed from birth. This gives both individuals a maximum amount of time to learn about one another. Second, one individual—the mother—literally programs the daughter with adaptive emotional and behavioral responses.

But any social bond, even the primary social bond between a mother and a daughter, is subject to serious difficulties. As any computer programmer could tell you, teaching anything to behave the way you want it to is rarely one hundred percent successful. Because the mother daughter bond is the single most influential primate social bond, problems within it can be catastrophic for the mother, the daughter, and the suitors as well. An example illustrates this point.

For the past several centuries, perhaps longer, Viennese mothers and daughters have formed highly visible, culturally important social bonds. Traditionally, mothers strongly influence their daughters well into adulthood. Mothers often dictate (or attempt to dictate) a daughter's career choice, mate choice, and choice of friends. In turn, a daughter is expected to support and pay homage to her mother throughout life. Vienna has always had a housing shortage; it is often expected that a daughter and her new husband move into her mother's flat. Moving in with or in close proximity to your wife's parents is called "matrilocality" by anthropologists. Frequently, though, the Viennese bride's parents will give their daughter their apartment and move into smaller, nearby accommodations. Austrian rent control laws actually favor this form of tenancy inheritance. Frequently, therefore, a Viennese marriage is a union of man, woman, and wife's mother.

Because the mother-daughter bond is especially intense in Vienna, problems within this bond can be especially troublesome. Some mothers exert pathological control of their daughters; some daughters respond with pathological hatred and rebellion toward their mothers. In such cases, the lesser male-female bond of romance is almost always affected negatively.

Understandably, the mother-daughter bond is a theme that runs through much Viennese literature. In an award-winning novel, The Piano Teacher, Viennese author Elfriede Jelinek describes a horrific conflict between a daughter, Erika Kohurt, and her mother. [7.9]

Erika's life is controlled by her mother. Hateful obedience to her mother distorts her world view; she is bathed in guilt and unfocused hatred simultaneously. Erika is incapable of pleasing her mother. No one is good enough for Erika; no career success is appreciated. In turn, Erika is incapable of pleasing herself. She strikes out against conforming to her mother's insatiable career and social demands by turning to masochism and sadistic sex. Erika is a teacher and stalker of men. "Lovers like haters," notes Viennese novelist Ingeborg Lauterstein, "are great stalkers." [7.10] Erika is socially dysfunctional because of a dysfunctional mother-daughter bond.

The negative impact on a daughter by a complaining, contemptuous mother is also a familiar subject in the American media. A recent television special highlights a teenager who is made to feel "not smart enough, not social enough and not quick enough" for her bitter, insecure mother. [7.11]

While parents often live vicarious lives through their offspring, this phenomenon is most acute between a mother and her daughter. A low-ranking (insecure, unhappy) human mother can be particularly demanding of her daughter. The daughter sometimes responds by becoming an insecure runaway.

Emotional abuse tends to run in matrilineages: the daughter who is abused by an insecure mother will, in turn, most likely become an abusing, insecure mother. Problems within a mother-daughter bond are not genetically inherited, but they are inherited nonetheless. For modern medicine, such mental problems are often more difficult to treat than genetically inherited problems. Even with an abusive mother-daughter bond, and the subsequent generations of abusive mothers and abused daughters that flow from it, abusive mothers may well produce as many or more offspring than their nonabusive counterparts in society.

While abusive people may fit poorly into our society, their genes are not at risk for survival. If true, then such child abuse is not maladaptive in a Darwinian sense. Such cases of emotional child abuse are therefore an ethically defined problem. That is, we have collectively said that child abuse is repugnant to us; we define it as a disorder, and we seek a cure. The same may be said of many mental disorders that do not affect the reproductive success of people who are called "diseased" or "mentally ill."

Because many mental problems do not limit the reproductive success of those who are ill, they will not automatically, biologically, be selected out of the human population. An abusive matrilineage can be persistent. The amelioration or continuance of abuse is entirely a matter of our own social priorities. Social priorities are not necessarily established by governments. How a social group personally defines and controls its code of conduct (its mores) can vary from democracy through totalitarian coercion regardless of the "isms" of the larger society. Most social codes are handed down from generation to generation in hunting bands, villages, and larger groupings. In America, our ethical views are increasingly derived not from personal contact and coercion, but from the mixed signals that flow from the impersonal, profit-oriented television screen. The human mother-daughter bond is certainly subject, for better or worse, to much external influence.

Not all mothers and daughters—Viennese or those elsewhere—should be painted with a black brush. Nonetheless, literature and television media have laid bare a painful theme of human life: a dysfunctional mother-daughter bond can damage all other social bonds that follow. Conversely, a functioning mother-daughter bond can facilitate and benefit all social bonds that follow it. The mother-daughter bond is *the* universal nuclear family. Most often, daughters grow up to be just like their mothers—or, in rebellion, their opposites. [7,12]

No other human bond is so influential. No other human bond has so much potential for good and evil. It is a bond backed by fifty million years of natural selection.

The Giant Step for Lemurkind

The tiny, bush-living mouse lemurs of fifty million years ago were extremely successful. They established their nocturnal territories in the bushes of a vast tropical and subtropical forest that extended from Western North America through Eastern Asia. But, they had their limitations. Their tiny size required them to avoid the harsh temperature and humidity changes that characterize the daytime. Their tiny size made them slaves to a miniature energy race, a quest for high-energy, quickly-digested resources. Seasonal changes affected them adversely. Their quest for food came to an abrupt halt in hibernation during the cool tropical winter.

The next step in lemur evolution was a relatively simple one. They got larger. In the course of a few million years, lemurs that weighed about 1.5 kilograms (little more than three pounds)—forty-five times larger than their ancestral mouse lemurs—appeared in what would later become Europe and North America.

As larger lemurs, they were no longer at the top of every predator's grocery list. Their larger infants had a better chance to survive. Their larger size gave them a more favorable ratio of surface area-to-volume; they gained and lost heat at a much slower rate than their smaller ancestors. Their metabolism slowed, enabling them to eat abundant foods such as leaves that were more difficult to digest and less rich in high-energy chemicals than the common, high-energy fruit and insect prey.

Relative to large mammals, small mammals have a high metabolism (energy turnover) and small digestive tract. A small digestive tract passes food quickly from the mouth to the anus—no time to ferment and digest leaves. So, small mammals must seek relatively uncommon, high-energy packages of food like insects or ripe fruit. A larger body size offers many advantages, not least of which is the ability to exploit the forest's most common potential resource—leaves.

The forest foliage supermarket enlarged before them. Larger lemurs could exploit these resources during the daytime, when their acute vision enabled them to spot ripening fruit and edible leaves from a distance. Daytime activity enabled these lemurs to use visual clues like posture (body language) and facial gestures for long-distance social interactions. Social communications could expand manyfold in complexity. With the possibility of more complex, more precise communication, social groupings could expand in size.

So, not long after the mouse lemurs first appeared, larger lemurs evolved. We have found the abundant, fossilized remains of many species in deposits from the Rocky Mountains, France, and Burma. Among the most common are the North American *Notharctus tenebrosus* and the European *Adapis parsiensis*. We classify them as prosimians; they are lemurs who belong to an extinct family group, the Adapidae.

The extremely successful adapid family persisted from about 50 million years Before Present until about 30 million years ago. For comparison, the human subfamily (Homininae) has endured only about four to six million years. A species of North American adapid (or, more likely, a species from a closely related family, the Omomyidae) probably is the ancestor of modern South American monkeys. A European adapid is most likely the common ancestor for all Old World monkeys, apes, and humans.

The living lemurs of Madagascar are also descendants of an extinct European adapid. The Malagasy lemurs became trapped on the island at least thirty or more million years ago. They survived while virtually all prosimians on the continents became extinct. Today, the Malagasy lemurs serve as scientifically invaluable relics of our distant past.

When alive, the abundant larger adapids weighed about one to two kilograms (2.2 to 4.4 pounds). They had a pointed, fox-like face. They gripped thick branches with hands and monkey-like feet. They walked on all fours and could jump between trees, probably swinging their long tails for balance in mid-air. In fact, in all crucial respects, they looked exactly like contemporary Malagasy brown lemurs and ring-tailed lemurs—creatures which serve well as models for the next step in our story of the evolution of human power, sex, and love.

CHAPTER 8

Sex and the Single Lemur

Jenny is a bright, happy fifteen-year-old. Today, as every day this past week, she has borrowed a dab of her mother's best perfume, donned her most fashionable blue jeans, pulled on a slightly revealing tank top, and, most importantly, placed a thin gold friendship band on her finger. She bounces from the house and joins Glenn who waits for her in his car. They will drive to the mall, meet with friends, share a laugh or two, then drive several miles distant to a secluded, sun-dappled spot beside the town reservoir. Jenny and Glenn have been going steady for a week now. Everyone in their social circle knows this.

A world away, in a Malagasy jungle, a young female ring-tailed lemur saunters some distance from the core of her troop. She anoints fallen tree limbs with her scent as she passes. Close behind, an obviously confident young male follows. He sniffs her scent, then marks the tree limbs in turn. Together, they journey some meters distant from the rest of the troop. They sit together, cuddle, and groom one another in the fading afternoon light. The two lemurs have formed a consort bond. Everyone in the troop that matters knows this.

RHIP and the Beneficent Rule of Females

The next stage of our ancestors' social evolution was that of the day-active lemur. A model for this stage is found today in the troops of day-active (diurnal) lemurs that live only on the island of Madagascar. Most diurnal lemurs live in social groups—troops—which number up to two dozen members.

One of the most beautiful and scientifically valuable of the diurnal lemurs is the *Lemur catta,* the ring-tail. It is named, appropriately enough, for its unmistakable, raccoon-like tail that it carries like a swaying question mark high above its back as it swaggers four-footed down a forest path. *Lemur catta* utter many vocalizations, including barks, grunts, and screams. But this gregarious lemur's scientific name reflects its cooing, mewing, catlike social contact call. It is the most common living prosimian and can frequently be seen in zoos throughout Europe and North America. Unlike other diurnal lemurs, ring-tails are partially terrestrial; they often move about the forest on the ground. Ring-tails eat leaves and fruit; they particularly favor the tamarind tree. They have been well-studied, both in captivity and in the wild.

Lemur catta *on the move.*

I have chosen to highlight the social behavior of ring-tailed lemurs in this chapter, in part because their behavior has been well-studied and is dramatic. Other diurnal lemur groups show considerable variation in their behavior from that of *Lemur catta*. Nonetheless, diurnal lemurs share essential similarities: female dominance, stable matrilines, and seasonally aggressive, migratory males. This social pattern appears to be the next rung beyond the mouse lemurs on the primate ladder of behavioral evolution that led to us.

As in the ancestral mouse lemur social pattern, the mother-daughter bond and the matrilineage persist as the strong base of the diurnal lemur troop. For diurnal lemurs, the mouse lemur's neighborhood of females has a new formality. The adult female diurnal lemurs are ranked in a pecking order from most dominant, called the alpha female, to most submissive, the omega female. Most females rank somewhere in between these poles. Three or four closest in rank to the alpha female, the beta females, together form a dynamic power coalition with the alpha female. They are the female oligarchy that controls the entire troop.

For the most part, maintaining dominance for these females does not involve overt acts of aggression. Everyone in the troop knows their place. When a high-ranking female wants to pass a low-ranking female on a branch, when she wants access to food or to grooming, the low-ranking female will move aside quickly. When the alpha female wants to move to another part of the forest, the troop moves with her. An alpha individual wears her rank by standing erect, staring coldly, and strutting with a confident swagger. The alpha female's confidence is not without support. She is backed in her demands by the powerful coalition of beta females who never venture too far from her side. RHIP: Rank Has Its Privileges. Its privileged feeding spots, its privileged resting spots, and its control over troop activities and movements.

If the dominant female's body language fails to impress a low-ranking individual, she may grab the lower-ranked lemur's fur and bite viciously or will swipe at her inferior with sharp fingernails. Diurnal lemurs have peculiar fingernails adapted for this. A strong, keeled ridge comes to a sharp point in the center of the nail. Both males and females fight by scratching their opponent with flailing, open hands. Like a cross between patty-cakes and a martial arts contest, two ring-tailed lemurs may square off on the ground or a branch, each attempting frantically to grab and hold the dangerous hands of the other.

In marked contrast to their ancestral mouse lemurs, an approximately equal number of diurnal lemur males as females live year-round in the same troop. Males within the troop are most often submissive to females. Yet the males, too, have a dominance hierarchy. The males in the troop have their own subgroup, known as the bachelor group. Males within the bachelor group devote much of their time to postural displays, to chasing, and to scent marking—moves directed to intimidate fellow males. The bachelor group is more internally contentious and aggressive than is the matriline, but all males, even the most dominant alpha and beta males, remain submissive to the members of the ruling matriline for most of the year.

Females lead the troop and determine its activity. The matrilineage, led by the alpha female, determines where the troop will go and when it will travel from one feeding and resting area to the next. The troop patrols a large area of the forest; the matriline in motion first, followed close at hand by the bachelor group.

The matriline will vociferously defend its foraging area—its home range—from adjacent troops. When another troop is encountered in a nearby tree, females bark and shout warnings across the gap in the forest canopy. The matriline is most active in defense of the troop's territory, but males participate as well. Males sit upright on their haunches and draw their tails across their chest and forearms, combining and depositing scent from special skin glands on their forearms and chest onto the fur of their bushy tail. The males then stand on all fours and, waving their tails like angry feather dusters, waft their scent in the direction of the potential interlopers. The encounter is noisy, animated, odoriferous, and usually bloodless.

At one time it was thought that scent marking was primarily a characteristic of nocturnal mammals who could not use visual displays for long-distance communication. Yet, contrary to initial expectations, diurnal lemurs have more scent glands and more scent-depositing rituals than nocturnal lemurs. The answer lies in a simple fact: diurnal lemurs are far more social than nocturnal lemurs. Diurnal lemurs use all of their senses—olfactory, visual, auditory, and tactile—to convey complex social information.

After the initial encounter with a foreign troop, within minutes the two troops will saunter off in opposite directions, tails held high, their respective home ranges inviolate. Female rule is neither unaggressive nor nonviolent. Yet, female lemur rule, in contrast with other male-dominated primate societies, is minimally aggressive and minimally violent both within the troop and between adjacent troops. Female rule is perhaps best characterized as a reign of beneficent despots. Most violence within the troop is avoided by a tacit recognition of everyone's rank on the part of all troop members. Squabbles now and then occur between animals of close—hence disputable—status. Dominance hierarchies are, within limits, fluid structures. For most of the year, males are the passive, unaggressive followers of the matriline. A troop of lemurs feeding in the forest's dappled sunlight is most often a pacific scene.

Beneath the tranquil surface of a lemur troop rests the seething disquiet of individual emotions, fears, and dominance ambitions—all codified, channeled, and made visible through complex hierarchies of rank. Only occasionally is the calm disturbed by a spat. An undercurrent of tension is inherent to all social mammals, from mice to men. Yet, perhaps nowhere in the primate world are such tensions less socially destructive than within the troops of female-dominated lemurs. It is a relative social calm that their descendants—the monkeys, apes, and humans—would not again enjoy.

Dominance plays a key role in our understanding of primate sexuality and human relationships. The social tools necessary to attain and maintain a high rank are, for the most part, behaviorally inherited; passed on passively as an infant watches the behavior of its mother. Most surprising, though, is that dominance *per se* comes to exist apart from mating considerations. The perks of rank seem fundamental to individual survival, not necessarily individual reproduction. Indeed, the first, the proximate benefit of high rank is survival—acquiring the best food, the safest resting place in the tree, and a modicum of control over activity. Yet, ultimately, considerations of rank are of prime importance in all human social behavior.

Motherhood, Child Care, and Social Castes

Diurnal lemurs, although large enough to tolerate the heat of day, cannot escape the impact of seasonal change on their lifestyles. There is only one time of year when infants can be born. Each dry season, when temperatures range from a mean high of 39°C to a mean low of about 17°C (102°–62.3°F), a new crop of offspring appear in the lemur troop. Females give birth to one infant, sometimes to twins. Most are born in time to grow into medium-sized juveniles before the cold damp of the rainy season, when temperatures can cool to as low as 7.5°C (45.5°F). A few, born too late, will die in the numbing, seasonal downpours. [8.1]

Most matings occur within a single month, April, with most births occurring four months later. However, matings can occur as late as July. Late matings often result in the birth of an infant who will not gain size and strength sufficient to survive the coming rains. Nevertheless, the larger size of diurnal lemurs, compared to mouse lemurs, allows their species some "slop" in timing their mating season that would prove invariably unproductive for smaller prosimians.

Infants are born helpless, save for a strong grip. They wrap themselves like a thin belt around their mother's waist. Their tiny fists and feet grasp their mother's fur for dear life as she walks along branches and leaps the gap between trees. The mother pauses frequently in her travels to allow her infant to suckle at her breasts.

Alpha and beta mothers with infants enjoy the special attention of all troop members. Young, inexperienced females—the two-and-a-half-year-old daughters of high-ranking females—remain close at a mother's side, grooming her and hoping for a chance to touch, groom, and hold the newborn infant. These young, ever-attentive females are called aunts. They are unrelenting in their solicitations to baby-sit the infant. The alpha or beta female will treat her infant with a tender, tolerant firmness. Under her ever-watchful eye, she will allow her infant to be held by others infrequently. Through close observation and trial-and-error, naive aunts learn how to be good mothers. They will succeed when their time for mating and child rearing is at hand. The matrilineage passes down its mothering techniques from mother to daughter, from generation to generation of females.

The infant diurnal lemur, like the infant mouse lemur, learns what to eat and how to behave by observation. But, in a troop of diurnal lemurs, there is more time to grow up and much more to observe. As the inevitable consequence of their larger body size, infant diurnal lemurs take longer to mature than the tiny infants of mouse lemurs. Not infrequently, diurnal lemurs live more than two dozen years. The longer childhood necessarily requires a longer period of maternal care. The infants have more time to learn how to be a lemur.

As the infant grows, it shifts its carrying position from its mother's waist to its mother's back. Perched high in the saddle, so to speak, it watches intently as its mother feeds. Occasionally and with increasing frequency, the infant reaches out to sample a leaf or fruit. After it is weaned, it will avoid fruit, flowers, and leaves not previously sampled.

Lemur catta *mother and child.*

From its lofty position atop its mother's back, the infant observes how other troop members behave toward its mother. The infant of an alpha or beta female sees that its mother struts confidently, and that all lemurs in the vicinity defer to her intentions with submissive postures. The high-ranking mother is groomed preferentially by a coterie of lower-ranking females and males. The infant sees all. As the infant matures and ventures for a time away from its mother, it struts confidently and demands the obeisance of others. It plays with nearby high-ranking infants and hones its dominance skills within a group of its peers. Thus, both the male and female infants of high-ranking females are privileged from birth, and from birth they learn how to exercise privilege. When they mature, these infants will most likely ascend to the top of their respective dominance hierarchies.

The infants of low-ranking females lead a hellish life by comparison. Their mother is continually abused by higher-ranking colleagues. Under almost continual stress, she is ever-vigilant for the approach of a more dominant animal. Not infrequently, a higher-ranking female will swipe at her. Her infant may be injured in these attacks or it may be pulled from her body by overeager, high-ranking juvenile females who aggressively solicit a chance to play aunt.

In Madagascar, my colleague and I rescued an infant ring-tailed lemur whose mother had been subjected to a vicious attack by two or three high-ranking females. The infant had fallen to the forest floor, with grievous wounds to her head and thigh. We adopted the abandoned tot and dubbed her "Little Orphan Annie." In time she recovered, and seemed well-adjusted to her life with people. Unfortunately, our attempts to reintroduce her to her troop proved difficult—she did not know how to relate to the dominance hierarchies of her own troop. While she displayed a cocky self-assurance around humans, Annie was terrified of any social relationships with her own kind.

Our experience with Annie in the forests of southern Madagascar have been mirrored countless times in zoos. Primates who must be reared by humans away from their social group are usually dominant to and aggressive toward humans, but almost hopeless social misfits when reintroduced to their own species.

In nature, the infant of a low-ranking female learns how to be submissive. It will be cowed by others and will assume non-threatening postures as a matter of course. The infant of a low-ranking female will be, if fortunate enough to grow to maturity, a low-ranking adult. The daughter of a low-ranking female will be a nervous, impatient, inept mother.

Gender Differences

As with the mouse lemurs that preceded them, the infants of diurnal lemurs begin to exhibit gender differences in behavior at an early age.

Presumably, these differences are induced by different hormones: testosterone in juvenile males and estradiol in juvenile females. Juvenile females remain close to their mothers. They are less inquisitive. Females remain in the troop throughout their lives; males will come and go. As a female matures, her rank will mirror that of her mother's. Females form the stable, permanent base of the diurnal lemur social group. As years pass, only the females will remain to mark the identity of the troop.

Unlike infant females, infant males are apt to venture longer and farther from their mother's side. They are more inquisitive. As juveniles, they wander away from their mother and the matriline, eventually joining the bachelor group. A juvenile male who is the son of a high-ranking female will fare well in play fights and dominance posturing. As he matures, he will likely be an alpha or beta male within the bachelor group. For most of the year, his high status within the bachelor group assures him a safe resting place, an abundance of food and grooming, and the deference of

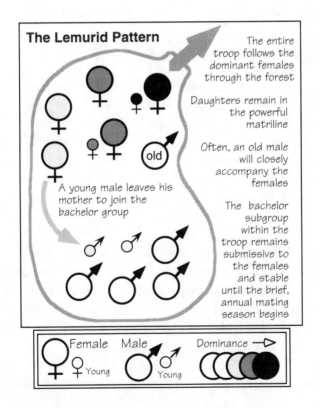

The Lemurid Pattern

The entire troop follows the dominant females through the forest

Daughters remain in the powerful matriline

Often, an old male will closely accompany the females

A young male leaves his mother to join the bachelor group

The bachelor subgroup within the troop remains submissive to the females and stable until the brief, annual mating season begins

Female   Male   Dominance →
Young   Young

his colleagues. But unlike the stable, nurturing matriline, the bachelor group violently self-destructs once each year. During a frenzied mating season, the status and the survival of males is turned topsy-turvy.

Unlike the composition of the stable matriline, the composition of the bachelor group is fluid. Every year, some males leave it and join other troops. Every year, a new crop of males enters the bachelor group and challenges the remaining members for access to estrus females. Only a few males remain within the same troop for more than a few years. Fortuitously, this pattern of migrating males and stable matrilines assures that inbreeding is kept to a minimum, even though no lemur that migrates or remains in the troop has the vaguest notion of such genetic perils.

The lemurid pattern of social organization is shown in the diagram above. Day-active lemurs live in troops of males and females. Females, in a stable, mother-daughter matriline, lead the troop. Males form an unstable, submissive bachelor group which is joined by juvenile males. Each year, some of the males will migrate to another troop in search of better mating opportunities. Females remain with the troop for life.

Consort Bonds and Chattel Goods

Once each year, in March, as the cool austral winter approaches, the mature females of the matriline undergo a profound internal change. Pre-gestational hormones course through their arteries, preparing their wombs for an egg, for a new generation of lemurs. Their vaginal lips swell and separate. These females mark twigs within their range with cast-off vaginal secretions and the broken parts of hormones in their urine. New scents alert all the lemurs within range that another mating season is at hand.

The males of the bachelor group are no less smitten by their internal biochemistry. The males smell and lick the marks made by the females. The females' pheromones entrain the males' internal annual clock. In perfect synchrony, the male's internal testosterone production increases. Their dormant testes quickly swell with sperm. Their behavioral restraints, their quiet assumption of their place within the hierarchy of males and females, is cast violently aside.

At first, a female coming into estrus is followed in her wanderings by one or more high-ranking males. The males threaten one another until eventually, only one male remains in close proximity to the female. If she accepts him, they will form a consort bond. The two will saunter through the forest together; they will sit and groom one another's fur, and they will cuddle together at rest. In some lemur species (most notably in the brown lemur, *Lemur fulvus fulvus*) consorts—both male and female—crawl across the backs of their prospective mate and urinate. This anointing is similar to territorial scent marking. It presages the prevalent, unromantic human concept that a mate is somehow "personal property."

In fact, many animals treat their mates as possessions, marking them and defending access to them from other members of their social group. This sort of chattel bond extends for the duration of the mating season and rarely beyond it. For our own lineage, the concept of a mate as a possession began with diurnal lemurs and has extended throughout their descendants—monkeys, apes, and humans.

While at first glance the concept that a mate is a possession is repugnant to many in our culture, the chattel nature of the consort bond has long-standing adaptive value. Vigorously defended access to the female assures the male mate that his genes and his alone will be present in her offspring. Conversely, vigorous insistence on monogamy insures the female that her male mate will help provide protection and perhaps food for her offspring.

Humans, like the lemurs before them, consider their mates as chattel. In a few progressive human cultures, the male-written laws that treat women as property have largely been revoked. Yet the concept of chattel consorts remains strong within our social conventions. Sexual infidelity and even alienation of affections are considered grounds for the dissolution of a consort (marriage) bond and often are grounds for punitive judgments as well. In many cultures, women are not unequivocally free to obtain an abortion, demonstrating that males exercise a form of chattel control over their bodies.

Since the time when our ancestral diurnal lemurs first developed this behavior more than forty million years ago, once any primate enters a consort bond, its choices of friends and lovers is severely curtailed. The concept that the affections and sexual favors of a partner belong to you—are *owed* to you—is deeply rooted in human evolution. It is a concept that we readily learn and more or less naturally accept. Interestingly, both we and our nonhuman cousins will engage in fleeting, often surreptitious sexual encounters without bonding. But any long-term, serious efforts at reproduction are almost always accompanied by consort bonding with all the implications that our mate is chattel.

Helter-Skelter

By their actions, a consort pair of diurnal lemurs announce their intentions to mate. But consort bonds are tenuous and in all cases temporary. With luck, the bond will last through the month. Often, the bond is lost in the male mating frenzy that follows.

The helter-skelter that marks the male mating frenzy is almost unimaginable. For the males, dominance ranks are quickly and summarily abandoned. Formerly high-ranking males find that their alpha or beta status is challenged continuously. Former alliances dissolve in the quest for a desirable female. Male consorts must continually defend their bond. Males square off against each other night and day. Tails flutter defiantly toward one another in countless spontaneous, provocative scent fights. Screams, chases, flailing limbs, swipes of razor-sharp fingernails, and slashes of stiletto-sharp canine teeth tear at both the flesh and the social fabric of the lemur troop.

This sudden, dramatic burst of male aggression is caused by a flood of androgynous hormones. Every mature male in the troop is affected. The hormones evolved primarily to initiate sperm production and, secondarily, to prepare the male for the competitive quest for a mate. But somewhere along the evolutionary line, priorities became distorted. Dominance, so useful a concept to gain advantage in day-to-day survival, often impedes successful mating. The most aggressive, most competitive lemur males are so concerned with asserting and defending their rank that, for them, the act of mating becomes a secondary consideration. The imprecise hormonal faucet can easily overload a male's system of social restraints and self-interest. Excessive concern about rank has a non-Darwinian, a non-reproductively adaptive, life of its own.

For example, field researchers Norman Budnitz and Kathryn Dainis observed a mating frenzy of wild ring-tailed lemurs where the quest for mating clearly impeded mating:

> The young males, that is, the males who are just reaching sexual maturity (2½ yr.), only get to mate with females when the older

males are occupied with some other activity. For example, Fifth male [a low-ranking young male] mated once when the other males had fallen out of a tree while fighting over an estrus female. Fifth male also mated another time when two females were in estrus at the same time and the other males were occupied with only one of them. [8.2]

And so it goes. Rank may have its privileges but a male's high rank is no assurance of mating success. In fact, the dominance position of males throughout eleven months of the year is subject to overturn during the mating season.

For their part, females appear beleaguered during the helter-skelter mating frenzy. Even an alpha or beta female's choice of a male consort may be no assurance of which male will actually impregnate her. We can, however, achieve some idea of a female's preference for a mate.

The most aggressive males have little time to mate; they spend nearly all their time fighting. Highly aggressive males even misdirect aggression toward potential mates. Every year, some defeated or otherwise unsuccessful males leave the troop in search of better mating possibilities. But each year, a few males strike a delicate balance between successful aggression against males and non-threatening allure toward females.

As with their mouse lemur predecessors, female diurnal lemurs prefer to associate with non-threatening, mellow, Falstaffian males. Some of these plump, older males spend virtually all their time in the matrilineage throughout the year. They are groomed and cuddled almost continuously. They are successful, year-round companions to the females. One such corpulent, mild-mannered male had one eye and a doddering gate; he was the unchallenged companion of a ring-tailed lemur matrilineage for more than a dozen years. We do not know whether they enjoy similar success during the annual mating frenzy. Such information can only come from long-term, intense studies in Madagascar (a political impossibility at present).

Consort Bonds and Mild-Mannered Males

Females, in estrus for the month, choose the most alluring males as mates. The most alluring males appear to be mild-mannered, sensitive males.

They are strong, confident, but not too aggressive. They are persistent, socially clever, and manipulative rather than threatening. They are uncommon. Somehow, these mild-mannered males achieve sexual allure and high status while restraining their hormonal urge to aggress all members of the troop. A female chooses such a male of closely-equivalent dominance rank. Successful, dominant females will form a consort bond with dominant, not-overly-aggressive males. Together, they have the best chance of producing a successful, similarly well-balanced baby.

Dominance status is crucial to every primate's choice of mates. For many years, scientists assumed that the higher the dominance rank of the male, the more offspring he produced. We now know that often this is not the case. The female lemur and the female human often pick less threatening, slightly less dominant males as their mates. While the particular male characteristics that human women select varies through time and between cultures, the most appealing males tend to be those who are less threatening—males who could potentially protect a female's family, but who offer that family no threat.[8.3]

The lemur story is reprised and amplified in virtually every society. The presidents, the generals, the legislators, the professors, and the leaders of business—dominant, highly-visible, alpha males to a man—almost never produce more offspring *per capita* than the nameless majority of less dominant citizens. There is an optimal, difficult to define level of male dominance and aggression that leads to reproductive success. In fact, the commonplace, excessive male drive for dominance may be detrimental to his individual reproduction. Ironically, the dominance drive of primate males, initiated biochemically to prepare males to mate, has assumed an agenda (the dominance for the sake of dominance game) that has little to do with a human individual's successful reproduction.

The latter phrase may seem a tad verbose, *i.e.,* "a human individual's successful reproduction," but there is a method in this wordplay. The dominance game of male humans has had a profound and positive impact on the successful reproduction of our *species*—to the reproductive detriment of many *individual* males. This paradox is explained in the chapters that follow.

A Lemur Legacy: The Balancing Act

The hormones that prepare primate males for sexual activity also trigger generalized, undirected male aggression. The hormones that prepare females for ovulation and sex do not initiate aggression. For a male, but not for a female, sexual desires are intertwined with aggressive thoughts and actions. Not surprisingly, aggressive fantasies and the domination of one partner by another are elements of human romantic love that differ considerably and markedly between men and women.

The nature and context of aggression differ between the genders. Females from lemurs to humans direct most of their aggression toward females of neighboring matrilines—potential interlopers on their resource territory. Females are aggressive in the defense of resources. Male lemurs direct most of their aggression toward rival males—potential despoilers of their reproductive success. Males aggress to assert and defend their status, their access to sex. Males and females differ in their definition of a threat and in their conception of an appropriate response to a threat. This fundamental difference in the focus and magnitude of male and female aggression has confounded and confused gender relationships since the time of the lemurs.

For more than fifty million years of primate evolution, males have had to aggressively seek, then aggressively defend their choice of mates. Females exercise mate choice as well, often showing sexual receptivity to bold, dominant males who represent no serious physical threat. For courtship to succeed, the amount of male aggression must strike a delicate, optimal balance. But aggression is a complex coloring of assertive behavior—in part hormonal, in part learned, in part a response to changing status within one or more dominance hierarchies. Few males can consistently meter, precisely direct, and adequately control their aggression. To make the matter more difficult, human societies (and human couples) constantly redefine the optimal level of aggression—as seen, for example, by their choice of passivity or violence in their art, laws, heroes, music, myths, and dramas.

The diffuse, intangible images of fifty million years of dominance battles cannot be erased completely by a few tens of thousands of years of cultural prohibitions. The degree to which human males necessarily link aggression to sexual performance is unknown. Some, as yet unquantified, level of dominance and aggression seems a necessary part of the male sexual response. At present, we only comment about male aggression in love and romance when the balance is pathologically unhinged.

Some men, especially those who consider their fantasies pathological, unique, or apart from society, will act upon them. Serial killer Ted Bundy discussed his inability to separate aggressive dominance from love only after killing dozens of women. Human societies will always contain some dangerous male sociopaths, a result of the complex web of social evolution where aggression, nurturing, romance, and status ride an ever-tottering balance beam. But to what extent and in what context is male aggression a natural part of human courtship?

Rape as a Male Reproductive Strategy

While female lemurs in estrus attempt to choose their mates, the actual mating act is often accomplished without their apparent consent. Further, low-ranking females and females who are temporarily lacking the protection of their consort male may be jumped and copulated with by other males. Rape—copulation without consent—is not uncommon in lemurs and this legacy of the lemurs can be seen in descendant primates, including humans.

Few acts seem more repugnant, socially disruptive, and alien to us than rape. The Federal Bureau of Investigation considers rape a crime of violence. The American Medical Association calls rape a "violent crime motivated by the need to dominate women . . . [it is a form] of abusive, dehumanizing behavior, being motivated by a profound hostility toward women. Rarely is rape sexually motivated; rape is a crime of dominance and anger, not of passion." [8.4]

Science writer Bettyann Kevles has noted that "[f]orced insemination in the animal world represents a breakdown of reproductive cooperation and compromise between the sexes." [8.5] Yet forced insemination—rape—is an integral part of many primate mating systems from lemurs to humans. Few female lemurs are serviced exclusively by their (apparently) preferred mate choice, their consort male. Instead, the chaos of the mating frenzy assures that many females will suffer insemination from interlopers, from unchosen males who seize an opportunity—perhaps their only chance—to mate.

For humans, rape is a fact in every culture. In the United States, there were 94,500 reported criminal rapes in 1989—a figure surely a mere fraction of the actual number.[8.6] Rape is probably the most underreported crime, a fact long known. Indeed, sex researcher Havelock Ellis stated that "[c]ertainly more rapes have been effected in marriage than outside it."[8.7] At the time Ellis wrote this hypothesis, marital rape was not considered possible by legal definition in most societies.

Even in Samoa, where fifty years ago famed anthropologist Margaret Mead asserted erroneously that forcible rapes were unknown, rapes have always been astonishingly commonplace. Anthropologist Derek Freeman reports that the rape rate in Samoa is probably 160 rapes per 100,000 people, a figure four times higher than that of the United States.[8.8]

Since rape is common from lemurs to humans, then it can be argued that rape as a means of reproduction has been selected for by natural selection. It is equally likely that rape has been ignored by natural selection because it confers no reproductive advantage or disadvantage. Rape may be selectively neutral. For most primates, rape is a consequence of the hormonal-behavioral complex that leads to male mating. This complex and its aberrations can be understood simply.

For males, successful mating entails two simultaneously successful behavioral acts. First, a male must be accepted by a female; he must be able to form a consort bond. Second, he must assert and defend his dominance over other, competing males. If he fails in either of these two behavioral acts, his mating success is in jeopardy.

Dominant males, especially those who pose no aggressive threat to females, are attractive to females. They have little difficulty forming a successful consort bond. Dominant males are successful in asserting their high rank over potential competitors. Their aggressive posturing toward potential competitors is sufficient. Dominant males have little need nor inclination to resort to rape.

Submissive males, on the other hand, have little or no success in forming either a consort bond or establishing a high rank among their peers. Submissive males are unattractive to females and are on the bottom of the pecking order. Their reproductive and dominance ambitions are frustrated. Their only real chance for mating success is rape.

Richard D. Alexander and Katharine M. Noonan have suggested that rape is a natural primate mating strategy for submissive males.[8.9] Submissive, hence unbonded, males have little to lose by rape, since rape may be their only chance at reproduction and since raped females rarely advertise the crime for fear that they will lose their consort's support. Further, a resisting female may unintentionally indicate to the potential rapist that she is part of a successful consort bond; hence, any offspring fathered through rape will receive the support of the unknowing cuckolded male.

The vast majority of primate males fall somewhere in between the alpha and the omega poles. For a subdominant male who has little success in enchanting a female, rape is a viable reproductive option. Likewise, even a subdominant male who has an established consort bond may become abusive toward females if he fails in his aggressions toward other males. This form of aggression—picking on someone non-threatening and close by when competitive success is thwarted elsewhere—is known as displacement aggression. Most mammals and all humans show some form of displacement aggression at one or more times in their lives. We can all probably name a half-dozen personal acts of displaced aggression without straining our memories. For humans, job and role frustrations are the most common stimuli for displaced aggression toward a mate. Here, displaced male aggression against a woman is a product of unfulfilled male dominance ambitions and a consequently poor self-image.

Since the time of the diurnal lemurs more than forty million years ago, males have had a profound problem balancing bellicosity toward other males and the tenacious pursuit of a mate with a non-threatening demeanor that is attractive to a female. Often, that delicate balance is not achieved, and rape or female abuse may be the result. Ultimately, then, rape and female abuse is an aggressive, violent product of testosterone-induced sexual passions and dominance frustrations.

For most human societies, rape is an unacceptable act, whether it is thought to be sexually inspired or the product of non-sexual rage and misogyny (a hatred of women). Yet, for many twentieth-century societies, rape is still not considered remarkable or particularly criminal. This is especially true for Latin American cultures. Until recently in America and Britain, marital rape was considered a husband's prerogative and not proper grounds for litigation.

There is no doubt that rape is a violent, frightening act that may permanently damage a woman's psyche. Rape is a crime against women and, in some cases, men. Human males presume that their consort bonds are inviolate (hence their mate's progeny are their own). Rape violates that consort bond and, if discovered, can measurably undermine the stability of a society. At the very least, rape is anathema to personal happiness, long-term human bonding, romance, and love.

While we have a superabundance of sound reasons to expose and extirpate rape, we will probably not understand rape until we place it in its proper evolutionary context. Rape is natural, fairly common, aggressive, and, for us, undesirable. If we are to reduce the incidence of rape in any human society, it seems crucial that we consider the natural origins of and the natural reasons for rape. As the great nineteenth-century German naturalist and poet Goethe counsels:

> Even what is most unnatural is Nature . . . [m]an obeys [natural] laws even in opposing them: he works with [nature] even when he wants to work against [nature]. [8.10]

Temporary Consorts

Lemurs introduced the consort bond to primate evolution. In a sense, a consort bond represents the context in which a mating is supposed to take place. Successful consort pairings in a primate group serve to reduce the level of tension. A consort pair signifies to one and all that a couple is compatible and that mate selection has taken place. A dominant male defends this bond against other males, but sometimes less-dominant males cannot sustain their consort bonds. Many, perhaps even most matings take place outside the boundaries of consent and the consort bond. Non-consensual sex works. Nature's way is ever pragmatic, not ideal.

Male lemurs (and males of all the primate species that evolved from ancient lemurs) are largely vagabonds. Males do not maintain lifelong allegiance to any particular matriline. Instead, they migrate from troop to troop in search of better dominance and mating opportunities. As primatologist D. L. Manzolillo puts it:

> Intergroup transfer [of males] has been observed in almost all species of primates studied in the wild. This behavior, often remarked upon in earlier studies as a rare event, is now consid-

ered a major factor in the reproductive activity of individuals, and an important process in the dynamic changes characteristic of social groups. [8,11]

The intergroup transfer of males, initiated more than forty million years ago by our ancestral diurnal lemurs, characterizes all extant diurnal lemur, monkey, ape, and human groups. Vagabond males are an important component of primate social systems.

After the lemur's mating season—after the socially catastrophic mating frenzy—male hormone levels decline precipitously and troop leadership returns to the female hierarchy. Consort bonds dissolve as quickly as they formed. The remaining males, now quite docile, reform a bachelor group. The submissive bachelor group follows the dominant females through the forest once more. The successfully mated females devote the remainder of the year to birthing and raising infants in relative peace and quiet.

Tender, long-lasting, caring relationships—an essential part of the human concept of love—remain the provenance of females through the mother-daughter bond and the infant-care attentions of aunts. Yet elements of a caring, consonant bond between males and females surface fleetingly each year as the consort bond. Sometimes, the same lemur couple will renew their bond for many years. Most often, though, the consort bond is temporary and non-renewable.

Significantly, a few old, unaggressive males may be welcomed into the hierarchy of females. These mellow Falstaffs are showered with affectionate grooming and are cuddled within the female sleeping groups year round. Sex is not necessarily an issue here, but reciprocal grooming, huddling, and caring is the key to access to the matrilineage for these privileged males. The largely platonic relationships between male and female lemurs presage yet another element of human love.

The roots of human romance were nurtured in a troop of day-active lemurs more than forty million years ago. They grow today in our modern world. By going steady, Jenny and Glenn are displaying to their social group. They, like their lemur ancestors long ago, have publicly declared a consort bond. Neither Jenny, Glenn, nor perhaps the ring-tail lemurs realize that this affectional bond is temporary. It is a hallmark of romance that we all form such bonds with unabashed optimism about their permanence. And we dissolve such bonds with regularity and, most often, unhappily. We, and probably the lemurs that preceded us, cycle repeatedly from the enthusiastic formation of a consort bond to its inevitable dissolution. For humans, we cycle from optimism to heartbreak time and again. It is a stressful and successful reproductive legacy that dates back more than forty million years.

There is, of course, much more to romance and social bonding than inevitable cycles of joy and sorrow. The next major development in the long adolescence of human power, sex, and love occurred in the jungles of Africa more than twenty million years ago. It was an exciting time when, if we had been present, we would have been able to recognize clearly many of the traits that characterize human relationships and societies today.

CHAPTER 9

The Day the
World Changed

For the first thirty million years of primate evolution, from 54 to about 24 million years B.P., females dominated primate societies. For all but an annual month-long mating season, they made the decisions that affected troop life. Today, there is only one small West African human society in which females are dominant. More than five billion humans live in societies overwhelmingly dominated by males. How, when, and why did this radical transition of power occur? How did the shift to male dominance affect the evolutionary course of love and romance? How does this ancient coup affect you?

Female dominance of troop life ended abruptly for the descendants of lemurs about twenty-four million years ago, when some populations of transitional African lemurs gave rise to a new, larger primate: the ape. These early apes, known as dryopithecines, were almost identical to the chimpanzees we see today. They were very successful and abundant. So abundant that paleontologists sometimes call the Miocene Epoch, the period in Earth history from 23.5 to 5.2 million years ago, "The Age of the Apes." Dryopithecines first evolved in Africa, then spread to Europe and Eurasia. The first specimens of *Dryopithecus,* the "oak nymph apes," were discovered in France in 1856 and were named after the oak leaves found in nearby paleontological sites. The dryopithecine apes were the immediate ancestors of modern chimpanzees, gorillas, orangutans, and ape-men.

History, evolutionary or otherwise, probably does not proceed by small changes piling atop small changes *ad infinitum.* History may be a series of small changes that suddenly and dramatically coalesce, propelling events in new, unexpected, often bizarre directions that are all out of proportion with the middling changes that came before them. Such apparently sudden leaps in the direction of events are termed emergent properties. History, it can be argued, is the study of past emergent properties. [9.1]

If we could take a time machine back to the jungles of northern Africa twenty-five million years ago, we'd probably see a troop of dryopithecines casually munching leaves and fruit beneath a large, broad-leafed tree. "So what?" we'd probably say. "They just look like chimpanzees to me." Today, with the power of twenty-twenty hindsight, we say something quite different. This event—the appearance of apes—heralded a time when the planet changed dramatically and forever. Power, sex, love, primate social order, and global ecology would never be the same again.

From Meek Bachelor Lemurs to Autocratic Apes

The dryopithecines inherited the lemur pattern of social organization, but evolved several crucial social changes all their own. The larger body of the ape—more than fifty times more massive than that of a diurnal lemur—was well-adapted to buffer seasonal changes in weather that would chill or overheat a smaller lemur infant or juvenile. Infant dryopithecines could survive well even during harsh weather. Accordingly, unlike female lemurs, female apes came into estrus every month throughout the year. The capability to produce infants at any time of the year allowed the ape to multiply many times faster than its ancestral lemur. Furthermore, the large-bodied dryopithecines could exploit subtropical, even partially temperate climates. In Darwinian terms, the year-round production of hardy babies was an extremely advantageous adaptation.

From this seemingly small change—a larger body size—extraordinary events in the path of human power, sex, love, and social organization were irreversibly predestined.

First, since female dryopithecines were sexually receptive every month of the year, it followed that, males, too, began to produce sperm year-round. Unlike their lemur ancestors, male apes were necessarily flooded with testosterone year-round in order to maintain their sperm count. Males, as they competed continuously for females, and with their year-round production of testosterone, became dangerously aggressive year-round. For our ancestral apes, the helter-skelter of male mating aggression now extended throughout the year. Aggressive, dominance-posturing males—not females—controlled the ape social group year-round.

Yet, it is doubtful that any primate society could long survive constant, unrelenting, socially disruptive male aggression. At least we are certain that none survived until the present day. Natural selection solved the problem of year-round male aggression in at least three ways: (1) some ape societies disintegrated into solitary males and females; (2) some apes adapted a harem social organization, a social group that contained only one adult male and many females; and (3) some ape societies—those that lead to chimpanzees and humans—developed male power coalitions.

For the dryopithecine ancestors of the modern orangutan, both males and females reverted to a solitary existence. [9.2] Huge males, some weighing more than 180 kilograms (almost 400 pounds), rarely met another male. Male-male aggression is avoided. Matrilineages—coalitions of related females—disappeared, replaced by a solitary mother and her dependent child. [9.3] Lactating females, carrying and caring for their large, dependent offspring, seldom came into estrus. Their reproductive hormones were suppressed by the rigors of long-term nursing and parental care. Modern orangutans have a very low reproductive rate, and, until humans recently invaded their world, they had no effective predators.

The dryopithecine ancestors of the modern African gorilla adopted another mechanism to prevent potentially lethal, socially chaotic male aggression. A single, gargantuan patriarch, called a "silver-backed male," controlled a submissive harem of females and their offspring. [9.4] The silver-back's dominance status was absolute and almost never challenged; he weighed in excess of 160 kilograms (350 pounds), nearly twice the body weight of an adult female. Within the harem, the patriarch governed his mates and offspring with little more effort than an infrequent withering stare. In the face of predators or in an infrequent encounter with a nearby patriarch, the formidable appearance of these huge animals and a few ritualistic thumps of their chests were usually sufficient to settle any dispute.

Upon the death of a ruling silver-back, one young male inherits its father's title. Other males leave their family group late in adolescence, to wander the forest in search of an elderly, enfeebled, or ailing patriarch to dethrone. But such youthful challenges to an autocrat's rule rarely occur. A powerful silver-back is virtually a tenured leader. [9.5] Today, leadership turnover in a gorilla's harem is uncommon. Gorilla harem life is, or at least was, largely tranquil. The chief cause of silver-back mortality was probably disease (until the twentieth century accelerated habitat destruction and slaughter by humans).

Both gorillas and orangutans have survived, relatively unchanged, for nearly twenty million years—hardly examples of evolutionary failures. Yet, for orangutans and gorillas, social peace prevails at an enormous survival cost. Both orangutans and gorillas mate infrequently. The unchallenged, dominant males have a greatly reduced libido. As yet, no one has measured the annual pattern of testosterone and serotonin (a brain hormone associated with dominance status) production in these free-ranging great apes. Levels of both these hormones are probably relatively low in gorillas and orangutans.

With few offspring, large territories, a low population density, and a placid, stable, unchallenged existence, orangutans and gorillas are ill-equipped to survive severe environmental change. Neither species is able to adapt to this century's rapacious human encroachment on their habitat.

Unlike the dryopithecine ancestors of orangutans or gorillas, a third group of dryopithecines—the ancestors of chimpanzees and humans—solved the problem of year-round male-male aggression and benefited from a vastly increased reproductive capacity.

The dryopithecine ancestors of chimpanzees and ape-men did not employ a social system which isolated individuals or banished males to singular, widely-dispersed harems. Instead, these dryopithecines transformed the lemur's submissive bachelor group into a single, dominant, all-male power coalition. This tense, aggressive coalition of males maintained an uneasy peace between its members by directing their pent-up aggressions outside the troop. Displaced aggression that spares the troop disruptive male-male mayhem has become *the* hallmark of chimpanzee and human reproductive and social success.

The dryopithecine ancestors of chimpanzees and humans redirected their aggression in two highly ritualized ways: through hunting and warfare. In both ways, the pent-up frustrations of males within a troop are displaced safely upon a victim outside the troop. Today, we can observe a model of the dryopithecine beginnings of these two crucial social institutions in the behavior of wild chimpanzees.

The Hunting Hypothesis

The myth of a courageous, crafty male venturing forth through hardships in search of prey for his hungry family is common to many modern cultures. The story is less a truth than a romanticized rationalization.

Organized, social hunting is characteristic of chimpanzees and humans. The practice probably began with our common dryopithecine ancestor more than 20 million years ago. It had little or nothing to do with acquiring nutrients. It had everything to do with releasing potentially harmful male aggression.

Six or so male chimpanzees jointly rule their troop of twenty females and fifteen or so offspring. They are a powerful coalition, lead by an alpha male. The alpha male retains his rank through the support of less dominant male colleagues. Individually, chimpanzee males are only slightly larger (about 10%) than chimpanzee females, a degree of sexual dimorphism not unlike that of humans. Chimpanzee male power, like human male power, is more a function of political power than individual might. In fact, the chimpanzee male coalition is a political organization in every sense of the term; it is rife with coups and conspiracies.[9.6]

Nothing divides the male coalition more than sexual access to females. Each member of this power coalition is a competitor whenever a female in the troop becomes sexually receptive. Accordingly, tensions within the male power coalition run very high. About once a month, the tensions build and threaten to physically pit each male against the other—potential pandemonium which would disrupt the entire troop with ruinous consequences. So, when the male tensions are palpable, the coalition joins together in what can only be described as a ritual of male bonding. Holding one another, they hoot and scream in near-sexual excitement. Then the males march off, away from the core of the troop's home range, in search of nearby prey. Their prey of choice—a lone infant deer or unguarded baby monkey—is never a match for a band of these 40-to-50-kilogram (88-to-110-pound) males. They violently and cooperatively dispatch the victim, pummeling the hapless creature with their fists, tearing

Alpha and beta male chimps survey their troop.

it apart with their powerful hands. When finished, they return together, prey in hand, to the core of the troop.

What follows is as socially important as the hunt. The male with the prey in hand will pass portions of the victim to the other males, high-ranking females, juveniles, and infants who beg a portion. The power coalition shares the meager spoils of the hunt. Importantly, chimpanzees normally forage independently; they do not share food. Sharing the spoils of the hunt has a social bonding function, primarily bonding the potentially divisive males together until tensions again make another bonding hunt necessary.

Calling the spoils of the hunt "food" would be a meaningless overstate-
ment. A few pounds of baby monkey meat a month, dispersed among
twenty-five or more adult chimpanzees—each weighing from 80 to 110
pounds—has almost no nutritional value whatsoever. Altogether, as many
as forty-five chimpanzees—adults, juveniles, and infants—will share tiny
pieces of the kill. Captive chimpanzees thrive nicely, reproduce, and grow
old without any animal protein in their diets.

Similarly, hunting in most human cultures provides few calories and
precious little nutrition. Consider the tragicomic Great White Hunter
syndrome of some American and European males. The GWH and his
buddies pile into a $14,000 Jeep, drive a hundred miles at eight miles per
gallon, camp in tents and gear worth more than $500, and shoot, using
$500 weapons, $200 worth of frightened, easily-ambushed meat (or
hook—using $200 tackle and a $1,900 boat—$50 worth of surprised and
helpless fish). The economics and the human energy expended for these
rituals far outvalue any catch. The story has changed little in a thousand
years, yet the myth that hunting is food-providing remains.

Prior to the advent of agriculture, the bulk of the human diet consisted
of fruit, grasses, insect grubs, and tubers—all acquired through individual
foraging or through the cooperative searching by the troop's females and
their offspring. After agriculture evolved, the bulk of the human diet
consisted of grains planted and cultivated by both women and men. Only
a few modern cultures presume the wealth to waste grain to feed livestock.
And, of these cultures, only the wealthiest members can acquire or profess
the need for animal protein in their diets. Humans and chimpanzees are
ritual carnivores. Dining in groups, for both apes and humans, can often
assume a greater social than nutritional function.

To be certain, hunting—and its close corollary, fishing—has provided
significant food stocks for marginally-distributed human groups. For
groups like the Arctic eskimos or African and Australian desert bushmen,
hunting has changed from a necessary male-bonding ritual into a necessary
male-bonding-and-food-acquiring ritual. Yet, it is apparent that a nutritional use for cooperative hunting followed long after hunting's social
origin. We can observe this in chimpanzees and we can logically infer it in
fossil ape-men.

The three-plus million-year-old fossils of the first humans—actually little
more than small, bipedally-erect African apes—are not found in associa-

tion with either prey or hunting tools. Frail, three-foot-tall, small-toothed ape-men would have needed a tool's mechanical advantage to regularly overpower a meaningful amount of prey. At most, ape-men, like their dryopithecine ancestors, were social hunters. Hunting almost certainly evolved in the first place to redirect male aggression and to socially bond overly-competitive males, not to provide a steady supply of food.

Unlike hunting, warfare, the most significant dryopithecine route for bonding males and redirecting their aggression, has changed little throughout more than twenty million years of subsequent evolution. The primitive roots of warfare, a legacy of our ancestral apes, run deep in every man and every human culture.

The Joy of War

Warfare evolved and persists as the most successful way to bond competitive males and redirect their aggression outside the larger social group.

In 1976, a surprised and saddened Jane Goodall reported that chimpanzees make war. She watched in horror as the male coalition of one troop huddled in excitement, "grinning hugely," then marched toward the edge of their territory in search of members of a neighboring chimpanzee troop. Upon locating a sufficiently small subgroup of their neighboring troop, the male coalition attacked them in merciless force, beating, biting, and slamming bodies against trees.

One such battle lasted no more than fifteen minutes. A six-member coalition, followed by a single female, had entered a neighboring troop's territory and attacked and brutally killed an outsider mother and her infant. For the next five minutes . . .

> . . . the . . . chimpanzees, in a state of excitement that bordered on frenzy, charged back and forth around the scene of conflict, dragging and hurling branches, throwing rocks, uttering the deep, low-pitched hooting calls that sound like roaring. Eventually, still in a noisy and boisterous mood, they turned and moved back the way they had come. [9.7]

The victory obtained, the coalition settles back in their territory, peacefully conducting troop life again and savoring their renewed alliances. The strongest male bonds come from shared victories. The next campaign will come soon, as sexual and competitive tensions within the coalition rise once more.

A chimpanzee coalition never picks a battle it cannot easily win. Most of the targets of aggression are single, old females wandering on the outskirts of their own territory. Sometimes, though, a holocaust is launched. One such slaughter killed all the males and infants in a neighboring troop. In each case, three to five males ganged up on each opponent, beating, biting, and slamming their victims to death without mercy. Later, the females of the decimated troop joined the conquering coalition.

The male coalition is almost always on guard. They are a patrol, leading their troop through their territory, protecting the troop from surprise attack, and attacking their neighbors whenever an opportunity presents. The creation of an outside enemy is crucial to successful male bonding and coexistence. Chimpanzees, like humans, divide the world into "us" versus "them." It matters not that the enemy poses no genuine threat to the coalition's survival. It matters that the coalition's survival is impossible without an enemy.

Warfare was the ultimate male bonding ritual for the dryopithecine ancestors of chimpanzees and humans. Male humans have extended this ritual to heights undreamt by our ancestors or evolutionary cousins.

Not surprisingly, the need for war is little understood by human females. Warfare threatens a woman and her children without enhancing her survival or her stature. To most women, warfare seems a terrible, wasteful, inefficient way to settle a dispute between groups. But war did not evolve to settle disputes. War evolved to displace in-group male aggression. Seen in that context, warfare becomes an adaptation central to preserving the peace within any ape or human troop that is composed year-round of aggressive males and tranquil female families. Warfare, more than any other social institution, clearly separates and clarifies the distinctly different goals of men and women. As primate evolution goes, it is only recently, through the rationalizations, vagaries, and deceptions made possible by human language, that male coalitions have convinced a majority of citizens that war is broadly beneficial or necessary.

The Female Family Group

Like the lemurs before, female apes still formed close bonds with their daughters. Our ancestral dryopithecine troop, like troops of modern chimpanzees, probably consisted of submissive, maternal families dominated by a nearby, tense male power coalition. The powerful matriline that distinguished a diurnal lemur troop had disappeared. In its place was a loose association of maternal families—neighbors to be sure, but not a politically effective matrilineage. As juvenile males matured, they left their families and joined the male coalition. Juvenile females became part of the submissive female family group. For adult females, the mother-daughter bond, the backbone of primate societies since the time of the mouse lemurs, remained intact.

Within the troop, individual matrilineages had their own dominance ranking. Some families were high-ranking, others appeased and entertained the higher-ranking families, while a few were low-ranking, social outcasts. The offspring of high-ranking females ascended to high rank themselves.

Like modern-day chimpanzees, it is likely that low-ranking dryopithecine mothers sometimes became child abusers; their children perpetuated the trait. Jane Goodall recounts a chilling story of a family of wild chimpanzees who, abused by their mother and following her lead, abused other members of their troop. [9.8] The mother, a low-ranking chimpanzee Goodall named Passion, was born about 1950. She was decidedly antisocial, cannibalizing at least three infants belonging to other mothers. Passion's daughter, Pom, was born in 1964. She was badly mothered and killed two infants belonging to other chimpanzees in the troop. Passion's son, Prof, born in 1971, shared in eating the murdered infants. Passion's offspring exhibited considerable fear of their mother. None attained high social rank and all exhibited extremely antisocial, disruptive behavior. The manifestations of a mother's love—or the lack thereof—is learned from the mother.

There is an unsettling lesson here. High social status—and concomitant high self-esteem—correlates well with tender, supportive mothering. Children raised by low-status mothers often mature to become unloving consorts and parents. It is a pattern that we can trace for more than twenty million years, from the extinct jungles of the human past to our homes within contemporary society.

In summary, the earliest apes, like modern chimpanzees, probably formed large groups of dominant males and submissive females. The lemur bachelor group evolved into a dominant all-male power coalition. The male coalitions survived by redirecting their aggressions outside the troop via hunting and warfare. Matrilineages became submissive, stable families of mothers and their offspring.

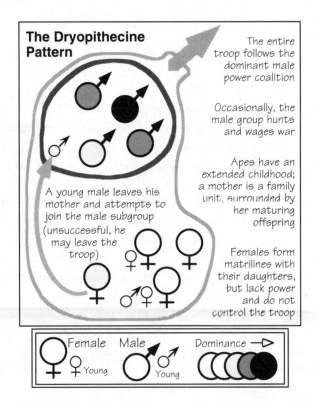

The Dryopithecine Pattern

The entire troop follows the dominant male power coalition

Occasionally, the male group hunts and wages war

Apes have an extended childhood; a mother is a family unit, surrounded by her maturing offspring

A young male leaves his mother and attempts to join the male subgroup (unsuccessful, he may leave the troop)

Females form matrilines with their daughters, but lack power and do not control the troop

Female Male Dominance
Young Young

The Oldest Profession and the Consort Bond

For the dryopithecine ancestors of humans and chimpanzees, adult, dominant males were not part of any family group, although some sons probably remained loyal supporters of their mother and sisters. Instead, high-ranking female families courted and enjoyed a close association with the most dominant males. Relatively long-lasting, warm, consonant bonds were formed between these high-ranking males and females. They sat together, embraced, and groomed one another. Often, these warm, caring relationships persisted when the female became sexually receptive. But any social bond, like the consort bond, is cemented by an exchange. The dryopithecine female, like the female common chimpanzee, exchanged sex for the protection provided her family by proximity to a powerful male.

In human groups, an exchange of an economic asset for sex is called prostitution. In the strictest sense, prostitution probably began more than twenty million years ago with the dryopithecine ancestors of modern apes and humans. Japanese researchers have discovered that modern female pygmy chimpanzees regularly exchange sex for food.[9.9]

It is highly likely that our dryopithecine ancestors began the practice of bartering sexual access for resources (like food) or intangibles (like proximity to power). The exchange trades upon a female's willingness to copulate for goods or services provided by males. As repugnant as this concept is to modern thought, it is likely that prostitution has a long history and is deeply ingrained in the male-female bonds of modern humans. Human prostitution takes many forms, but to the degree that a woman provides herself and her family protection and survival through prostitution, the behavior can hardly be called ignoble.

Prostitution is a cold, hard, amoral fact of ape and human life. Prostitution, the exchange of sex for desired benefits, is simply another facet of our evolutionary heritage—a heritage we may take umbrage with or praise. Some contemporary thinkers extend the definition of prostitution to extremes. For them, every woman who accepts a gift from a man is engaged in prostitution. Philosopher Alison Jaggar asserts that a woman who merely attends a candlelight dinner with a man is a prostitute—and hence, contemptible. Many feminists despise the image of prostitution.[9.10] Yet, a female's exchange of sex for goods and services seems a keynote of ape and human male-female bonding. The disparity between natural, amoral realities and ever-changing, arbitrary human ideals is a by-product of our enormous and often troubling brain. It is likely that we are a species capable of far too much thought (some of it logical) to be truly happy or even satisfied with our lot.

Dryopithecine females probably had some choice of sexual partners. Females attempted to consort with a few desirable, high-ranking males.

But the dominant males had their way whenever a female entered estrus. High-ranking females were chosen by (and in part, chose) high-ranking males. Low-ranking females were submissive to any powerful male.

Dryopithecines, like their descendants, chimpanzees, were promiscuous. That is, some females and most males mated with more than one partner. Monogamy was not a requisite for the formation or continuance of a consort bond. Humans are much like their evolutionary cousins, a fact that many find troubling to admit.

The Ape's Legacy to Human Relationships

The ancestral ape pattern of social organization appears like a parody of some forms of human social organization. Actually, human social organization has been inherited with only slight modifications from that of our ape ancestors. Humans are risen apes, not descended angels. Our societies echo strongly the troops of ancient apes. Social dominance of males has been characteristic of human evolution, and is characteristic of virtually every human culture. Social rank is largely inherited, primarily through offspring learning their place in society by observing their mother's behavior.

Dominance position matters as much, perhaps more than, sexual satisfaction. Our difficult game of courtship is layered each day with the complexities of power struggles, preferential treatment, leadership, and survival. Who you are seen with, who prefers you, who grooms you, becomes more important than mere sex. Male chimpanzees and humans establish and retain their rank by association.

Mate choice is governed by these social rankings. For the male human or chimpanzee, it is important to mate with the highest-ranking female. The proper choice of a mate affirms his dominance position. For the female, gaining the protection of and privileged association with a high-ranking male will both confirm her social rank and insure the safety of her family. For the male, caring for a female is a requirement for dominance. Abusive, frightening males are avoided by females as much as possible. Consequently, they have less reproductive success than those males who offer females protection and solace. For the female, caring for a male is a pragmatic extension of maternal nurturing. Neither love nor romance can be considered apart from dominance and social rank. Human mates are usually chosen from social ranks close to one another.

Underlying the complex requirements of dominance and rank are the basic, opposed reproductive strategies of males and females. These reproductive strategies remain little changed from that of the ancestral mouse lemur; that is, the optimal female strategy is to mate with the most successful male, and to care for offspring (preferentially, daughters); the optimal male strategy is to mate with as many females as possible, and to invest as little care in females or their young as possible. Females seek stable families; males seek novel females. Females seek goods and services (such as protection) in exchange for sex. Males seek sex.

Since the days of our ape ancestors, courtship has never been a simple matter. Our dryopithecine ancestors canalized many of the more complex dominance considerations of human society and romantic love. Profound, divisive gender differences ranging from the nature of status through the importance of ritualized killing—hunting and warfare—have separated the romantic goals and life expectations of men and women ever since the days of our ancestral dryopithecine ape. Love, expressed as some form of egalitarian ideal that works for both men and women, must work hard to conquer all the evolutionary legacies of our past.

PART III

The Human Veneer

CHAPTER 10

The Brave New World
of Articulate Apes

The dryopithecine apes of African jungles and forests were the ancestors of African ape-humans, the next stage of our own evolution. Dryopithecines were quadrupedal (they walked on all fours). At best, dryopithecines, like modern apes, could move on their two hind limbs with difficulty. Their longest bipedal amble of a few dozen meters would have resembled an awkward, crouching, splay-footed, hands-out balancing act.

The earliest walking ape-humans were creatures called australopithecines; they first appeared almost four million years ago on the savannahs of Africa. The earliest known australopithecine is called *Australopithecus afarensis* after the region where it was discovered, the Afar triangle of Ethiopia. It had a medium-sized brain, scarcely larger than that of an ape. The brains of australopithecines averaged about 440 cubic centimeters (27 cubic inches) displacement. For comparison, the brains of chimpanzees and gorillas displace approximately 390 to 465 cubic centimeters (24 to 28 cubic inches). [10.1]

Australopithecines closely resembled other apes, save they stood erect on their two hind limbs and walked with our easy, familiar, striding, two-legged gate. Bipedality afforded them two principal advantages: walking is a relatively energy-conserving means of covering long distances, and walking liberates the hands—all the better for carrying things long distances. Australopithecines were the first truly vagabond primates, free from the confines of the forests. They could follow herds, scavenge food,

and extend their range across the African savannahs with relative ease.
Their unique form of locomotion proved highly advantageous; australopithecines created a unique primate ecological niche.

An australopithecine stood erect, much as we do, and it walked much
like you and me. It probably behaved much like a common chimpanzee
with troops consisting of a dominant male coalition and a number of
female families. Like modern chimpanzees, the members of the australopithecine power coalition would have sublimated their aggression
through periodic warfare and hunting rituals.

Unlike modern chimpanzees, the australopithecines exploited a more
forbidding habitat, the open savannahs and scrub grassland forests. Any
creature that walked upright through the treeless, grassy plain was visible
to a host of predators. Our ancestors faced predators such as lions and
cheetahs without the luxury of trees to climb. Their safety net was the
bluster and bluff of the dominant males—a tactic seen today in their
cousins, the savannah-dwelling baboons. Australopithecines, like modern
humans, had small, unimposing canine teeth. An australopithecine threat
probably consisted of hoots and wild gesticulations with flailing arms.
Further, australopithecines have been found in association with crude
stone tools called Olduvai choppers. These roughly finished rocks, used
primarily for husking plants, smashing nuts, and rending carcasses, may
have been hurled in desperation at threatening predators and in anger at
neighboring troops. It is unlikely, though, that the crude, heavy choppers
were routinely carried as weapons.

We can reasonably infer that australopithecine male coalitions func-
tioned sometimes to protect their highly visible troop from predators. If
so, then the male power coalition served a useful role beyond that of
redirecting their own internal aggression. Humans have romanticized this
role of the "male protector." Yet, these male protectors often protect
females and infants from the aggressive males of neighboring troops. It is
an irony of our evolution that females and infants would not need much
protection *by* males were it not for the aggression *of* males. In that regard,
the coalition of males has always been largely self-serving and self-per-
petuating.

Of Bipedality, Buns, and Bonds

While australopithecine social life probably differed little from that of the chimpanzee, there were a few likely innovations. Dryopithecine females, like their chimpanzee counterparts, displayed estrus vividly through a great, cauliflower-like swelling of the perineal region—the rump surrounding both the anus and the genitalia. In common chimpanzees, the perineal swelling turns vivid pink and red near ovulation—a clear sign to males that impregnation is possible. This perineal "estrus flag" necessarily disappeared when the dryopithecine evolved into a walking australopithecine.

The reason for the disappearance of the estrus swelling is easily envisioned. The tailless, quadrupedal dryopithecine held its rump region high as all quadrupedal mammals must. From behind, both its anus and the genitals were clearly visible. But for an australopithecine (and for us), standing erect forced the anus and genitalia to rotate downward, not rearward. Physical changes in the pelvis and upper leg that permit walking included a massive increase in size of the muscles of the posterior pelvis and upper legs, [10.2] further obscuring the perineal region. These enlarged muscles are the gluteal muscles—more commonly called the buttocks. Chimpanzees and other quadrupedal apes have almost no buttocks. A bipedal australopithecine, like a modern human, had large buttocks that effectively obscured both its anus and genitals. "Once [humans became upright]," notes New York University anthropologists Frederick Szalay and Robert Costello, "there was a problem with the signalling system." [10.3]

Lacking a perineal estrus flag, the australopithecines would have probably mated frequently to ensure that conception would occur. Today, we see that Pygmy chimpanzees, *Pan paniscus,* show little perineal swelling and, as a likely consequence, they are much more sexual than their close relatives, the Common chimpanzees, *Pan troglodytes.* Pygmy chimpanzees possess a relatively larger penis and clitoris and mate far more often during each day, during each month, and during each year than do other apes. [10.4]

Australopithecines were probably far sexier than their dryopithecine ancestors as well. Of course we have no way of knowing whether australopithecines considered their bulging buttocks—the consequence of their adaptation of walking—an erogenous zone. Many modern men and women consider the buttocks an erogenous zone. Then again, we are such a sexually-oriented species that there's hardly a square inch of the visible

human anatomy that some group somewhere hasn't considered an erogenous zone at one time or another. The whole-body approach to sexuality
is a human trait.

Anthropologist Marvin Harris has suggested that the loss of a clear-cut
sign of ovulation (the estrus flag) led to intense sexuality and to the
formation of longer lasting male-female bonds. If so, then sexual uncertainty—ambiguity about when is the best time to mate—abets the longer-
term consort bonds we see today in humans. Literally, we mate frequently
because we are more ignorant about the timing of sex than the common
chimpanzee.

Naturalist Jared Diamond, citing anthropologists and other biologists,
listed six other hypotheses regarding the selective advantages of concealed
ovulation in the human lineage: [10.5]

1. Concealed ovulation evolved to enhance cooperation between
   males and reduce male-male aggression. A blatantly obvious sign
   of female ovulation would disrupt society.
2. Concealed ovulation requires females to be sexually receptive at all
   times, cementing the male-female bond.
3. Concealed ovulation requires males to be constantly attentive to
   females, supplying them with protection and resources such as
   food.
4. Concealed ovulation forces males into permanent (or at least long-
   lasting) consort bonds with females (a variation of hypothesis 3
   above).
5. Concealed ovulation conceals male parentage, forcing males to be
   attentive to the offspring of their mates (after all, the child *could*
   be theirs).
6. Concealed ovulation allows females who are aware of their ovulatory cycles (a dubious assumption at best) to elicit copulations and
   gain the favor of powerful males without the dangers and burdens
   of childbirth and parenting. This unlikely hypothesis pictures the
   protohuman female as a primate who consciously used birth control knowledge to manipulate her political fortunes.

Regardless of which, or how many, of the preceding hypotheses are
ultimately rejected, the fact remains that potentially long-lasting human

male-female bonds are fostered by relatively long-lasting, constant, and insatiable sexual appetites. Humans are the sexiest—or at least most sexually active—primates.

The evolutionary trend of increasing sexuality from apes to humans spans more than mere behavior. The human penis is the longest and thickest of any primate species; human testes are larger and heavier than those of either the gorilla or the orangutan. Our physiology requires us to savor our copulations longer than any other primate. As Harris states, natural selection has "endowed us with sexual needs and appetites so strong that people are predisposed to tolerate, if not to crave, sex every day of the month, every day of the year over a span of many years." [10.6]

The March of Australopithecines

Walking on savannahs was such a successful adaptation that the Genus *Australopithecus* evolved several species. *Australopithecus afarensis,* the ancestral australopithecine "Afarensis," thrived from about 4.2 until about 3.8 million years Before Present. It produced at least two new lineages: *Australopithecus africanus* ("Africanus") and *Australopithecus robustus* ("Robustus"). Africanus was gracile in form and stood barely more than four feet tall. It differed little from Afarensis and resembled a walking chimpanzee. It probably ate seeds, nuts, tubers, and, occasionally, caught small game and scavenged carcasses along with hyenas and other, lesser predators. Robustus, which may have evolved from a population of Africanus, was stout and powerful. It resembled a small, walking gorilla. It probably ate mostly leaves.

Africanus survived from about 2.8 until about 2.2 million years B.P. For a time, it may have stalked the savannahs near populations of Robustus, which lived from about 2.2 until about 1.0 million years B.P. Most anthropologists now believe that both Africanus and Robustus produced no further descendent species. They became extinct without issue. Instead, they trace our origins from Afarensis to a different African lineage of ape-humans called habilines, after the species *Homo habilis:* [10.7]

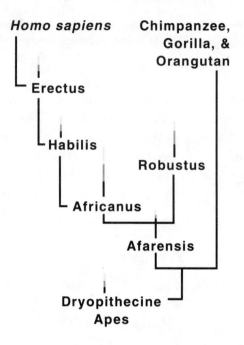

Since australopithecines were first described in the 1950s, phylogenetic trees of australopithecine evolution have come and gone about every half-dozen years or so. Sometimes, a new family tree is constructed following a new fossil discovery (although most often the tree is reshuffled without any new data). Anthropologists will probably never agree on who begat whom. Nonetheless, some essential points are common to all family trees. Namely, australopithecine evolution displays a radiation—a proliferation of species—indicative of the adaptive success of the central behavioral and anatomical feature of australopithecines, walking.

The australopithecines of two million years ago inherited the dryopithecine social system of dominant male coalitions and female extended family groups (matrilines). Physically and probably behaviorally as well, they were little more than bipedal dryopithecines. The wandering australopithecines built upon the dryopithecine social pattern. Bonds between males and females were presumably strong and relatively long-lasting—a product of their intense sexual drive, their enlarged sexual equipment, and their uncertainty about the optimal time to mate.

Like extant male apes, australopithecine males probably did not participate in parenting. Mothers and their daughters undoubtedly formed the
strongest, most enduring bonds within the australopithecine troop. Mothers socialized infants. Mothers programmed daughters. Juvenile males
were socialized primarily by the bachelor group. This social pattern—the
mother-daughter bond coupled with the bachelor group of young males—
has persisted from the time of the mouse lemurs. Variations of it persist
in social groups today—in the lemurs, the apes, and humans.

The public's interest in the australopithecines is great. National Geographic documentaries about the work of the late Louis S. B. Leakey and
his family (wife Mary and son Richard) at Olduvai gorge have piqued a
fascination with the human past. Popular books about the life and times
of australopithecines attain best seller status each decade even though
there is almost nothing to suggest that australopithecines were more than
bipedal apes. Significant changes in the ape social pattern occurred far
more recently than the time of the australopithecines. Major alterations in
the ape pattern occurred as a consequence of a dramatic increase in brain
size—an increase, first seen in the habilines, that led to the human mind.

The Bloating Brain and the Origin of Language

Afarensis, Africanus, and Robustus had ape-sized brains which averaged
about 442 cubic centimeters (27 cubic inches) displacement. [10.8] The brain
of *Homo habilis* averaged about 642 cubic centimeters (39 cubic inches).
Habilines were larger than australopithecines: they weighed about 40
kilograms (88 pounds) versus about 30 kilograms (66 pounds). Their
larger brain would have given them somewhat greater computing power
than their australopithecine forebearers. How much greater, we cannot
say. But we do know that the tools associated with habilines are no more
sophisticated than the slightly modified river rocks that are found with
australopithecines. Despite its somewhat larger brain, there is little reason
to consider *Homo habilis* a major behavioral step away from australopithecines.

About 1.5 million years ago, larger-brained descendants of habilines
appeared in Africa. These creatures, called *Homo erectus* ("Erectus"), had
a brain case that averaged 941 cubic centimeters (57 cubic inches)—a
figure within the lowest range of modern human brain sizes. They were

larger than habilines and weighed about 50 kilograms (110 pounds), about 10 kilograms (22 pounds) more than *Homo habilis*.

In life, Erectus must have appeared the archetype of the popular Hollywood "cave man." Its face was chinless and had a sloping forehead. It viewed its world through eyes shaded beneath a massive, bony brow ridge. Yet it stood as erect as you or me, it carried objects, and walked and ran with the grace of a modern athlete.

Erectus was clearly smarter than the australopithecines or habilines that preceded them. Their brains were fully 40% larger than those of their predecessors. Erectus made many stone tools, ranging from elaborately flaked hand axes to hide-scrapers. Erectus males hunted large game cooperatively, piling the bones of their prey near their campsites. There is excellent evidence that Erectus made use of fire. Some Erectus skulls have been found with the base of the skull removed—evidence that the brains of these hapless individuals had been removed by other Erectus, an act which suggests a ritual. In short, Erectus was the first truly culture-bearing primate, a significant break with the ape-humans of the past.

If Erectus hunted cooperatively, passed the knowledge of tool manufacture from generation to generation, and conducted brain removal rituals (perhaps cannibalistic, more likely, religious), then it is reasonable to conclude that their mode of communication was an order of magnitude more sophisticated than the emotive communicative systems of apes and australopithecines. It is likely, but by no means certain, that Erectus communicated using human language. Since language is the sine qua non of humanness, Erectus was probably the first truly human primate.

Scholars are entitled to disagreements about when language first appeared. Language leaves no fossil clues, save evidence that we use to infer its presence. Jared Diamond, for example, argues that language appeared about 35,000 years ago with modern *Homo sapiens*. [10.9] Even if Diamond is correct and *Homo erectus* did not use language, the argument presented here regarding the evolution of human social behavior and romance would not change much. In fact, Diamond's argument suggests that the ape model of social behavior remained with us until 35,000 years ago, not 1,500,000 years ago as I have stated.

Eventually, inevitably, *Homo erectus* changed. Through evolution, no species lasts forever, no matter how successful it appears to be. About half a million years ago, larger-brained descendants of Erectus appeared: *Homo sapiens*—us. One or more populations of Erectus was ancestral to our species in one of several possible ways. Some anthropologists maintain that only one group of Erectus gave rise to all *Homo sapiens*. According to this hypothesis, other Erectus populations scattered about the globe became extinct without issue. An older hypothesis, becoming popular once again, states that modern humans evolved in different places and at different times from different populations of Erectus. In other words, the present, globally-distributed population of humans that we now consider a single species *(Homo sapiens)* is, in fact, a conglomeration of many different species. Whichever hypothesis survives closer scrutiny, a singular fact remains: modern humans evolved from Erectus. [10.10]

It is likely that once language had evolved, selection favored those Erectus who had the capacity of mind to store, retrieve, and weave words. Language ushered in an ongoing selective pressure that favors larger brains, ever better adapted to use language.

One theory, currently in vogue, states that the relatively large primate

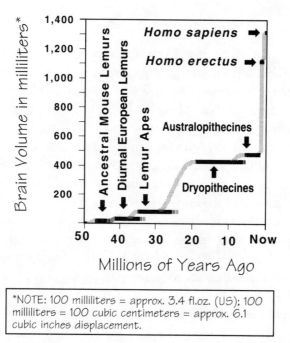

*NOTE: 100 milliliters = approx. 3.4 fl.oz. (US); 100 milliliters = 100 cubic centimeters = approx. 6.1 cubic inches displacement.

brain is larger than the brains of most mammals because primates have sophisticated social systems and natural selection has chosen large brains to make social calculations. [10,11] To some extent, this is probably true. But the enormous increases in brain size from Habilis to Erectus and from Erectus to *Homo sapiens* cannot be explained away by a presumed increase in the complexity of social arrangements. It is more likely that language—with its storage requirements for object names and metaphorical relationships—spurred the geometrical increase in brain size within the human family.

Our species is merely the most recent stage in an evolutionary trend of larger and larger brains within our lineage. Our brain averages about 1,400 cubic centimeters displacement (85 cubic inches). It is a marked improvement over the brain size of Erectus. But the human brain's storage and retrieval capabilities have already been surpassed by one of our inventions: the silicon brains of digital computers. We are, in a sense, designing the next, out-of-body stage of brain evolution. Perhaps we are designing our successors.

Language and the Population Explosion

Language is uniquely human. All social species communicate, but only we can speak. The difference is significant. With language, we can arbitrarily name objects in our environment. We can label our feelings and discuss them. We can communicate about the future and the past. We can devise and act upon artificial classifications of the world. Language enables us to create many different metaphorical worlds—places, times, and events that have never actually existed. Language is the prerequisite for religion, art, mathematics, music, and for many of the social institutions that distinguish human societies from those of other animals.

For the ancestors of modern humans, the immediate benefit of language was to empower the aggressive, dominant male group to engage in verbal, not physical, aggression. At once, much larger, less physically violent social groups became possible. A single troop, formerly limited to perhaps a dozen or so adult males, could now contain hundreds of arbitrarily defined, competitive male groups. Language redefined the game of aggression.

With language, the genus *Homo* quickly populated the connected continents of the Eastern hemisphere. The African Erectus spread to Asia and Europe. Erectus thrived for more than half a million years. *Homo sapiens,* its immediate descendant, extended its range and its numbers throughout the globe. Our species' population explosion was made possible by language, a system of communication which fosters the creation of many competing male subgroups within a single society.

Language enabled humans to exist in population densities unthinkable for any other primate. Tens of thousands of humans can coexist relatively peaceably in areas that can only support dozens or hundreds of nonhuman primates. For example, at most, only about 400 small nocturnal *Lepilemur* or about seven human-sized chimpanzees inhabit a resource-rich, one-square-kilometer forest patch. Yet, each day more than seven million people coexist relatively peacefully in New York City, an astounding density of more than 9,300 humans per square kilometer. Population densities of people stacked atop one another in skyscrapers in other major cities exceed this figure. Even vast regions of the globe hostile to most primate life sustain large populations of the human primate. Barren Ethiopia, for example, now supports more than 39 people per square kilometer. [10,12]

The Origin of Marriage

With so many males now existing in close proximity, the competition for mates could easily have become a year-round, deadly recapitulation of the diurnal lemur's month-long mating frenzy. The adoption of relatively permanent consort bonds insured social stability for the Erectus group.

Language enabled Erectus to arbitrarily define the nature and limits of the consort bond. We have a power to control the shape of social bonds far beyond that afforded any other creature. The universal, arbitrary, human consort bond is marriage.

Marriage is proclaimed publicly so all members of the social group are aware that an inviolate consort bond has been established. Marriage bonds are negotiated. As for our ancestors, the formation of this sexual bond requires an exchange of goods: a man gives money, food, property, or the promise of protection and security in exchange for sexual access to a woman. Often, an initial exchange of goods is given between a man and his bride's family. In any case, the human marriage bond is more than a sexual link between two people. A marriage cements two lineages within a larger bond of relatedness.

Marriage bonds stabilize society in two ways. First, individuals bound by marriage have restricted public sexual access to all other sexually active individuals in society. Members of a marriage bond are publicly acknowledged to be taken or spoken for. Sexual violation of the marriage bond is universally considered punishable. This arbitrary prohibition serves to reduce public promiscuity. As we have seen, public promiscuity (*e.g.,* the mating frenzy of lemurs) can lead to socially disruptive violence. Humans must be privately promiscuous or risk social approbation.

Secondly, marriage bonds join two unrelated families together in a social relationship. An ape or australopithecine troop was a loose association of female families and a single, changing, dominant male power coalition. The human troop, at least locally, is bound together by a web of kinship and marital relationships. For humans, genetically unrelated in-laws become de facto "kin."

Human "troops" are controlled by many competitive male coalitions (one is drawn at the left of the diagram, below). More or less permanent consort bonds—marriages—reduce aggression between males. Dominant females tend to pair with dominant males. Daughters tend to stay with (and be influenced most strongly by) mothers. Sons join bachelor groups and receive much of their socialization from peers outside the family unit. Later, adult males join various power coalitions ranging from networks of kin to corporations. There are many minor cultural variations on this basic human pattern of social organization. Even so, the basic pattern of human social organization remains remarkably close to that of modern chimpanzees and of the common ancestors of humans and chimpanzees, the dryopithecine apes:

The Human Pattern

Societies are led by powerful male subgroups who redirect aggression outside their group or society. Some males, bonded to near-ranking females in marriage, are part of a family and a larger kin group (unmarried males often retain kin ties to parents).

Daughters are socialized primarily by their mother; sons join other male (bachelor) subgroups.

Many male power coalitions exist in every society; an individual may belong to several simultaneously. Recent widespread trends: females join male groups or form their own power groups; serial monogamy; single-parent families.

Female   Male   Dominance →
Young   Young

Language—the adaptation that allows the human primate to prosper in large societies composed of many potentially disruptive male subgroups—evolved primarily to foster social harmony. As such, language is not necessarily a communicative system that fosters truth, beauty, or honesty. In fact, language is a system well-adapted to deception.

CHAPTER 11

Monogamy, Language, and Lies

Language distinguishes us from our ape ancestors. Language has enabled our species to conquer the earth and to reach for the stars. Yet, perhaps most importantly, language enables us to deceive ourselves and others. If human relationships differ from those of contemporary apes, they differ most in their fundamental deceptions. Perhaps most fundamental is the often stated monogamous ideal that hides a polygamous reality. There are two sorts of polygamy: a male has more than one female mate, which is polygyny, or polyandry, where a female has more than one male mate.

Polygamy in Disguise

For most mammal species, males mate with more than one female. Males are more promiscuous than females. Most mammals are therefore polygynous. There is ample evidence that humans, too, are biologically polygynous. Human males usually mate with more than one female. While individual human males, on average, produce fewer offspring than individual human females, *some* males will produce more offspring than any female. In short, human males have productive copulations with different females (are promiscuous) more often than the reverse is true. [11.1]

Along with the observation that males are more promiscuous than females, polygynous species such as ours show other adaptations in their physical form and behavior. As for other polygynous species, human males

174

are larger and take longer to mature than females. Human males are conceived in greater numbers than females, but they die in greater numbers than females as embryos, as juveniles, and as adults. Males age more rapidly and die sooner than females. All signs point to polygyny.

In practice, though, a formal marriage rule that allows multiple spouses at the same time is extremely rare. Formal polygyny (multiple wives, one husband) and its even rarer converse, formal polyandry (one wife, multiple husbands), are uncommon, highly specialized human mating systems. While humans are a promiscuous, polygynous species in practice, formally sanctioned polygyny and polyandry are rare because they threaten group stability.

Polyandry is strongly selected against in nature because it defies the biological imperatives of the puddle-where-sex-was-born, *i.e.,* males have the capacity and adaptive drive to impregnate more than one female; polyandry requires many men to bond to a single woman. Polygyny is likewise selected against because it reduces the number of available females, thus increasing disruptive male competition and aggression. Further, polygamy of any sort "builds disproportionately large and powerful lineages of close relatives"—a direct threat to pre-existing male power coalitions. [11.2]

Anthropologists have long pointed out that both polygyny and polyandry are short-term, adaptive responses to extreme environmental circumstances. Today, polygyny is practiced widely only by West African, sub-Saharan peoples. There, women and children work the land, and land is held in common by a clan or lineage. The more offspring a woman has, the more surplus food she can produce for her clan. Men may have children with more than one woman; women may have children with more than one man. Fathers provide little child support. A mother and her children form the basic family unit, although children are thought to belong to an extended family (the clan), rather than to a particular man or woman. These supporting factors, claim health care workers John and Pat Caldwell, "may increase fertility by reducing the direct cost of a man's decision to have more children." [11.3]

Ecologically, polygyny in West Africa worked well. The population grew quickly and exploited land more rapidly than could have been the case with monogamous child production. But today, the sub-Saharan population has grown to exceed the agricultural support capacity of the land. The

people, unable or unwilling to switch to less productive means of reproduction, face starvation or decimation by diseases associated with promiscuity. Ultimately, changing circumstances and natural selection determine
the viability of human mating systems.

Monogamy: Selection Against an Ancient Reproductive Strategy

Monogamy, an oft-stated ideal mating system, has always been at variance
with the reproductive strategy of male primates. The fictive, monogamous
human mating system has recently come under highly visible, social attack.
As Danny DeVito stated in a recent motion picture: "Maybe it's not
natural to stay married to one person for life. My parents did it. Sixty-three
years. A few of 'em good." [11.4]

Perhaps nowhere was the difference between the cultural ideal of monogamy and the biological fact of polygyny more in evidence than in
Vienna at the turn of this century. In Vienna, then as now, the ideal
monogamous progression is vaingloriously celebrated: romance, love, marriage, children, and the kind companionship of old age. But Vienna was
(and remains) a practical, pragmatic city. A daughter is often influenced
greatly by her mother in her choice of a suitable mate. A man almost always
chooses a wife who will reflect well upon his ambitions—ambitions honed
in bachelor groups. The mother-daughter bond, and the male dominance
(status) hierarchy are well preserved here. A marriage in Vienna and
elsewhere is a formal joining of two lineages, two dominance hierarchies.

Vienna's pragmatic approach to romance and love extended to the
evolution of marriage as well. The progression was simple, well understood, almost inevitable, and never idealized:

1. Boy meets girl.
2. Families approve, a marriage occurs.
3. Wife has babies.
4. "Happily married" husband goes out at night in search of other
   lovers.

In 1873, Austria, a staunchly Roman Catholic land, came to terms with
this "natural" progression: prostitution was legalized. At the century's

turn, more than 10,000 prostitutes satisfied the needs of men acting out stage four. In typical Viennese fashion, the often untrue nature of monogamy and the proliferation of mistresses were made the subjects of light entertainment in plays and operas, *e.g.,* Strauss's *Die Fledermaus.* The comic premise of *Die Fledermaus* ("The Bat") reveals much about Viennese society's approach to monogamy. In the drama, a man attends a costume ball and fails to recognize his own wife. Thinking she is someone else, he attempts to woo her. In the end, the surprised husband and the unmasked wife laugh at the attempted adultery, kiss, and sing happily ever after.

The "Vienna Waltz" is repeated in almost every culture, and in every epoch of humanity's history. Monogamy is rarely monogamous. The ancient, primate, sociobiological heritage is repeated by humans: the optimal mating strategy for males is to mate with many females; for females, the optimal strategy is to mate with a dominant (successful) male, and to insure the survival of offspring. Children in schoolyards throughout the globe learn this sociobiological imperative. In turn-of-the-century Vienna, boys boasted of their numerous, sometimes apocryphal sexual conquests, while girls talked excitedly about the beauty of fashions, weddings, and child-rearing. The games of children become the lifestyles of adults. Every culture adds variations to the Vienna Waltz, but the waltz remains essentially, biologically the same.

Anthropologist David Maybury-Lewis recounts the story of Wodaabe marriage and adultery, which, though different in detail from Viennese marriage and adultery, is similar in kind. The Wodaabe people are West African nomads who practice formal polygynous marriages they call "kobgal." A man has many kobgal mates, and these wives and their children belong to him. A kobgal marriage legitimizes children and establishes kinship networks; love considerations are decidedly secondary within a kobgal marriage.

The married man may conduct many amorous, extramarital affairs, as long as the liaisons are short-lived and discreet. So far, except for the formal choice of monogamy by the Viennese and polygyny by the Wodaabe, the mating practices of the two cultures seem similar. But the Wodaabe carry the Vienna Waltz one step farther. A married man may decide to conduct a longer, more intense affair with someone else's wife. Should she feel passionate enough about him, she will abandon her own kobgal marriage (as well as her children and kin network) to join her new lover's polygynous family. Such a marriage—a marriage for passion—is called a "teegal" marriage. Maybury-Lewis writes: "The Wodaabe have dealt effectively with the age-old problem of trying to reconcile marriage with passion by instituting these two kinds of marriage." [11.5] Both the Viennese and Wodaabe are well and truly polygynous; only the two cultures' ability to rationalize their behavior via cultural rules and values differ.

Like the Viennese and Wodaabe examples, everywhere we turn in human cultures we find similar behavioral practices that differ only in detail, not in form. The human species is united in its broad practices of gender roles, love, war, child care, population growth, and so forth. We are one species, bound in our behavior by our common ancestry of lemurs, apes, and prehumans.

Today, in many cultures, women have expressed dissatisfaction with the status quo. Young girls sometimes boast of their sexual conquests; unfaithful wives are the stuff of sympathetic soap operas. Increasingly, women refuse to turn a blind eye to male promiscuity. Many women have demanded equality in sexual affairs. The unstable, perhaps undesirable cultural proscriptions of both monogamy and of exclusive male promiscuity are everywhere affirmed in many different ways. Many of the cultural and biological underpinnings and definitions of romantic love are being tested socially.

Troubling questions arise repeatedly. If monogamous, romantic love is so frequently violated and so difficult to maintain, should we hold monogamy as an ideal? Wouldn't an honest assessment of our genders' conflicting, evolutionary paths release us all from harmful guilt and self-doubts? If the ideal of monogamy is deemed worthy of our efforts, how can we avoid the Vienna Waltz, the sad, often disruptive dissolution of a monogamous ideal? Ultimately, the solution to these questions rests individually with each of us.

Deceptive, Adaptive Monogamy

Although monogamy has always been at variance with the reproductive strategy of male primates, monogamy is characteristic of most human societies, including many Asiatic, some Amerindian, and virtually all European societies. Of all the earth's creatures, only humans, a few other mammals, and some birds consistently practice monogamy—and all for similar, adaptive reasons.

First, monogamy reduces the duration of helter-skelter competition for mates. Monogamous pairs, once they are formally proclaimed as such, are reproductively off-limits.

Second, monogamy promises that the male will share significantly the costs of raising offspring. In fact, paternal care is biologically required if the mother alone cannot successfully raise her offspring. If the offspring dies, both the mother and the father lose their genetic contribution to the next generation.

A third adaptive reason for monogamy is that it gives each male and each female in society the opportunity to form a mating bond (assuming, of course, that there are approximately as many males as females in the society). Monogamy limits the size of the kin network that any individual male can accumulate. Monogamy is the only potentially egalitarian mating system.

And finally, monogamy is not a permanent impediment to polygyny. Serial monogamy—marriage, followed by divorce and remarriage—is a consistent human practice. Monogamy is a grand biological and cultural illusion of faithfulness to a single mate. The illusion works. Monogamous consort bonds, no matter how temporary, produce the most human offspring with the least social disruption.

In the human monogamous mating system, consort pairs form ritually announced, supposedly permanent, marriage bonds. The female's offspring belong to this bonded unit. Mothers—and to a variable, lesser extent, fathers—socialize the children produced within this bond. Lifelong fatherhood is a behavioral pattern unique to us. It has recently evolved, perhaps by *Homo erectus* less than a million years ago. Therefore, the precise role of fatherhood is poorly defined and varies greatly between different cultures. In many cultures, children (and the wife) belong to the father. Islamic law, for example, provides that both the wife and children are the property of the husband. In other cultures, the female almost always gains custody of the children whenever the marriage bond dissolves. Divorce cases in Western law favor the retention of mother-child bonds to the usual exclusion of the father.

For humans, monogamy is an adaptation to relieve courtship stress (predominantly male-male aggression) within the social group. As an important secondary benefit, monogamy assures that two adults will attempt to provide care and resources to a female's offspring. Marriage and monogamy provides the offspring with a family name—a formal brandmark of social stature. Monogamy is the most successful male-female bonding strategy ever employed by a primate; it is largely responsible for densely packing the planet with more than five billion humans.

Monogamy, as a formal, culturally prescribed bonding system, works. It produces many children and it reduces social tensions. Yet, matings frequently occur outside the monogamous bond. Monogamy conceals polygyny.

Imperatives for Monogamy

Humans are biologically equipped to form loving, close, consonant consort bonds. Human skin has the richest array of sensory nerve endings of any mammal. We are satisfied as much by the familiar touch of a lover as a pet dog is satisfied by a hand stroking its fur. We are primates who need to be cuddled and touched year-round, whether or not we are in estrus. [11.6] And we are mammals who are almost always in estrus; we desire sexual release whether or not sexual behavior will result in offspring. Uniquely, the human female shows no certain outward sign nor inward knowledge of ovulation; hence, in principle, copulation is encouraged at all times. We seek sexual gratification on a regular basis throughout much of our juvenile and adult lives.

Strong, relatively long-lived consort bonds are essential to our species' reproductive success. Accordingly, humans invest more mental energy to establish a consort bond than does any other primate species. Romantic images, like other mental acquisitions, cost real biological energy to obtain, maintain, store, and retrieve. This investment in getting to know a partner creates its own inertia.

After we form a consort bond, we resist its dissolution if only because a lost bond represents too many lost, costly images and emotions. It is as if each consort pair has made an enormous investment in specialized software programs for their personal, mental computers. Only if new, far better software can be inexpensively obtained will one or both partners dissolve the bond and discard the older programs. But, if the old programs prove extraordinarily unsatisfying, the bond may be severed.

Yet, for all the selective pressures to form strong male-female bonds, monogamy and its product, the male-female family, are recent human developments. For most of the 54-million-year course of primate evolution, males and females pursued distinctly different reproductive goals and social commitments. Mothers bonded to daughters. Males bonded to males. Mothers socialized daughters. Males acquired social and other survival skills as part of an all-male subgroup. The mother-daughter bond has endured and developed for more than 50 million years. Male sub-

A Brief History of Human Bonds

Tens of millions of years	**Solitary females & solitary males**
About 15 million years	**Dominant mother-daughter matrilines; solitary males outside the female social group**
About 18 million years	**A dominant matriline & a submissive male "bachelor" group within a single troop**
About 23 million years	**A dominant male subgroup (a ruling power coalition) & submissive female families (matrilines) within a single troop**
less than the last 2 million years	**Mother-father families; monogamy; many competitive male subgroups within a large society**

groups have persisted and perfected their politics for more than 40 million years. Male dominance coalitions have existed for more than 20 million years. Monogamy and the concepts of fatherhood and family have a heritage of less than one million years.

Some bonding elements essential for monogamy have a long evolutionary history in our lineage. The formation of brief consort bonds during estrus dates back more than forty million years, a legacy of diurnal lemurs. The formation of strong, close, consonant, caring bonds have many of the qualities of ancient mother-daughter bonds that were present at the origin of the Primate Order more than fifty million years ago. The formation of lasting social bonds is not an entirely new concept for us. Even so, the monogamous bond is a dynamic, changing, ongoing experiment in human behavior.

As with our ape ancestors, human males still form dominant, competitive subgroups outside the monogamous bond. Males dominate human society and their allegiance to one or more of these power coalitions is often more important to them than their allegiance to their consort. Politics, religion, science, and business have, until recently, been populated by almost exclusively male subgroups. In turn, each of these major male playing fields is crowded by competing male subgroups. For example, in business, IBM competes with Apple, Toyota with Ford, and so forth.

These adult male subgroups are populated by apprentices—recruited, juvenile males. Various male subgroups—ranging from street gangs to the Cub Scouts, from varsity teams to the armed forces—initially socialize the juvenile males. The ability of a single human troop to tolerate more than one male power coalition is the hallmark of human social organization, and its principal distinction from that of chimpanzee social organization.

In marked contrast to a male who leaves the matrilineage as he matures, a daughter is socialized by her mother for an extended period of time. For females, socialization is accomplished by close relatives. Until recently, the only female bond formed outside her matriline was a temporary consort bond. The matriline has been the primary and most enduring primate social group since the time of the ancestral mouse lemurs more than fifty million years ago.

Serial Monogamy and Concepts of Romance and Love

Serial monogamy is a fact of human life. Marriages, on average, don't last long; men, more often than women, remarry. Male promiscuity is likewise a fact. In America (and elsewhere), men are twice as apt as women to engage in an extramarital affair. Furthermore, humans now live almost twice as long as they did a century ago. They enjoy reasonably good health, a sexual appetite, and increased mating opportunities for many more years than ever before. [11.7] Conditions for serial monogamy could not be more propitious.

There is ample evidence that Occidentals are dispensing with formal marriage bonds and practicing short-term, rapid turnover, serial monogamy. In First World countries, where the birth rate is declining overall, births to unmarried women are increasing. The single-parent family has become the fastest increasing family type everywhere but in Japan. [11.8] Note that boys in single-parent families tend to receive almost all their socialization from the bachelor group, a fact reflected by the remarkable increase in gang activity in recent years. [11.9]

These facts, however, are almost never in evidence when two lovers form a consort bond. Romance requires deception, most often self-deception. A man is not often a cynic who enters into love with one woman with the design to bed her, then find another. Language and socialization accomplish the deception that enables two lovers to bond, optimistic that this love and this romance will last for all time. It is the myth of Romeo and Juliet, fostered in many ways by nearly all cultures.

In reality, when and if Romeo and Juliet part, most often Romeo will find another Juliet and father additional children. The original Juliet may also find another lover, but she will be less likely to bear additional offspring. Thus, a serially monogamous bonding system hides a polygynous mating system that favors some successful, promiscuous males.

With this culturally adaptive system in place for nearly a million years, it is understandable that inequities of the human bonding and mating systems have rarely (and only recently) come under discussion or debate. Humans have long endured (and biologically benefited from) the double standard, the concept that men are entitled to greater sexual promiscuity than women.

Language, Socialization, and Our Mental Image of Love

We differ from our nonhuman primate predecessors in one very crucial behavioral trait. Our ancestor of two million years ago, *Homo erectus,* developed language. Language enabled these early humans to define monogamy and to create non-lethal, competitive, multiple-male subgroups within a larger society. As a direct consequence, human population densities could increase beyond the aggregations seen in any mammal before or since.

Today, humans are the only animals that communicate using language. Language is more than mere object-naming, syntax, and grammar. Language is our way of organizing information. In large measure, we think linguistically. Language specifies the rules for the culturally defined, monogamous bond, marriage.

How does language shape the concept of romance? When we put a discrete, arbitrary, universally understood name upon any object, it is likely that the name itself is a small label that refers to a larger image stored within memory—within a matrix of cells in our brain. Attached to each mental image are memories of emotions, of sounds and perhaps scents. Each mental image is formed from different experiences, and every person's images are unique to some variable extent.

Socialization—the learning process—links name labels to mental images. Names allow us to retrieve mental images quickly—to conjure up feelings and emotions much like your bank teller retrieves a massive financial record and personal record using a small account number. For example, if I tell you: "Whatever you do, don't think of a ball," I suspect that you momentarily saw or will soon see the image of a ball. Note that some people might first see the image of elegantly-clad dancers in a ballroom rather than a baseball. Our mental database has very flexible pointers—a boon to creativity and individuality. In any case, the tiny word "ball" fetches a collage of different spherical images for our mind's eye. This linkage between words and images (or retrieved emotions) is almost impossible for us to ignore.

Although we can all generally describe what a sphere should look like, we encounter serious difficulties when we try to explain and agree upon complex images such as love and romance. Our complex romantic images come to us from many sources, but two sources are paramount: mothers teach daughters, and male subgroups teach males. Mothers emphasize words and images of a stable, supportive mate. Male subgroups encourage visions of multiple sexual conquests. Romeo and Juliet saw and felt quite different things when they gazed into each other's eyes.

The linguistic concepts and the mental image of love and romance differs crucially between the sexes. Further, linguists have found that men and women structure their conversations differently, frequently talking past one another with little exchange of understanding. The primate dominance game, played anew by each couple, has men and women talking different words from different worlds, with distinctly different styles, and with the cross purposes of different goals of dominance and control. [11.10]

Despite profound perceptual differences that exist between the genders, most societies have graced monogamy with a myriad of praiseworthy terms, linguistic metaphors, idealized images, plays, edicts, and poems. In essence, most societies tell their members that monogamy is good and normal—regardless of any individual mental images to the contrary. Consequently, anthropologists classify most human mating systems as socially-enforced monogamy. Societies promote monogamy because it insures a reduction of wasteful competition for mates and therefore a measure of social stability.

Regardless of social conventions, monogamy is under consistent attack. An attack is waged from *within* each of us; from a calculus of fifty million years of self-serving, me-first, approaches of primate courtship; from fifty million years of mother-daughter bonds, aggressive males, and status-conscious males and females. Little wonder that the most fragile pattern of human behavior is monogamous love. Romance is the most delicate rose in the human garden of social behavior. It requires herculean efforts to grow, and it can be killed by the slightest chill.

Deception and the Nature of Language

For our non-linguistic ancestors, courtship and mating were stereotyped, public displays of dominance, power, and copulation. At best, the apes could only act out the patterns of courtship they learned as observant juveniles. For our ape ancestors, courtship was straightforward and, apart from status-posturing feints, honest.

Probably due to our adaptation of monogamy as a bonding system, we have driven courtship and mating into dark corners and private dwellings. It is doubtful that monogamy could survive if humans, like their polygynous ape ancestors, made love consistently in public view. Hiding our intimacies reduces comparisons and competition. For human males especially, the consort bond is a proclamation of social (dominance) status. Any *visible* weakening of that bond would engender violent instability—as much for the cuckolding of genes as for the denigration of rank and status. Of course, behind closed doors, away from view, the monogamous consort bond is often violated.

Self- and social deception is essential to human reproductive success and social stability. An initial public flourish announces the formation of a consort bond. That flourish may include exchanging friendship rings, holding hands in public, marriage ceremonies, or even passionate or erotic public displays. After the announcement, human romantic love retreats behind closed doors. There, any fiction in our monogamy cannot disturb social orderliness. Humans, alone amongst the primates, have divided behavior into public posturing and private realities. Humans can lie to each other and to themselves. Often, in our attempt to conform to society's norms, we willingly accept biologically unrealistic images of love and romance.

Overall, human romance and love resembles a fantastic, Rube Goldberg machine. All that matters is that it works. Reproductive success is everything in the cosmic calculation of evolutionary success. Natural selection strives for neither truth nor beauty—unless truth or beauty begets more children or insures the requisite social stability to beget. Fortunately, as thinking individuals, we can strive for whatever goals we can realistically formulate. Couples can arrange their bond according to whatever values they can communicate. We need not follow blindly all the dictates from our evolutionary past.

Language has been a double-edged sword for our communications. Thanks to language, we humans are the most communicative animals the globe has ever seen. We can verbalize our feelings—however poorly we may understand them. Theoretically, we can negotiate our courtship to achieve mutual satisfaction. Yet, not surprisingly, our language reflects the repressed nature of romance and love. Our communication of the private side of romance is couched in obfuscations and euphemisms. For example, it has been estimated that the living English language contains no fewer than 300 euphemisms for the word "penis," a clear indication of our preoccupation with sex and our attempts to keep communications about that important subject private, imprecise, and obscure. We have evolved a communication system—hence a way of thinking—that is fraught with taboo subjects, with unspeakable words, with fantasies that ought not see the light of day, and with metaphors that communicate at the expense of accurate analyses.

Humans are metaphorical mammals. Metaphors must have been highly adaptive constructs; they allow a few words, placed in proximity, to imply whole paragraphs or stories. Metaphors carry more information than their individual parts could possibly convey in isolation. Metaphors allow us to economically communicate moods, emotions, and opinions, often at the expense of directness and accuracy. We have developed metaphors beyond speech and extended them to music, art, and dramas.

As a result, we dwell in a world filtered through our limited senses and recreated anew, often metaphorically, in our minds. We easily blur the distinction between tangible, external realities and the metaphors we build. The system of human thought and communication is the richest in obfuscations of any yet evolved. It is likely, then, that human language evolved not to communicate more accurately, but to satisfy the everpresent pressure of natural selection to better achieve reproduction through social stability.

For primates, a good communication is not necessarily an accurate one. Communicating deceptively in matters of dominance and love was a powerful force that shaped the initial development of human language. Indeed, the vast majority of animal communication systems have been shaped by sexual deception. [11.11]

Language, more than any other animal communication system, encourages deceptive interactions. Indeed, more than mere deception between two people, language encourages self-deception. "What sets human beings apart [from other animals]," said anthropologist Robert W. Sussman, "is our ability to deceive ourselves . . . Culture is by definition self-deceptive, but it is essential for human existence." [11.12]

Philosopher Ludwig Wittgenstein recognized the duplicitous nature of language. He proposed that all human social problems arise from misunderstandings and mistakes in logical grammar. Wittgenstein viewed philosophy as an ongoing "battle against the bewitchment of our intelligence by language." [11,13] Gender relationships, by affecting the primary design of language, have always played a major role in that bewitchment.

In less than two million years, humans have evolved from public anthropoid lovers into private human lovers that time and again inaccurately communicate heartfelt thoughts about love and romance.

Imperatives for Romance

The human species created the concept of romantic love. It is an imprecise, changeable metaphor, precisely what we might expect for a concept that depends upon no small amount of deception to succeed. The many behaviors—caring, love, bonding, sex—that comprise romantic love manipulate both partners. Even so, romantic love is arguably one of our more important linguistic adaptations. The metaphor promotes successful mating and child rearing. The metaphor fuels much of the creative genius that has been essential for the survival of our species. The metaphor defuses aggression and promotes cooperation. The metaphor can be (and often is) applied to magnificent advantage far beyond the particular person or pair that spawned it.

For all language's shortcomings, language offers the only hope of analyzing, understanding, mitigating, changing, or using the biological imperatives and cultural rules of the past to advantage. The careful use of language is our only hope for restructuring our received mating and bonding systems into systems that foster any personal desires for egalitarian, lasting, exciting, beneficial relationships.

CHAPTER 12

Natural Selection in Our Time

Gender differences in bonding, aggression, and reproductive goals have been millions of years in development. Human power, sex, and love is steered today by the legacies of ancestral lemurs, dryopithecines, australopithecines, habilines, and *Homo erectus*. The evolutionary imperatives that canalized the behavior of our ancestors are apparent in the present human approach to war, civil unrest, child abuse, altruism, monogamy, changing gender roles, fatherhood, the population crises, and AIDS. These examples, briefly highlighted in this chapter, show the long-standing influence of past evolutionary events in crafting our behavior. The examples also reveal a precarious balancing act between our past and our present, for humans—as well the selective pressures that operate upon us—continue to evolve. Evolutionary psychology strives to understand the past, interpret the present, and reasonably predict the future of human social behavior.

The Perfection of War

War was the adaptation of our ape ancestors to bind the male power coalition together and redirect its members' lethal aggression outside the troop. Humans did not invent war, but humans have perfected war. The quintessential human adaptation is war.

There are many theories about why war exists. [12.1] Anthropologists have

189

proposed more than a dozen theories. These recent, anthropocentric (human-centered) theories have concentrated on war as a process initiated to achieve some tangible, proximate goal—territory, spoils, wives, revenge, and so forth.

Here, based upon a survey of evolutionary psychology, I present a different hypothesis. War is not a means to solve a problem, but a means to direct natural, intra-group aggressions (and to defuse other social problems) outside a society. War is not a conversation with extreme prejudice, but a bellowing shout. A shout—an obscene belch, really—issued not to impress war's victims, but to relieve the aggressors. Cast in this light, war cannot be replaced easily with logical, reasoned discourse—a fact humans have observed throughout recorded history. In yet another example of how language intentionally communicates inaccuracies, the public rationalizations and the announced goals of warfare do not correspond with the adaptive reason for warfare.

Stripped of the bells and whistles of rationalizations, human war is precisely like chimpanzee war. A male power coalition redirects its internal aggression outside its troop's boundaries. The enemy is almost always easily overcome or is *presumably* easy to bluff into defeat. But, for twenty million years, the uncertainty of war has proven a powerful lure. In principle, the leaders of the coalition pick an opponent that they know the social group can easily conquer. However, the leaders are sometimes incorrect—consider the misjudgments shown by Adolf Hitler, Lyndon Johnson, Richard Nixon, or Saddam Hussein.

Measured uncertainty about the outcome fuels the game of war, since human males (and perhaps nonhuman primate males as well) are especially attracted to risky adventures. The unbridled joy that Goodall witnessed when her chimpanzee troop had ravished a neighboring troop [see Chapter 9, pp. 151–52] may well have been the same adrenaline rush that follows the survival of an uncertain adventure or accident. If this is so, then warfare may be addictive in the same physiological sense as jogging (where a rush of feel-good neurohormones flood the brain following strenuous exercise). In any case, warfare usually involves little perceived risk for the aggressors. At the conclusion of a successful war, the male power coalition is socially bound together and is stronger than before.

Language dramatically increased the scope and the adaptive significance of war. Prior to language, only one male power coalition could exist within a troop. Through language, an infinite number of male power coalitions could be defined within a single group. Language enabled us to redefine successful aggression from lethal outcome to some arbitrary, non-lethal, competitive victory.

Since males could now coexist in high population densities without lethal social disruption, the human population swelled and spread across the face of the planet. Arbitrary, competitive male power coalitions served to increase the chance for their group's survival. The human social group expanded from a troop of dozens, to a tribe of thousands, to a nation-state of millions. Only time will tell whether we have achieved yet another plateau in our arbitrary ordering of social structures. The corporate state is superseding the nation-state in the government of vast numbers of people. Today, government by corporate state is in some ways a shadow, de facto government, since the oligarchies that lead nation-states frequently conform both internal and external policy to benefit multinational corporations, whose interests may not coincide with the interests of the nation-state. The state's cohesion—national, corporate, or otherwise—is assured through its interlocked, competing male subgroups.

The sizes and competitive agendas of human subgroups are extremely diverse. Some groups define themselves as businesses (in non-lethal competition with other businesses). Some groups are easily observed: athletic teams that compete for points against other teams. Other subgroups define themselves and their victories along more ethereal lines. For example, organizations of pacifists, conservationists, educators, therapists, and religionists—all of whom are locked in non-lethal combat with other such groups—compete to acquire the most followers, the most funds. Still other competitive subgroups define victory in several ways, *e.g.,* publishers, it is said, count both readers and profits. Significantly, victory is almost always defined in relative terms: the winner acquires more members or points or dollars at the expense of the loser.

Historically, the most successful definition of a non-lethal victory has been financial success. The quest for wealth is arbitrary victory at its finest; an exchange of intrinsically worthless pieces of paper distinguishes the winner from the loser. Financial warfare, some might argue, has integrated vast numbers of competitive male subgroups and built modern science, technology, medical care, education, arts, and social programs that invite non-kin to care for one another. Financial warfare has also created rank-

ings from the rich to the abject poor, measurements of individual dominance status unknown to our ancestral australopithecines or to *Homo
erectus.*

Regardless of how many male subgroups exist within a society, the most
dominant male power coalition remains the one that attempts to control
the entire social group. So it was for our ape ancestors and so it remains
for us. For modern humans, the most dominant male coalition is the
oligarchy that leads the nation-state. This oligarchy, in turn, is composed
of competitive subgroups. For the most part, the oligarchy's internal strife
is non-violent. Nonetheless, one crucial atavism from the days of our ape
ancestors persists. The oligarchy that leads the nation-state ultimately
retains power (in the face of internal aggression, dissent, financial hard-
ship, etc.) by redefining the entire social group's pent-up frustrations. The
power coalition redirects potentially disruptive aggression outside its
nation-state. It creates war.

Great leaders of these power coalitions are great precisely because they
can redirect their social group's aggression toward arbitrarily defined
scapegoats (thus sparing their society disruptive internal strife). For example, Hitler and Saddam Hussein were masters of social manipulation, as
were their conquerors. Churchill, DeGaulle, Roosevelt, and Bush united
their societies and focused their aggression outward, at least temporarily.

For every war, there is at least one aggressor. Sometimes, there are
two—two power coalitions that engage in a battle against one another to
redirect their social group's aggression and insure their own survival. Most
often, there is an aggressor and an aggressee. The latter human group is
a hapless victim that fights for survival, much the same as the surprised
chimpanzee must fight or flee an approaching group of males from another
troop.

The Adaptive Benefits of War

Throughout recorded history, warfare has been overwhelmingly beneficial
to the human species. Following a war, populations of victors (and often
the vanquished) increase. The deaths attributed to war are far exceeded
by the exponential baby booms that characterize postwar population
growth. The internal tensions that led to warfare disperse, in part because
new problems consume social energies and, in part, because the most

dangerously aggressive members of society—the young males—have satiated their aggressions outside their troop (or have been killed in battle). The male power coalition—the group that defines the reasons for the war—remains in power, directing the battle, out of harm's way. Leaders almost never pick a fight in which they might be harmed.

Leaders are those who convince young males to leave their pursuits of dominance positions and reproductive success to kill other young men outside their social group. Anthropologist R. Brian Ferguson's assertion that "[w]ar is not the human condition" because leaders must convince soldiers that the enemy is inhuman or because people do not naturally love violence is irrelevant. [12.2] War remains the human condition precisely because we can be readily convinced it is necessary. War is a universal human condition whether or not some people like or do not like war.

Young, naive males often march to war filled with heroic notions about noble combat. Sometimes, they return disillusioned with violence and resigned to the survival of the coalition that sent them into battle. Some men, however, are unable to return to society after combat—they retain their aggressions or direct them toward society. In either case, their ability to challenge the ruling oligarchy is limited by their experience of war. War, for twenty million years, has served the needs of the ruling oligarchy above all other considerations.

Warfare is a reliable way for power coalitions to consolidate their power. Social tensions never disappear for long. Warfare is usually cyclic, especially for societies with well-defined, permanent military subgroups. Cycles of war and peace define human progress; we mark our culture's time in history books by first one war, then another.

Warfare shapes the politics of human groups to the advantage of males more than any other social adaptation:

> Because men fought the wars, it was they who reaffirmed the right to decide between war and peace. Such decisions required high political authority . . . Men are above women in politics because men are warriors and not because men were in some societies breadwinners. [12.3]

Ultimately, warfare produces more than it destroys. Warfare, better than any other social competition, spurs male subgroups to design new technologies. Spin-offs of these lethal technologies further fuel non-lethal competition within the social group. That is, the inventions of war and the subgroups spawned by war are often transformed into, respectively, the toys and tools of peacetime economies. Victors (and sometimes the vanquished) often experience Golden Ages following wars.

The End Game

If evolution has shown us anything it is this: nothing lasts forever. While warfare served us well for millions of years, the environment changed radically fifty years ago. The game of war works adaptively as long as the competition is only partially lethal. When warfare becomes a lose-lose game, a game that both the aggressor and the aggressee lose, it is maladaptive. Inevitably, the technology that led to weapons of combat destruction led to weapons of mass destruction led to weapons of potential extinction. Doomsday is, for the first time in the history of life on earth, immediately before us. The game is lose-lose. Despite much soothing rhetoric, few societies have acknowledged this fact, and none have acted fully upon it. Doomsday weapons continue to proliferate.

So far, our species has shown little ability to deal with these new environmental realities. Since 1945 alone, about 20 million people have died in wars; countless more have been injured. [12.4]

Even America, the society that first invented and deployed the nuclear doomsday machine, has engaged in no less than six post-invention wars. America has killed enemies in Korea, Vietnam, Grenada, Libya, Panama, and Iraq since it observed the nuclear destruction that ended World War II. Humans are apparently unable to disengage themselves quickly from a social adaptation that has succeeded so well for more than twenty million years. The human species continues to grow at an exponential rate—proof that nuclear doomsday is not a selective agent until it occurs, and by then, it is too late to circumvent.

For millions of years, war has been *the* human adaptation. Our perfection of war characterizes our species and separates it from all other species of life on Earth. We have become exceedingly good at destruction. Ironically, we are so good at destruction that we have created a technology that renders a survivable major war impossible. Crucially, we have yet to devise an adequate and absolute social replacement for war. We have no workable substitute for redirecting the aggressions of the most dominant hierarchies within our societies.

So, we march into the twenty-first century much like the Giant Stag trotted across the heaths of Europe a hundred centuries ago. The Giant Stag was a magnificent, proud deer with 100-pound antlers ten feet across. A creature at the pinnacle of its evolutionary success. The male deer's formidable antlers—fully one-seventh the weight of its entire body—made it well and truly a king of Europe's heath-dotted plains.

But the climate changed. The heaths became bogs. The antlers—the reason for the Stag's success—became a burden to grow and a burden to bear in the ever-expanding quagmire beneath its hooves. The Stag could not change. It died where it stuck. It became extinct. Only its antlers remain to tell us of the dangerous reversals natural selection sometimes takes.

Riots Revisited

A legal institution hands down a verdict, and a group of concerned citizens protests the ruling. Next, the streets of the city erupt into spontaneous violence. Many buildings are burned; rioters, defenders, and non-participants alike are set upon, injured and killed. Rioters loot shops and liquor stores. The riots last less than a week. The damage affects the society for years to come; the supposed issues that spawned the unrest are barely addressed in its aftermath.

The preceding scenario describes the riots that beset the city of Los Angeles in 1992. They also describe the riots that rocked the city of London in 1780, and, with only minor modifications, countless other social upheavals that have characterized human societies since records have been unearthed. [12.5]

Rioting, anarchy, civil disobedience are terms that conjure a society out of control, a society whose social contract is rent. At first glance, a riot would seem to be the antithesis of a war. Wars, at least at their outset, are well-organized. Wars, like equally well-organized competitive games, seem to have only two sides. Riots, on the other hand, seem to contain unorganized mobs in opposition to organized power structures. Riots seem to happen, wars are planned.

In fact, wars and riots have much the same organization; the same

ancient evolutionary imperatives guide their formation and their out-
comes. Wars and riots are common human social adaptations that owe
their origins and the reasons for their existence to our ancient ancestors,
the dryopithecine apes of twenty-odd million years ago.

Riots have always marked human societies. They share the same structure. A male-dominated subgroup (or subgroups) redirects its aggression
outside its members and toward individuals or subgroups outside its
perceived larger social group. In the end, the oligarchy that institutes the
riot usually benefits by having its internal aggressions mollified, and by
having its power structure—its dominance hierarchy—reaffirmed and
strengthened. Dryopithecines most likely did this. Chimpanzees do this.
So do humans.

Riots and wars involve an element of risk to the subgroups that initiate
them. Sometimes, riots backfire. The subgroup may attack another subgroup that can defend against the attack and, in turn, inflict fatal damage
to the initiating subgroup. Nevertheless, risk-taking behavior is characteristic of most young male primates, from lemurs to humans. Few secure,
elderly male oligarchies risk rioting.

Most riots have a vocalized cause—a seed, if you will, much like a
snowflake that develops around a speck of high-flying dust. The Gordon
Riots that rocked London in 1780 erupted because the British Parliament
passed the Catholic Relief act; this infuriated Protestant subgroups. The
L.A. riots erupted because a non-African-American jury acquitted a team
of European-American policemen of charges that they unjustly beat an
African-American male. The seeds for both these and most other riots are
the same: racism, economic deprivation, social injustice. These are easy
seeds for humans to wrap their aggressions around. These seeds are
convenient and enduring nuclei for male subgroups; their utterance identi-
fies "us" as a group versus "them" as a group. It is of little importance that
the group identified as "them" may or may not be an appropriate target.
Neither riots nor wars often succeed in eliminating either the seeds or the
subgroups that form around them.

The seeds that are said to cause human riots and wars obscure the root
causes of such behavior. The roots run millions of years into the human
past. Until and unless we come to grips with the ancient imperatives that
guide male subgroups, riots and wars will remain a common part of the
human adaptation.

We know, for example, that male subgroup formation is a natural part of human societies. The males within a power coalition have high levels of aggression, partly hormonal and partly derived from endless jostling for a high rank within the coalition. To keep the coalition intact, individual, pent-up aggressions are periodically redirected outside the coalition. Any reasonable-sounding seed can be used to redirect this aggression.

For young males living in the impoverished conditions of a south central Los Angeles ghetto, economic or racial inequities are all that is necessary to rally their subgroups to action. The larger society, distinct from ghetto society, views the resulting acts as "socially disruptive." The ghetto-bred subgroups view the resulting riots as an affirmation of their existence; their internal dominance hierarchies are strengthened at relatively little cost.

Male subgroups abound in every human society. Most redirect their internal aggression using socially acceptable channels. Consider the management staff of a computer firm. Internally, this ruling hierarchy may be rife with competition. Underlings are scratching and clawing their way to a higher position on the dominance hierarchy; high-ranking officials are holding on to their positions of power using every trick known to management. The corporate pecking order is visibly defined, in this case, by the absolute quantity of greenback pieces of paper each individual pockets for a salary or perk. Periodically, the management of this subgroup redirects these internal aggressions outwards, either by developing a new product that will defeat a competing subgroup's products or by organizing a corporate takeover of another subgroup's company. Either strategy channels the subgroups' energies to a target outside the subgroup. The members of the corporate group expend their aggressions outside their own management circle. The seeds—product competition or corporate takeovers—are deemed socially acceptable by the society at large.

Most members of our society would argue that the corporate subgroups are behaving in ways beneficial to the larger society, while the ghetto subgroups are behaving in a manner detrimental to the larger society. The task, then, for the evolutionary psychologist might be to redirect the disenfranchised subgroup's aggressions toward socially acceptable ends. That is, to *empower the subgroups with a substantial and acceptable outlet for the internal aggressions* that we know will develop within this or any other male subgroup. Internal male-male aggressions occur naturally and frequently in boardrooms, barrios, pulpits, and parliament halls.

As an integral part of this approach to social engineering, we should also reduce many of the social grievances—the seeds of economic, racial, and social injustice—that formed the focus for the subgroups' redirected aggressions in the first place. It is clear, though, that merely addressing the seeds—the proximate issues or resource needs—while ignoring the subgroups' need to redirect internal aggressions will always leave male subgroups in search of further, potentially disruptive means to redirect their aggressions.

Suffer the Little Child

Children are the ultimate products of romantic love. It is likely that only our species intellectualizes the process of parenting. Our attitudes toward children, the products of our quest for reproductive advantage, have been shaped by our evolutionary history and long-standing biological imperatives. Not surprisingly, then, we seem to regard children in some combination of four ways: they are objects for abuse, for murder, for sex, and as objects of affection for our survival beyond the grave.

Some people physically abuse children (their own or those of others). In many cases, this abuse is redirected aggression. Abuse of offspring has been observed in most non-human primate species. Usually, the instigator is submissive and is said to hold a poor self-image. The objects of aggression are children because they are easily subdued. Because virtually all societies have individuals on this bottom dominance rung, pathological abuse of children will always occur with some frequency. Fortunately, this attitude toward children is uncommon and clearly pathological. It enhances no one's reproductive success.

Some cases of infant murder may hide a gruesome reproductive strategy. Some people may knowingly or unknowingly view other people's children as competitors in the endless struggle for relative genetic supremacy. Each child born to someone else reduces your relative contribution to the next generation. Primate species have been shown to apparently act on this biological truism. Male African and Asiatic leaf-eater monkeys (colobines) often kill the infants of a troop they invade. [12.6] After the slaughter, the lactating females quickly become sexually receptive and propagate a new generation—this one bristling with the genes of the conquering males.

Infanticide increases the relative genetic contribution of invading males to the next generation at the expense of the female's relative contribution. Infanticide of this sort is widespread in the animal kingdom. [12.7] It has been observed in some species of African and South American monkeys, and some instances of gorilla and chimpanzee infant killing may fall into this category. To what degree humans practice this reproductive strategy is largely unexamined, but it is not uncommon for a stepparent to resent a stepchild (and vice versa). Reproductively-based infanticide may well be an evolutionary ghost in the human psyche.

Assets or Burdens?

Children are assets. They can increase a family's productivity and wealth. Children can increase a parent's kinship network. On the other hand, children that do not contribute measurably to a family's wealth or that present a burden are often expendable. Humans routinely abandon or kill unwanted infants.

Between half and three-quarters of all sampled preindustrial societies customarily practice infanticide. Subsistence-level Australian aborigines commonly kill half of their infants. In India, boys can outnumber girls four to one, since the "less valuable" girls have been killed. Between 30 and 40 percent of all live female births have been destroyed in some regions of China. In France during the decade 1824–1833, over 300,000 infants were abandoned to foundling hospitals where 80 to 90% of them eventually died. In America today, children fill strained orphanages and foster parent programs. Newborns are occasionally recovered from trash cans. In Latin America, street children are almost as common as parented ones. It would appear that the fabled mother-infant bond may be easily abandoned in favor of pragmatic economic considerations. [12.8] Ultimately, the survival of the mother may take precedence over the survival of the child.

Some parents view their offspring as potential or actual mates. Such sexual activity is probably widespread; it is a form of child abuse that has been called a modern epidemic. Almost all human societies view matings between close relatives—mother-son, father-daughter, brother-sister—as incestuous, hence wrong.

Freud viewed the Incest Taboo as a purely cultural proscription. [12.9] He failed to note several sound biological imperatives that sponsor the cultural taboo. There are, in fact, at least two genetic reasons that nature would select against inbreeding. Inbreeding eliminates genetic variety, technically known as a "loss of alleles" or an "increase in homozygosity." Genetic variety sometimes enables a population to survive when the environment changes. Genetic variety is the stuff that natural selection acts upon. Variety is indeed the spice of life, the grist that favors species' survival.

Secondly, matings between close kin tend to produce less viable off-spring. Combinations of closely related genes tend to allow two deleterious genes to pair together, often producing a weak or defective offspring. Finally, matings between close kin are much less fertile than matings between distant relatives. Some of the best data for the effects of inbreed-ing on fertility and infant survival is seen in controlled matings of domestic dogs: [12.10]

Degree of Inbreeding (1.00 = completely inbred)	Number of Pups Produced	% Who Survived Ten Days
0.008-0.186	636	75
0.251-0.578	565	51
over 0.673	39	25

All wild mammals studied to date avoid mating with close relatives. How does this biological constraint work? Do mammals from mice to men recognize and calculate degrees of relatedness before they copulate? Prob-ably not. Incest avoidance is no more complicated than avoiding sex with individuals with whom we are extremely familiar, a hypothesis first pro-posed by anthropologist Edward Westermarch in 1891. [12.11]

All mammals, it appears, find that familiarity begets impotence. Mam-mals are turned on by novel sexual stimuli, and turned off by sights, sounds, and smells they are used to. Usually, mothers, fathers, brothers, and sisters are too familiar; they are just not novel enough to be sexually exciting. Studies of human mating avoidance among Israeli kibbutzim-raised non-kin support this hypothesis. [12.12]

Because sexual desire probably relies on some perceived level of novelty, it is easy to see how incest occurs. A human parent, blessed with a large and imaginative brain, can sometimes (or one time) view (or fantasize) their child as a novel sexual stimulus. Brothers and sisters often see themselves as different people as puberty erupts and distorts their formerly familiar physiques. It is likely that only learned prohibitions (a sense of culturally mandated right and wrong) prevent widespread incest in these circumstances. Incest is further reduced in most human societies because our children move away from home soon after they complete puberty. They take their novel sexual stimuli elsewhere in search of biologically sound mates.

Fortunately for the continuation of our species, we most often regard children as an extension of ourselves. They are proper objects for our affections, for our love, for bonding. They are surrogates of us. They are our genes (or, at least, tangible signs of our nose and eyes and hair) marching into a future that will soon bury us. Not surprisingly, then, most parents attempt to mold children in their own image. Some try to live their lives vicariously through their child. We argue that we want only the best for them. We want them to avoid our sorrows and to experience joys that we denied ourselves. A child is our hope for immortality.

This attitude—the child as our future—is an ideal. It is likely to occur when the parent's resource conditions are optimal or at least adequate. Proper parenting requires a level of obtainable resources that are rapidly diminishing worldwide. If push comes to shove, it is likely that the children will be the first to suffer.

The Paradox of Self-Interested Altruism

Language makes the human species unique in many ways. For one, we believe (although we cannot demonstrate unequivocally) that humans are the only individuals on the planet that can rationally analyze their own bonds. This ability can cause us anguish unknown to other species. Particularly troubling, we can and often do analyze our own consort bond as Karen does in the example that follows.

Karen is perplexed. All her life, she believed that when she fell in love, she would be "totally devoted" to pleasing her man, to raising her family. She's thirty-five years old now, she met and married her true love, and she has two children. Yet, deep in her heart, she realizes that she has pleasureless sex with her husband twice a week rather than risk a confrontation that would divide the family. Worse, she believes that her outward devotion to her husband is a sham that allows her to maintain her social position, her comfortable home, and her not inconsiderable buying power. This isn't the way it should be, is it? Karen believes that her feelings toward her husband reveal that she is unnaturally cynical at worst or, at best, portend a divorce.

Karen suffers a common guilt and a cynicism that often follows logical analysis of a mythic ideal. She has been endowed, as have we all, with the faculty to analyze her bond. If she were a chimpanzee, her guilt trip would be necessarily much shorter. But, as a human, she uses language and logic for introspection—to assess her position in space and time and to discern and reshape her feelings. Karen cannot blindly follow her hormones, her genes, and her socialization. She has determined that selfless caring and self-sacrifice (altruism), essential parts of her image of love and romance, have become acts of calculated self-interest.

Karen need not despair. She is normal. Human romance is, more often than not, reducible logically to negotiated compromises motivated by enlightened self-interest. Sadly, her ideal image of love conflicts badly with the reality of our evolutionary-derived romance. And, with this dissolution of her mythic, romantic ideal, Karen has experienced one of the ways that deceptive language can hurt us. With time and further introspection, Karen could reformulate an ideal that better reflects the sociobiological reality of her consort bond. Perhaps she will realize after all that acknowledging legitimate self-interest is compatible with a satisfying romance and love.

In fact, the jury is still out with respect to the existence of altruism. Altruism may not exist for any relationship, let alone the consort bond. Some sociobiologists have argued that an animal will sacrifice itself only if in doing so, the sacrifice saves more of its genetic material than would be lost by its death. What appears as altruism is in fact genetic self-interest. In other words, a mother (or father) will risk its life to save two or more of its own offspring, or twelve or more of its cousins, and so forth. Furthermore, since your mate is not closely related to you genetically, it follows that lovers will not, as a rule, behave altruistically toward one another.

Actually, the calculus of genetic self-interest is sloppy at best. Humans have evolved within close-knit, cooperative social groups. Millions of years of cooperative living have reprogrammed us to behave in an altruistic manner toward those to whom we bond. Sacrificing oneself for the good of a mate is an essential part of the bonding process; obviously selfish individuals have less success at bonding than do those who are willing to self-sacrifice (or *seem* willing to). It is likely, therefore, that some elements of altruism exist occasionally between individuals, and that romance can potentially bring out the altruist in us all. If so, then altruism must be truly an uncommon act that runs counter to self-interest—an act that is biologically unsound. Put another way, altruism may exist infrequently, but cannot be commonplace.

Natural selection has not been circumvented here. Altruism that inevitably lowers an individual's reproductive success cannot exist long in a species. If lethal altruism was required often in social interactions, then altruists (and the concept of altruism) would disappear as surely as did the Shakers, a religious sect that eschewed reproduction while other religions promoted childbearing.

Changing Gender Roles

Women in many modern societies have postponed a decision to have children and have entered the work force as the equals of males. The often predictable results of this ascendancy can be seen as we enter a warmly lit living room and eavesdrop on a pair of lovers.

We stand behind a sofa that is positioned before a crackling fire. A couple is seated on a rug before the fireplace. Both are holding wine glasses and are gazing at one another, talking softly. The strikingly sensuous woman is wearing a tasteful negligee; the man is wrapped in a velour robe. The romantic scene is suddenly shattered by the harsh ring of a telephone. The woman rises quickly and leaves the room to answer it. The man shakes his head and slowly clenches his fist at the intrusion.

We hear the woman say, "Thanks for calling."

Her voice rises to a commanding tone: "Look, you tell Harold and John that if they can't straighten that account out by the time I'm in my office tomorrow, they'll be looking for someone else to work for! I'll see you tomorrow, too. Yes, at 9:15. Thank you, good night."

The woman returns to the scene, sits down, and smiles. But, the man appears uneasy. His amorousness seems as flaccid as a newspaper caught in a rainstorm.

"I just remembered," he says, dryly, "I have some work to do myself. Maybe we can get away this weekend, okay, honey?"

He places his half-empty wine glass down, and starts to rise. The woman appears stunned by his abrupt departure.

Why did he leave? Variations on this scene have become commonplace. It has been less than a century since women have, in large numbers, joined the traditionally male work force. Women have assumed a role within the traditional male dominance hierarchies. But many males—burdened by the evolutionary heritage of twenty million years of dominance struggles within exclusive male groups—have difficulty accepting the object of their desire as an equal or superior competitor. Often, male impotence and female anomie are the price the human sexes pay for having equal brain power and nearly equal social roles. Estimates suggest that as many as half of all males in Western societies may experience impotence and feel threatened by competitive females.

Gender roles, established through more than fifty million years of primate evolution, cannot be trifled with lightly. Ethologist John Hurrell Crook writes:

> Young women appear to be attractive to young men owing to the combination of [childlike] and secondary sexual characteristics which they present to them initially at a distance. Hairlessness, voice tone, complexion and girlish behavior all have a childlike character that in ethological terms appear to lower the probability of a male aggressive response or to appease if one is present. These same characteristics are likely to reduce male fear and anxiety on closer approach and to permit sexual expression. [12,13]

Many women—politically more powerful today than at any time in human history—are adopting traditionally male aggressive postures and selecting for nonaggressive, non-threatening men. To observe the reversal in selective priorities, reread Crook's quote, substituting "men" for "women," "female" for "male."

The juggling act of dominance, submission, and gender identification is a considerable burden for both men and women. It is not a question of social justice; no one can argue (logically, at least) that gender should limit anyone's freedom or access to social justice. Instead, rapid cultural change is introducing new variables into an ancient dominance game. Our biology—our emotional and sexual responses to conflicting dominance and submission signals—has not had time to adjust. How will we, as individuals and as a species, accommodate to these rapid cultural changes in male-female dominance and social and sexual roles?

The twentieth century changes in gender roles and dominance are unprecedented, although women have obtained (and lost) a small measure of political power at many times in the past. In the third century B.C., Roman women were "more out of hand than in hand, or so . . . male contemporaries complained." [12.14]

Roman males did not long suffer the political ascent of women. In 215 B.C., Cato the Censor argued before his Senate colleagues that the Oppian Law, repressive to women, must be maintained because "[S]uffer women once to arrive at an equality with you, and they from that moment become your superiors." [12.15]

Most contemporary men are no less threatened by female bids for political equality. The vision of women posturing as equals within the male coalition is threatening to men both because it increases competition and because the aggressive postures that are necessarily adopted by politically active women destroy most of the non-threatening behavioral signals that males require from their mates for successful copulation.

It is possible, of course, that we are witness to the troubled dawn of a new, more egalitarian definition of love and romance. If so, it would be a true biological revolution, not merely a simple alteration in cultural rules or learned individual preferences. Changes in established gender roles will not come about easily. But, evolution is nothing if not change. And no primate is more capable of behavioral change than the human primate.

Strangers in a Strange Land: Males within Female Families

More than twenty years ago, I observed that some captive lemur males behaved differently toward certain infants and juveniles within their enclosure. Infants and juveniles that they had fathered were permitted great license: they would pull their father's tail and frequently disturb his slumber without penalty of rebuke. Non-kin youngsters were dealt harsh rebuffs. In spite of his paternal beneficence, it is likely that the male lemur had no concept whatsoever of fatherhood or genetic relatedness. He merely responded pacifically to any juvenile who looked or perhaps smelled similar to himself.

Fatherhood is not a well-developed primate characteristic. Amongst some other, nonhuman primates, males are often brutal toward non-kin youngsters. When Hanuman langur males enter a new troop, they sometimes kill the existing juveniles and infants. They supposedly practice infanticide as a reproductive strategy to enhance their relative genetic contribution to the next generation. The offspring they father later are tolerated, but otherwise ignored. Only a few primates like the tiny South American marmoset monkey, the Barbary macaque, and the siamang (a gibbon) show any inclination to care for infants and juveniles. [12,16]

Neither was fatherhood a trait known to our primate ancestors. It is doubtful that human fathers could associate the sex act with genetic progeny until less than a hundred thousand years ago. But female primates have always known who their offspring were. The act of birth and the requisite formation of caring, mother-infant bonds assured that more than fifty million years ago. The maternal family has a momentous evolutionary head start on fatherhood. That fact translates into a stable role for mothers, and a questionable, ever-changing, experimental role for fathers within the monogamous family group.

Not surprisingly, the modern human father is often confused. A question most important for the shape of human relationships: what fathering qualities are deemed desirable by potential lovers? What, exactly, is his role in family life? For millions of years, infants have been nurtured exclusively by mothers. Should a father adopt the nurturing behavior of a mother? Should a father become a peer role model, emulating the venerable bachelor group? If a father enters into a consort bond from a posture of dominance, should he assert dominance over his offspring as well? If so, how?

There are no pat answers to any of these questions. Fatherhood is simply too new an adaptation to have developed significant biological roots. As such, it conforms to whatever role is deemed appropriate by a particular culture at a particular moment in time. In Western societies, fathers range from absentee breadwinners, to beneficent entertainment directors, to judgmental jailers. It is likely that today's definitions of fatherhood will differ significantly from tomorrow's. Radical philosopher Alison Jaggar claims that human societies are "phallocentric." She would like to abolish all existing concepts of fatherhood and family and, with the aid of technology, "one woman could inseminate another . . . men could lactate . . . and fertilized ova could be transferred into women's or even men's bodies." [12.17]

At present, some females still opt for a father in their family and choose the potential father with whom they will mate. For such a romance to succeed, a man must adopt or feign the fatherhood role desired by the woman of his choice. Natural selection will favor only the most adaptable men, although in the United States, an increasing number of single-parent women have accepted that male sexual partners will not remain within the family. Fatherhood is, in principle, an adaptive biological trait and a common romantic virtue when more than one adult must provide the goods and services to raise children. In America, single-parent families struggle with fewer resources (food, shelter, clothing, health care, and education) than two-parent families.

Quixotically, single-parent families are increasing in numbers. In the United States in 1989, only 58.1% of our children lived in natural, two-parent families; 20.9% lived with their mothers, 2.5% lived with their fathers, the rest resided in orphanages, with relatives, or with foster care families. Single-parent families have increased from 9.1% of all families in 1960 to 24.3% in 1989. [12.18]

Meanwhile, births to single mothers doubled to more than one million each year; half of these births were to African-Americans—a fact which indicates that ethnic and socioeconomic variations on the human theme of love, romance, and family are significant. American society's stated romantic and family values are badly out of synchronization with social reality and perhaps with our biological needs as well.

Iron Men and Rusted Sons: Finding a Father's Role

For most of the fifty-odd million years of primate evolution, mothers socialized daughters. Daughters, always in close proximity to their mothers, patterned their behavior on that of their mothers. If the mother was a high-ranking, dominant female, then the daughter would copy her successful behavior postures and, in adulthood, would almost invariably be treated as a high-ranking female herself.

The sons of high-ranking female primates also copied their mothers' behavior. But, unlike their female siblings, juvenile sons left mother early in their development to join an all-male, bachelor group. Here, in the bachelor group, their future dominance (or submission) postures were honed. Once again, sons of high-ranking females had learned how to behave like a dominant animal from their childhood observations of their dominant mother. Often, but not always, they ascended the troop's pecking order and became dominant individuals in adulthood.

Poet Robert Bly, father of the currently popular, strongly metaphysical Men's Movement, has suggested forcefully that men need a father figure. [12.19] He claims that men don't bond with their fathers until they are in their forties. Without an older "male mentor," a developing young man is "lost." "A woman," Bly notes, "cannot bring a boy to be a man, only other men can do that." [12.20]

Yet, Bly argues most forcibly not for father-son bonding, but for the formation of all-male groups where men can go to other men for comfort, and where men can bond to each other without the stress attendant in adult dominance and mating competition. Ironically, his prescription is for a mellow, socially acceptable men's group patterned (unknowingly) after the adolescent bachelor group that has dwelt within virtually every nonhuman primate troop for the past fifty million years. Bly's men's movement is another example of evolutionary déjà vu. Unwittingly, the men's movement is playing to very ancient primate social imperatives.

Given that human fatherhood is a relatively recent social invention, it is remarkable that fathers can and do influence greatly their progeny's dominance behavior and success. But, unlike the simple female family groups that have prevailed for most of primate evolution, the human male-female family provides offspring with two adult dominance role models. The potential parental pairings include: a strong (dominant) father and a weak (submissive) mother; a weak or absentee father and a strong mother; a weak or absentee father and a weak mother; a strong father and a strong mother, and all variations of dominance posturing in between.

The sons (and daughters) of any generation grow up in family groups that vary both in their parental composition and in the matrix of possible dominance positions of fathers and mothers. How might these combinations of parental rank affect the quest for power, sex, and love of sons and daughters? At present, we have little systematic information to answer this important question. Until evolutionary psychologists test the role of fathers in families, the influence of fatherhood on the social organization of the human primate will remain extremely speculative.

Love in the Time of the Population Glut

"Men and women are not alike," writes Gore Vidal. "They have different sexual roles to perform. Despite the best efforts of theologians and philosophers to disguise our condition, there is no point to us, or to any species, except proliferation and survival . . . Men and women are dispensable carriers, respectively, of seeds and eggs; programmed to mate and die, mate and die, mate and die." [12.21]

Producing offspring has always been the ultimate goal of romantic love. Three billion years of natural selection has programmed all creatures to maximize their fitness, their genetic contribution to the next generation. How will love and gender relations change on an increasingly over-populated planet? Each day, a quarter of a million humans are born. Already, our planet may have exceeded its carrying capacity, its ability to sustain our species. We face an immediate challenge to the pretense for sexual relationships—to the principal biological and cultural *raison d'être* for the consort bond, for marriage, for sexuality, and for romantic love.

With regard to human population control (or its lack), two different kinds of selection appear to be operating on humans at present. The first universal selective pressure drives individuals to reproduce. The second selective pressure operates on social groups. Those social groups that limit their population growth in the face of diminished resources thrive; those societies that continue to produce an overabundance of offspring may decline or die off entirely.

Robert Thomas Malthus's *Essay on the Principle of Population* was the foundation of Charles Darwin's and Alfred Russel Wallace's concept of natural selection. In 1798, Malthus suggested that human misery is a product of our fertility combined with irresponsibility. Our resources, he concluded, increase at best arithmetically, while our population can easily increase geometrically. The three horseman of Thomas Malthus—starva-

Malagasy mother and child face an uncertain future.

tion, disease, and warfare—limit the success of overpopulated societies. Three hundred years later, the horsemen have quickened their pace. Ultimately, our fate as individuals is a function of the fate of our group.

Selection can affect us in subtle ways. In First World economies, individual greed (euphemized as enlightened self-interest) effectively limits the number of offspring that couples produce. Affluence coincides with a decline in fecundity. Stress, engendered by increasing competition for limited resources, can also limit fertility (the ability of individuals to reproduce successfully). For those living in poverty, the course of romance is often abbreviated and violent; progeny, often abundant, have a greatly reduced chance of survival (for a tragic example, see Somalia during the 1980s and 1990s). Love among the ruins is noteworthy in that aggression and dominance predominate over caring and affection.

Political pressures can curtail or enhance individual reproductive efforts. Some societies provide tax incentives for parenting; others impose surcharges for children. A few decades ago, the Soviet, Japanese, Chinese, and Malagasy governments (to name but a few) publicly awarded productive parents. Now, these societies and many others encourage families to limit their number of offspring. Predictably, older members of these societies are confused.

Religious pressures to reproduce abundantly have always existed. Religions, in competition with each other, require their followers to add significantly to their number of recruits. Religious power is directly proportional to the number of believers. Many religions stipulate that caressing and copulation can be justified only to produce children—an infallible mandate for overpopulation. The clash of traditional religious mandates and the newer notions of parishioners is nowhere more in evidence than in the struggle by some Roman Catholics for the right to practice birth control and, when such efforts fail, abortion.

These turbulent social currents affect deeply our personal conception of romance and love. Because social values are in a continual state of rapid change, not all members of a society will believe in either large or small families. Cultural lag occurs frequently when one institution, such as a fundamentalist religion, promotes sexual activity solely for reproductive purposes while another institution promotes sexual activity for recreational purposes, but not reproductive ones. Cultural lag introduces additional strains on individual human relationships. Will the object of your affections desire many, few, or no children? Will the object of your affections view romantic love, caressing, and sex as merely a means to produce a child? Do you agree on birth control? Abortion? Your personal concepts about reproduction and sex can potentially clash sharply with those of your intended mate, your religious society, and your government.

None of these questions concerned our primate ancestors. Our ability to forecast the effects of overpopulation (and to adjust our behavior accordingly) introduces an unprecedented selective pressure on our species' relationships. Forecasting the future in detail is an imaginative act, unknown to other life-forms. Only the human species can potentially adjust its fecundity by hearkening to the demands of its imagination. Imaginative concerns, romantic hang-ups, and relational analyses themselves are strictly recent, human, cultural inventions, made possible by language. In Western societies—arguably home to the most inquisitive peoples on the planet—a bewildering multitude of conflicting, rapidly changing cultural values, rules, and self-analyses are a primary source of difficulties for gender relationships.

Love in the Age of AIDS

Several decades ago, some scholars argued that human biological evolution was essentially dead. Culture, not natural selection, they said, would determine humanity's future. Such pronouncements were incorrect. In fact, it is biological constraints that ultimately shape cultural values. Usually, biological pressures are subtle and poorly understood. Occasionally, a cataclysmic incident points out the fact that we are very much a part of nature. One such incident occurred prior to the 1970s in central Africa, when a heretofore mundane, minuscule snippet of genetic material called STLV (Simian T-cell Leukemia Virus) gained parasitic access to a single human. The ramifications of that unheralded event grew and continues to grow in exponential proportions.

Today, humanity faces its first genuine threat of extinction because this parasite has, without thought, plan, or malice, evolved a lifestyle that can potentially out-compete and defeat every human's essential immunological defense. No one is immune to HIV—the STLV-derived, sexually transmitted, Human Immunodeficiency Virus. Throughout human history, culture has been altered dramatically by pandemics: bubonic plague, malaria, smallpox, syphilis, typhoid, tuberculosis, influenza, and poliomyelitis. All but the latter two were bacteria or larger organisms, and none were completely invulnerable to our body's defense system. HIV is unique amongst pathogens.

To make matters worse, the always-lethal virus employs a virtually flawless method to gain access to us. HIV relies upon sexual behavior for transmission. To unequivocally stop the spread of HIV, humans would have to forsake copulation—an unlikely event that would harbinger extinction anyway.

HIV is pernicious. It is difficult to detect and can effectively hide from view for a decade or more, allowing countless carrier lovers to spread the infection. At present, we are in the infancy of the HIV pandemic. AIDS, the disease syndrome that follows HIV infection, has just begun. To date, only Africa, the pandemic's epicenter, has been obviously decimated; there, some Central African human communities are extinct. In some cities in Tanzania, 40% of the population is infected and dying. The infection rate in Kigalli, Uganda's capital, is 30.3% and rising. [12.22]

The World Health Organization warns that AIDS is increasing at an alarming, exponential rate worldwide. For example, no HIV infections were observed in Asia in 1988; 500,000 were reported by 1990. [12.23] Health organizations revise their estimates of HIV/AIDS infection upwards almost every quarter. Worldwide, an estimated eight to thirteen million adults presently carry HIV; that number is expected to exceed 100 million by the year 2000. [12.24]

At present, fewer than 200,000 Americans have contracted the AIDS disease while upwards of three million Americans are probably now infected with the HIV virus. Many in Western societies foolishly consider the pathogen to be specific to homosexuals, drug users, minorities, and prostitutes, even though 75% of the individuals infected with the virus worldwide have contracted it through heterosexual sex. [12.25]

Worldwide, heterosexual humans are in a state of profound and dangerous denial. HIV, like other sexually transmitted diseases that came before, has assumed incorrectly the status of a social identifier and morality play. This form of stereotyping and self-denial *could* (but probably will not) lead to the extinction of the human species.

Humans are not the only animals that face possible extinction via a sexually transmitted disease. *Chlamydia,* a bacterial pathogen also found in humans, now threatens the survival of China's panda and Australia's koala.

But, unlike the panda or koala, humans can identify the threat to their survival and can potentially take measures to limit their mortality. For the foreseeable future, our only partial defense against HIV is behavioral. Those who will survive the pandemic and reproduce will be those who drastically alter the present human patterns of promiscuity, romance, and love. AIDS, the disease manifestation of HIV, is truly the Black Death of Love.

No society on earth will escape the profound changes associated with AIDS. Unstable economies will likely collapse under the weight of medical costs and the decimation of their work forces. The federal Agency for Health Care Policy and Research estimates medical treatment for each AIDS patient will cost $32,000 per year. In 1991, the United States spent $5.8 billion treating HIV-infected individuals and AIDS patients; that figure will nearly double to $10.4 billion in 1994. [12.26] The medical budgets of most nations were already dangerously strained before AIDS appeared.

The mating systems of every culture will be altered; unalterable cultures will simply perish. Many New World and Polynesian societies were ravaged or became extinct through the introduction of European syphilis, a considerably less virulent bacterial disease.

The concept of romantic love will undergo the most drastic, rapid alteration. Promiscuity and adultery (the Vienna Waltz), long characteristic of human societies, may soon decline. The only members of the sexually active human population that are likely to survive the HIV epidemic will be those individuals who are celibate or who share a single, long-term, unbroken, monogamous relationship. That message has clearly not yet impacted America's sexually active juveniles. The American Center for Disease Control reports that teenage premarital sex nearly doubled between 1970 and 1988. One out of two girls under eighteen is sexually active; one in four under the age of fifteen engages in intercourse. [12.27]

These data bode ill for their future.

Encouragingly, a RAND survey conducted between October, 1989, and January, 1990, showed that almost one-third of all American, adult, heterosexual respondents reported that they have changed their sexual activities because of AIDS. More than one-fifth reduced their number of sex partners, while 3% were frightened into celibacy. A nationwide *Los Angeles Times* poll conducted in November, 1991, reported that almost half the teenagers surveyed claim they have changed their sexual habits as a result of AIDS. [12,28] The latter survey was conducted shortly after basketball star Magic Johnson announced that he was HIV-infected. Interestingly, adult respondents reported no significant increase in either their concern about HIV or their willingness to alter their sexual behavior to avoid the disease.

HIV is an especially pernicious pathogen. An individual infected with HIV today may show no symptoms of the infection for a decade or more. This lag time between infection and disease is particularly difficult for young people, the most sexually active portion of our species, to grasp. In the past, human disease epidemics were far more direct. People who contracted yellow fever, for example, sickened or died within days of their infection. It remains to be seen, then, what public announcement or what population level of infection will serve as a threshold beyond which the majority of people in any particular culture will alter their behavior or even admit their vulnerability to HIV.

A willingness to change sexual habits can mean as little as a reduction in the number of promiscuous matings or as much as celibacy. Neither celibacy (nor homosexual monogamy) are viable species options, because a non-reproductive population leaves no descendants. Evolutionary success, after all, is simply a tally of offspring. Therefore, the probable, proximate destiny of humankind is enforced monogamy and the consequences of enforced monogamy. I suggest that surviving cultures will adopt several or many of the following patterns of behavior:

- Lovers will question seriously the sexual background of prospective mates. Such questions may spawn an industry of specialized detectives, testing centers, and certifying agencies.
- An increase in marriages; a decline in the number of singles.
- Arranged marriages: pre-pubescents become engaged.
- Preference for virgins (both male and female) in marriage, in extramarital affairs, or in pubescent sexual experimentation.
- An increase in pedophilia (sex with known or presumed virgins).
- An increase in incest (all forms).
- An increase in or change in the nature of extramarital affairs. For example, preference will be given to the choice of a partner already engaged in a long-term, monogamous relationship (or to a presumably inexperienced pubescent).

- An increase in polygamy; an increase in polyandry where the number of males exceed females in the society.
- A precipitous decline (or the eventual disappearance) of heterosexual and homosexual prostitution.
- A decline in promiscuous bisexuality and homosexuality; an increase in monogamous homosexuality.
- A decline of casual sex in all forms, *e.g.,* job-related, singles bars, swing clubs, etc.
- Mate selection will favor individuals who are mildly obese and who do not appear to be playboys or party girls.
- Pornographic movies and literature will gain a greater measure of social acceptance as couples attempt to stimulate their fantasy life within the narrow confines of a long-term, monogamous bond.
- Single females (including lesbians) will choose artificial insemination; single, relatively safe copulations; and adoption as a means to have children and reduce the chance of contracting sexually transmitted diseases. Ironically, this trend, already in evidence, marks a return to the mouse lemur pattern of mother-daughter bonds and nurturing matrilines.

Some of the preceding predictions read like the worst nightmare of a humanist, the rantings of a Bible-belt preacher, or the antithesis of a romantic's dreams. Romance, in many of its mental images, conjures visions of free will, spontaneity, and egalitarianism. But HIV does not respect even the best of intentions. If love is to survive the Era of AIDS, then extraordinary individual and societal efforts will prove necessary. Love and romance will necessarily become a less spontaneous, less casual, more thoughtful human activity. Successful humans will temper their hormones with their cerebral hemispheres.

HIV is not the only human sexually transmitted disease showing a marked increase during the latter years of this century. Gonorrhea, syphilis, chlamydia, hepatitis B virus, herpes simplex 2 virus, and Human Papilloma Virus are dramatically increasing worldwide. Many of these pathogens are mutating to strains resistant to known treatments. Some scholars attribute the unprecedented increase in sexually transmitted diseases to social conditions such as rampant promiscuity and intravenous drug use. [12.29]

Social conditions certainly fuel pandemics, but they should be considered in light of a larger picture. The human population has grown so large that our numbers provide an enormous, expanding Petri dish—a perfect and abundant environment for the growth and rapid evolution of parasitic microorganisms. The increase in STDs, sexually transmitted diseases, may be a natural consequence of the exponential increase in the number of humans and their exponentially-increasing sexual encounters. There are more people and more sexual acts; there are absolutely more humans for STDs to infect and absolutely more sexual acts that STDs use to gain access to humans. The reproductive success of these STD organisms, in turn, reduces the fertility and survival of their hosts (us). STD organisms are the predators, humans are the prey.

Technically, this sort of interaction between populations of humans and STD organisms is called "density dependent natural selection." Density dependent selection is the way that very large populations like ours are reduced in the natural world of ecological checks and balances. Our species, less than a million years in development, is being changed and culled dramatically. Darwinian natural selection is alive and well.

CHAPTER 13

Therapy and Free Will

The new scientific view of human behavior, evolutionary psychology, is a view grounded in an old, well-tested, but continually developing science: evolutionary biology. It is a view that expands to consider not only where we came from, but where we are now and where we are going. It is a view that updates its paradigm continually with pertinent information about how we think (from cognitive science and neuroscience) and how we behave (from primatology, sociobiology, sociology and anthropology). Evolutionary psychology promises to help us attain a more realistic appraisal of all human behavior. It is a revolutionary idea that began with the work of shy English gentlemen more than a century and a half ago—when Charles Darwin and Alfred Russel Wallace presented the theory of evolution by means of natural selection.

It is likely that, had biologists continued on the path Darwin and Wallace plowed, we would have achieved our present understanding of the evolution of human behavior decades sooner. But, at the turn of the century, some biologists overextended Darwinian theory into an unacceptable political movement—eugenics. Proponents of eugenics advocated the controlled breeding of humans. Their autocratic, elitist, Orwellian proposals created such public furor that all biologists quickly abandoned statements of any sort that referred to humans. Biologists tacitly agreed to stick to the analysis of behavior in nonhuman animals; the human social sciences developed quickly to fill the void.

Darwin's concept of evolutionary change, though, inspired initially all the behavioral sciences that followed: psychology, anthropology, and sociology. Each discipline quickly followed its own course of development, placing its own stamp on similar subject matters. Psychologists, anthropologists, and sociologists attempted to describe and explain human behavior. While each discipline acknowledged that nature was dynamic and that behavior evolved, each harbored measurable animosity for the notion that man was a mere animal.

Each discipline set out to demonstrate that their particular brand of investigation (and theirs alone) could best explain human behavior. Each investigator, locked into the restrictive mold of methods and theories of his or her specialized discipline, described and explained the same human social relationships differently. Each of the social science disciplines soon cashiered biology and behavioral evolution and veered rapidly away from biological science.

Social scientists viewed evolution's legacies, if they considered them at all, as remote and unnecessary mechanisms for understanding human power, sex, and love. Freud proposed other mechanisms. Crucially, he revolutionized the doctor's bedside manner by insisting that the best way to first treat a patient was to listen to him or her; psychotherapy— couchside counseling—was born. Psychotherapy offered hope that, with professional counseling, troubled individuals could understand their hidden motivations, exorcise repressed childhood demons, and modify their behavior.

The Rise of Therapy

Freud, his followers, and his detractors launched dozens of "schools" of therapy differing in their mental models as well as therapeutic techniques. [13.1] Professional therapists ranging from trained medical practitioners to self-taught gurus appeared. Some schools have had some success at making patients feel better. Many have not.

Nevertheless, since Freud's time, Westerners have turned to psychology to understand human relationships. Within the twentieth century, psychology and psychiatry have provided the paradigm and have affected dramatically how each of us thinks about ourselves and our interactions with others. Psychiatry in general and psychoanalysis in particular have been extended to anthropology, sociology, art and literary criticism, political theory, biographical writing, mythology, and language. Its influence on human thought has extended from the European asylum to the White House, to every bedroom in the land.

We interpret the correctness of our behavior and the behavior of others through many terms and concepts of psychiatry. Psychiatry has told us what is normal and abnormal behavior. Most of us have struggled with our putative "subconscious." We have worried about our ego; wondered whether our dreams reveal some hidden mental desire or disorder; vexed over our attachment to our parents ("Am I Oedipal?"); and pondered the vitality of our "psychic energy." Subjective psychiatry has defined and given names to our "neuroses," "psychoses," "paranoias," "complexes," and "dementias"—and perhaps, through self-fulfilling prophecies, even caused a few.

Psychiatry has clearly struck a chord with the American people. In 1985, Americans made 27,800,000 visits to psychiatrists; by the year 2000, that number is expected to swell to more than 33 million. [13.2] The power of this profession to influence our culture's view of behavior is remarkable.

All the more remarkable is the observation that the fundamental paradigms used by many professional therapists to guide a client's behavior are based on the emotional problems of Viennese housewives at the turn of this century. [13.3] (The case studies that formed the base of theory-building in psychiatry did extend to some French and a few middle Europeans, but psychiatry retains a peculiarly Viennese stamp.) Modern psychiatry has been enmeshed largely in a starched, cultural straitjacket since the time of Freud. Psychiatry has largely ignored both evolution and comparative studies of our close relatives, the nonhuman primates. This narrow focus has had unfortunate consequences for our understanding of human behavior.

Consider, for example, many psychiatrists' stock-in-trade response to one small aspect of human love—jealousy. "Jealousy," we are told by some psychiatrists, stems from the loss of "self-esteem" and the "self-criticism in which the person blames himself for the loss" of the loved object. Furthermore, the jealous reaction is "not completely rational, for it is disproportionate to the real circumstances, not completely under the control of the conscious ego, and not derived from the actual situation." [13.4] Dr. Joyce Brothers, expanding on this definition in her syndicated newspaper column, said that "all jealousy springs from a basic insecurity and dissatisfaction with self." [13.5]

Basically, then, much of contemporary psychiatry views jealousy as an antisocial, diseased state. Jealousy is harbored by individuals who think badly of themselves, who are out of touch with reality, who are out of sync with those of us who are "well adjusted" and "normal." To most psychiatrists, jealousy is unremittingly bad and undesirable; jealousy is a harmful emotion that ought to be eliminated.

How different our view of jealousy becomes when we use a broad, evolutionary perspective. Jealous behavior evolved millions of years ago, in creatures with few neurons with which to feel "dissatisfied with self." Jealousy, more strongly developed in males than females, evolved to promote and defend one's genetic contribution to the next generation. With the evolution of diurnal lemurs (Chapter 8), mates defined one another as a possession (as chattel) within a consort bond. The descendants of lemurs—apes, prehumans, and us—have continued to lay claim to their mates.

Jealousy, then, is a normal human emotional response. It is biologically wired into our brain; it is a natural part of our romantic thought process. Jealousy is one crucial part of the human romantic response that is not to be trifled with lightly. Jealousy, on its face, is neither good nor bad, wrong nor right, but it is a real part of human behavior that must be understood. Depending on its expression and social context, jealousy can be adaptive or maladaptive. Therapy, properly applied, can discourage maladaptive (dysfunctional) jealousy by considering contemporary ethical and social mores and the patient's needs and social relationship. But no amount of therapy is likely to eliminate the primate predisposition to view one's mate jealously as a possession.

Contemporary psychiatry is not without merit or grains of pragmatic truths. Yet, it is unclear whether a person suffering mental anguish could obtain equal or better results from talking with no one or with a sympathetic friend or a school or religious counselor. For example, as of 1988, Tokyo had only four practicing psychotherapists. It is doubtful that its citizens suffer more mental anguish or are any crazier than those in comparable American cities.

In 1952, English psychiatrist Hans Eysenck found that patients undergoing psychoanalysis improve at a rate of 44%; those subject to psychotherapy recover at a rate of 64%, while those people who avoid professional treatment are cured at a rate of 72%. [13.6] Eysenck's findings were substantially confirmed by other psychiatrists in the 1970s. [13.7]

Some people may even suffer harm through psychiatric counseling. In our example, a jealous person, told that he or she is harboring a deep "unconscious" feeling of inadequacy, may be talked into a poor self-image that he or she doesn't have. As British psychiatrist Sidney Crown noted: "Any practicing psychotherapist must recognize the truth of this observation—we do make some patients worse." [13.8] Given the uncertain benefits of current psychotherapy, the high costs of professional treatment seem outlandish. A classic therapy regime may consist of four or five hourly sessions each week for more than five years for treatment of most common mental disorders. [13.9]

The problem, I think, is not with the dedication or concern of most therapists. It lies with their fundamental precepts. Diagnosing behavioral problems and prescribing cures through outmoded science can be hazardous. As satisfying and perhaps useful as Freudian psychotherapy's journalese, "just-so" models [13.10] have been to generations of admirers, neither Freud's mental maps nor mythic metaphors have been verified in the human brain nor identified empirically in patterns of human behavior. Even Freud doubted his models' scientific validity. In a private letter, he conceded that "it's hard to say whether [the models of psychoanalytic theory] should be regarded as postulates or as products of our researches." [13.11]

Contemporary psychiatry has largely failed to employ precise, current definitions, tested information, and a prehistorical and historical perspective to understand human behavior. But, this situation may change. Psychology led the way away from biology. Significantly, then, psychology, with a new, multidisciplinary approach to human behavior, may lead the way back. Once again: it is not Freud's approach to the patient that has failed. Freud pioneered the medical practice of an exchange of information between the therapist and the patient. I suggest that it is the information that has failed, not the act of therapy. Evolutionary psychology offers better information about the underlying causes of human behavior—a picture that spans cultures, time, and species.

A New, Deterministic View of the Human Social Machine

According to evolutionary psychology, none of us are born facing life's problems entirely as individuals. We do not fall in love, clamor for sexual gratification, or seek power or alliances as independent beings. We are first and last social beings, enmeshed in a gigantic social machine. The machine has been running, with extensive modifications, for a billion or more years. During the past fifty million years, our ancestral primates—lemurs, apes, and prehumans—have largely established the shape of this machine. Each of us is born as an expendable, behaving cog in a pre-existing, human social machine. Some of the grooves and lands in our individual gears are formed before birth, others develop as we age. To some extent, as our behavioral gears fit in or clash, we all minutely change the shape of the contemporary human social machine. Throughout our lives, some individual cogs grow, others shrink, but inevitably, all are replaced. Life goes on; the social machine continues to churn; our species evolves.

Our present social behavior is, in large measure, a legacy of the behavior of our primate ancestors. In a way, we are puppets, crafted by natural selection and motivated by the products of our genes. Human power, sex, and love relationships dance to tens of millions of years of evolutionary tunes.

Many of us would like to believe, for example, that love is a bastion of human choice, of free will, of egalitarianism, and serendipity in action. Yet, love is a behavioral concept and action that embodies brain chemistry, sexuality, mate choice, and dominance. Lovers unwittingly relive the evolutionary adaptations of our species' evolutionary past. Who we fall in love with, how we fall in love, and what love means has been bequeathed to us by countless ancient ancestors. Evolutionary psychologists can see many of the scars and triumphs of this long evolutionary journey through time in our behavior today.

From the puddle where sexual reproduction was born, we inherited significant gender differences in our romantic goals. The male reproductive strategy is to seek, win, and mate with many females. A man, driven to continually seek new sexual partners, may be obsessed with romance. Men readily engage in intense, brief, often impractical, love affairs. A woman, on the other hand, tends to seek a deeper, more enduring, more pragmatic bond.

The female reproductive strategy is to seek stability; to protect and insure her survival and the survival of children (especially her daughters). For males, romance is a continual, testosterone-driven quest—indeed, conquests. For females, romance is a more reasoned choice. Females must seek resources not only for themselves, but for their offspring as well. Both a man and a woman seek to insure the favored survival of their genes, but "favored survival" means different things to the genders—a man is pre-programmed to seek multiple partners; a woman seeks stable support for her maternal family group.

Our earliest primate ancestors, the mouse lemurs, bequeathed us a strong mother-daughter bond and female families (matrilineages), and reaffirmed the expendable, predatory nature of the male reproductive quest. Later lemur groups struck a tenuous balance between the need for male-male aggression and the need for compassion toward females in romance. It is a balance that, fifty million years later, is often unhinged.

The lemur introduced the temporary consort bond to primate behavior—a bond that has become formalized in human societies. The lemur consort bond, as that of all the primates that followed, is formed between individuals of near-equal rank. Social status in primate societies is a function of the status at birth, then as now. Dominance status plays a key role in our choice of partners.

Our ape ancestors transformed a female-dominated primate society to male domination. They solidified female family groups and the structure of the all-important male dominance hierarchy. Female apes receive most of their concepts about mate selection, dominance, and bonding from their mothers; male apes learn about mating from the dominant male groups. This is largely the same gender-divided way that humans learn about social behavior. Gender differences in socialization and in hormonal responses were emphatically demonstrated by the ape adaptation of war: males fight often to redirect their aggression outside the group; females seldom engage in physical violence, and only then to protect their resources. This paradigm of war is a legacy that humans have followed to this day.

A human male seeks to form power alliances with other men. Dominance status in these coalitions may be even more important than sex or love. A man will cooperate with some men in a power alliance, but will view other men as competitors. Male-male bonding is based on redirected aggression and shared risks—a form of bonding not previously practiced by females.

A woman who joins a traditional male dominance hierarchy will be viewed as a potential threat by men. A woman who joins a male dominance hierarchy will necessarily adopt male social signals. A career woman often engenders a conflicting "sexual approach–competitor withdrawal" response from men.

A woman naturally forms long-lasting bonds with her daughters, with other women, and lastly, with her male consort. A man will form many (temporary) bonds with other men; a woman forms fewer, more permanent bonds with other women. The male-female consort bond is temporary—yet neither a man nor a woman enters into this bond with its dissolution on their minds.

Even the consort bond itself means different things to the genders. A man's consort bond corroborates his dominance status within his male group (or groups). For a woman, the consort bond protects her social status and provides a measure of insurance for her family.

A man will likely endure a "bad marriage" rather than end it and suffer a diminished dominance rank. A woman will likely endure an unsatisfying or abusive relationship because it appears to offer some measure of social stability and survivability for her offspring. It is remarkable how much unhappiness humans can endure in search of social stability. Romance and love often play little or no role in determining the permanence of consort bonds.

Fatherhood and monogamous marriage are new, cultural inventions. Both fatherhood and monogamy are weak, poorly-defined bonds, but often socially important ones. Because these bonds are new, "experimental," and non-instinctive, many men and women will disagree fundamentally on their precise form. Serial polygyny—impermanent monogamy—is the human bonding adaptation. Yet most of us are repelled by the thought that love will not last forever. It is a reality that sharply contradicts our romantic myths.

Since the Age of the Apes, then, gender loyalties have been necessarily divided. Men serve their individual reproductive interests, the social demands of their male power coalition, and the particular needs of their consort. Women serve their genes, their maternal lineages, their offspring, and, lastly, their mates. A successful relationship is one that concedes the importance of and the differences between these divided loyalties. For example, an assertion that altruism is a basis of romantic love is not a cudgel that can make all other personal and social interests null and void. True altruism, in fact, may only rarely exist in any social relationship.

Humans recently introduced language to the mixture of millions of years of biological imperatives. Through language, humans arbitrarily define, negotiate, and rearrange love and romance. Language, a deceptive form of communication, conceals mating strategies from our mates and ourselves. Language formalizes and institutionalizes dominance hierarchies and consort bonds.

But we should not fool ourselves by equating linguistically created cultural values with free will. Cultural values and the rules that spring from them are, more often than not, "directed at maximizing the reproductive success of the individual members of societies."[13.12] Cultural values and rules, subject to natural selection as are any other aspect of human behavior, are mostly the tools of natural selection. Cultural rules do not subvert ancient, evolutionary imperatives. Married men, publicly touting their culture's ideal of monogamy, still commit adultery.

Psychological studies, evolutionary or otherwise, remove most free will from human behavior. Before evolutionary psychology, psychologists attributed our actions to mysterious, subconscious desires and mental images that responded to childhood insults by issuing a variety of adulthood psychoses and neuroses. In contrast, evolutionary psychology attributes our actions to behavioral patterns established by ancestors in our evolutionary past. Evolutionary psychologists see the format of childhood socialization itself as partially derived from our evolutionary past.

Fortunately, the strings that bind us to our genetical, ancestral puppeteers are often long and flexible. Our ability to modify biological and cultural proscriptions is directly proportional to our knowledge of those proscriptions. We can act to alter our behavior more than can the individuals of any other species. Nowhere is the human struggle to understand and modify behavior more sharply defined than in our unending attempt to balance changing cultural rules with conflicting biological imperatives. The information supplied by evolutionary psychologists could help us all juggle these rules and imperatives in our lives.

Can Therapy Work?

It is remarkable that we study a manual, practice, and often enroll in classes to obtain a driver's license, but we are content to acquire virtually all our skills for the profound complexities of romance, love, parenting, and social relationships from informal, haphazard sources. Neither driving a car nor achieving a workable relationship is "intuitively obvious" for a human, so it would seem logical that counseling would improve a person's performance both driving a car and performing socially.

But if, unlike driving a car, major aspects of social behavior have already been determined by our biology, then what role does the profession of psychology have in producing meaningful behavioral change? Can social counseling—the principal technology of psychotherapy—work? Does our evolutionary past and our genetically-determined present place us in an unenviable position as bit players in our own evolutionary play? We now face the crux of the matter for evolutionary psychologists: can an individual, or even a small group of individuals, take charge and genuinely change behavior? This question is the heart of the issue of free will.

Language, evolved as it did to foster deceptive communication, makes it relatively easy to deny our predicament and avoid the issue of free will altogether. But, unless such self-deception is highly adaptive, the issue will not disappear. We are either individually or collectively capable of some measure of free will, or we are not the responsible agents of our own actions. Without a modicum of free will in human behavior, psychotherapy is unlikely to work.

To some, the fact that twentieth-century science cannot accurately describe all the nuances of design in the human social machine is somehow comforting. For example, we know that a single human thought is a chorus of ten thousand million nerve cells. We barely perceive the anatomical complexity of a single human thought, let alone the behavior that a thought might generate. Behavior's complexity defies all but the simplest deterministic predictions—at least for now. But free will is a false concept, a linguistic deception, if it is merely a label for our present inability to predict complex behavior.

The concept of free will is perhaps more a heartfelt, human wish than a reality. Most of us would like to believe that we choose our affairs of the heart and design our relationships through our own volition. But, as we have seen, human social relationships are severely canalized—limited and sharply constrained—aspects of our repertoire of behavior. Little evidence of free will is seen in social behavior.

Free Will?

Seventeenth-century British philosopher Thomas Hobbes expressed a view of free will closely in line with current concepts in evolutionary psychology. Hobbes stated that ideas, sensations, and all psychological processes are motions or modifications of materials in the brain. For Hobbes, voluntary human actions—acts of free will—were caused by a mental struggle between desire and aversion. The mental struggle itself could be traced to physical actions within the brain. [13.13] In short, free will is not free; it is ultimately determined by biology. Today, neurophysiologists are some distance from tracing complex thought patterns within the brain, but we can state unequivocally that the brain and its workings are the result of millions of years of evolution.

What can remain of free will in a brain whose structure has been determined by chance historical accidents and natural selection? Our expanding knowledge of evolutionary psychology has apparently rendered the realm of "free will" tiny indeed. Cognitive scientist Marvin Minsky suggests that "Free Will" represents a tiny box that dwells between deterministic "Chance" and "Cause." A slight modification of Minsky's boxes is appropriate here: [13.14]

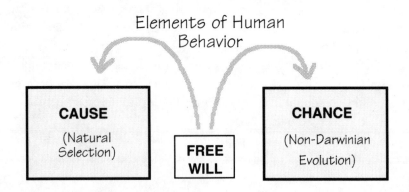

The more we know about life, the more concepts we pull from the box of Free Will and place into the deterministic boxes of either Chance or Cause. "In ancient times," Minsky notes, "[the realm of Free Will] was huge, when every planet had its god, and every storm or animal did manifest some spirit's wish. But now for many centuries, we've had to watch that empire shrink . . . [Yet] [t]oo much of our psychology is based on [the concept of free will] for us to ever give it up."

Minsky argues that free will is an illusion necessary for the proper functioning of human societies. Many would agree that social interactions like romance may require an unexamined belief in Free Will. Others have argued that there is a "necessity for a little stupidity in social life."

In 1894, Benjamin Kidd, in his book *Social Evolution,* argued cogently that nonrational social institutions like religion serve an integrating function; they are a necessary prop—a crutch—for proper conduct. Kidd's critics (who were legion) felt his theory justified untenable stupidity in social life. According to Kidd, natural selection selects for a degree of irrationality in human conduct. Perhaps, nearly a century later, it should be conceded that "man cannot survive on a pure diet of scientific rationality" after all. [13.15]

Scientific realism can be painful. The world view presented through deterministic logic is often stark. Even the simple terminology of evolutionary psychology is fulsome to some. Curmudgeon Ian Shoales notes that "[t]he word relationship best refers to the connection between a parasite and a host, or a shark and remora. It's a biological term. I'd rather be a jerk than a scientist when it comes to love."

Fran Lebowitz concurs and presents a popular, probably accurate notion that self-deception is a requisite of romantic love:

> Romantic Love is a mental illness . . . It's a drug. It distorts
> reality, and that's the point of it. It would be impossible to fall
> in love with someone that you really saw. [13.16]

The dogged persistence of the belief in free will in scholarly circles requires an additional explanation. As nineteenth-century philosopher Friedrich Nietzsche suggested:

> It is certainly not the least charm of a theory that it is refutable:
> it is with precisely this charm that it entices subtler minds. It

seems that the hundred times refuted theory of "free will" owes its continued existence to this charm alone—: again and again there comes along someone who feels he is strong enough to refute it. [13.17]

To a measurable extent, science and philosophy are merely word games played by humans. Science and philosophy constitute a form of adult play, much like a game of poker. It is not unreasonable to suggest that those hands which offer the most sport—like the concept of free will—are played over again many times.

Regardless, with each new study of human relationships, the box of Free Will shrinks and the boxes of Cause and Chance fill. The concept of free will and its antithesis, determinism, have been vigorously debated for centuries. Philosophers define determinism simply: for everything that happens there are conditions such that, given them, nothing else can happen. In this strict, philosophical sense, if human behavior is biologically determined, then no one can help being what he or she is, and doing what he or she does.

Yet, few processes in biology are this rigidly determined. Behavior is displayed more as a range of actions, and, at any particular time, any particular behavior is either a strong or weak probability. Consider that the brain is, amongst other things, an information gathering and information processing device. New information can alter the brain's response. Memories—previously stored and subsequently retrieved information—can further alter a brain's response. A brain is a complex device—a social computer, if you will—whose response can be altered by information. If a smidgen of free will is to be found at all in human behavior, it is in what information we gather and how we process that information once we receive it.

In the final analysis, the choice to understand and modify our behavior is probably the last bastion of human free will. [13.18] Evolutionary psychology can play an enormously beneficial role in these regards. Perhaps a mutually satisfying, long-lasting relationship is the most emphatic display of free will in a species whose behavior seems governed by conflicting, deterministic motivations from its past. As primatologist Sarah Blaffer Hrdy proclaims, humans can "intellectually draw up guidelines to overcome our biology." [13,19] We can challenge the present forces of natural selection—in an extreme example, a person can commit suicide (an act that usually denigrates or destroys an individual's reproductive success). Despite the prevalence of the past in determining our present, our biology allows us considerable slack—slack that includes some behavioral capabilities that we all can use for our betterment.

Hypothetically, then, *individuals* are capable of considerable choice and change. Yet individuals are part of a larger social group, a long-standing social machine that inevitably curbs individual choices. The structure of a larger social group is itself canalized by the evolutionary and present-day biological selective forces we've discussed previously. We are all programmed by our societies to an extent that most conceivable individual choices are simply not visible to us. Once again, evolutionary psychology can serve us: it shows us how societies mold individuals and what individual choices are likely, unlikely, possible, or virtually impossible. Evolutionary psychology may be the ultimate reality check.

Future Relationships: A Thump on the Box of Free Will?

When we wake in the morning and roll out of bed, our feet strike the floor with a resounding thump. We do not fall up to the ceiling, we do not sail above the floor, bleary-eyed, toward the door. We are constrained by the forces that pull objects together, just as our ancestors were constrained. But humans are clever animals. By understanding the forces that bind objects together, and those that allow objects to float, we have built wings. We can soar, not in defiance of gravity, but in concert with it. Together, men and women have understood natural forces and have built machines that today carry them toward the stars.

The social machine that we humans have inherited is a sort of natural force, much like that of gravity. Evolutionary psychologists are working toward a better understanding of the biological forces that have shaped and continue to shape our behavior. With that understanding, we may be able to craft social relationships and societies to overcome what we see now as evolutionary constraints.

In principle, we can decide not to have children (or to limit the number of children we have). Abusive parents can take stock of their actions and, if motivated and educated, change. We can choose to define and support families of any sort—single parent, two-parent, multiple-parent, heterosexual, or homosexual.

An empowered and knowledgable woman can exercise control over mothering. She need not have children. Unlike the dryopithecine apes that came before our species, women today can join together and define their own power coalitions. Similarly, a man can defy millions of years of social evolution and choose to act as an individual, not as a member of a power coalition. [13,20] Although job and social pressures may force most men to join groups, men do not *have* to band together and redirect their aggression upon scapegoats outside their social group. Even men (and increasingly, women) who choose to sublimate their individuality for an in-group identity can and sometimes do find socially cohesive, cooperative outlets for aggression.

The possibilities for the limited exercise of free will are constrained only by our imagination—even though the range and character of our imagination itself are products of millions of years of our evolution. While intelligent and satisfying behavioral choices are possible, they are only likely through a realistic appraisal of the biological forces that shape human society.

Who and what will shape our gender images in the future? For much of the global village, television now provides the prime focus of socialization for our youth. This change is unprecedented in primate evolution. The electronic media has assumed a collective role in socializing the next generation that rested exclusively with individual mothers and with individual bachelor groups for tens of millions of years. This change is crucial, since the media is largely responsive to proximate economic pressures, not ultimate social concerns.

There is little evidence that electronic media packagers comprehend their power, their pivotal role, or the dangers inherent in shaping the next generation of humans. Or, in a more cynical analysis, media mavens understand their role in socializing humans and simply don't care. In either case, the media—citing a concern for freedom of speech—wants no programming policy whatsoever to provide adaptive direction, guidance, or education. Today and for the foreseeable future, whatever images can be assembled quickly and sold in quantity will prevail. Media players prevail (compete with each other) by manufacturing a supply of ever-escalating, supernormal stimuli for their audience (us). A supernormal stimulus is a stimulus that elicits a greater than expected response; here, it is an image, concept, or a metaphor that produces ever-greater product sales. [13.21]

It is likely, therefore, that gender relationships in the future will be troubled by even more conflicting images of aggression, nurturing, discrimination, and egalitarianism. Given the media's lack of logical guidelines and penchant for maximizing the stimulation of its audience, future socialization will continue to contain bizarrely exaggerated images—supernormal stimuli—from the legacies of lemurs, apes, and prehumans. At the least, few such presentations are likely to realistically explore or increase our understanding of gender relationships.

Our children's images of relationships will undoubtedly differ from ours. Will they realistically reflect evolutionary constraints? Will our children's training at the hands of educators, peers, writers, producers, directors, and rock stars help them adapt to the increasing pace of cultural change? Or will present offerings introduce additional conflicts between cultural values and our biology? Will future lovers resolve romance with egalitarianism, meaningful fatherhood, and faithful monogamy? Will society foster single-parent families that fulfill the needs of both mothers and children? Will our children avoid AIDS or perish? Will they find love without the repeated goal of childbearing—or will the crush of children continue to surpass the limits of the earth's long-suffering ecosystems?

All these questions are obviously rhetorical. An optimist would answer them positively, a pessimist would cite prevalent trends and predict gloom. As a scientist who has studied these issues for many years, I am pessimistic. For example, with regard to the crush of humanity, I think that professional cynic Kurt Vonnegut has said it best. Humanity, he writes, has become "an unstoppable glacier of hot meat, which [eats] up everything in sight and then [makes] love, and [doubles] in size again." [13.22] Glaciers are probably impossible to stop. Novelists and essayists like Vonnegut often serve as canaries in societies' coal mines. When they go belly up, it is well to pay close attention to the social environment.

Of course, anyone can be a futurologist. But, while the future is largely speculative, there are two certainties about it. Gender relations will change in the future as they have changed in the past. And, collectively, our understanding of human relationships will change. We will perceive ourselves differently tomorrow than we do today. In the near future, we may understand ourselves better, or, should some transient Dark Age descend upon our society, we may understand even less about human relationships tomorrow than we do now. Changing perceptions and changing values are a grand part of never-ending evolutionary change. Change is a given in the paradigm of evolutionary psychology.

At present, the more we learn about behavior, the more we see that human behavior does not differ greatly from the behavior of our evolutionary cousins, notably the chimpanzees. Even with language distinguishing us from all other primates, language has only enabled our species to garnish the basic social organization that was established first by the dryopithecine apes millions of years ago. Our behavior is to chimpanzee behavior as a great and garish rococo cathedral is to a simple, one-room Presbyterian church. The plans and purposes are similar; only the scale and ornamentation differ. Further, the most revolutionary change in social organization occurred not when speaking humans became distinct from grunting proto-humans, but when apes evolved male-dominated societies from the female-dominated lemur societies that preceded them. These observations are—or at least should be—humbling.

Today, more than 50 million years since the first lemurs scrambled about the bushes, more than 20 million years since the Age of the Apes, more than a million years since our bipedal ancestor began to speak, we face a momentous crossroad in human evolution. Unlike any species that evolved before us, we must soon choose whether or not we'll continue to increase our numbers and destroy our global habitat. This choice will likely determine whether our species will continue to evolve, or will become extinct without issue. This decision is—or at least should be—humbling.

The Untimely End of Evolutionary Psychology?

How would you react to the knowledge that someone was systematically entering libraries around the world and burning books? The books incinerated were virtually the entire storehouse of human knowledge about nature and its history. Within a generation, you are told, almost all the world's books on the subject will be lost forever. With their destruction, the promising new science of evolutionary psychology will draw to a halt. The scenario sounds worse than the burning of the ancient library at Alexandria. Not even the book burnings of all the twentieth-century megalomaniacs put together could compare with the scope of such a hypothetical disaster.

Tragically, this sort of disaster is by no means hypothetical. It is happening now. The pace of destruction is increasing exponentially. Its unchecked climax—a pile of unusable, unreadable cinders: knowledge forever lost—is in sight. Books are not being burned. Trees are burning. They are burning because humans are clearing the primary tropical forests of the world. They are burning because humans, who pride themselves on being the most intelligent creatures on earth, exhibit rapacious greed, shortsightedness, and stupidity more often than wisdom. No single human ethnic or social group is exemplary: the destroyers range from tribesmen to chief executive officers.

Entire ecological systems, millions of years in creation, are being leveled overnight. To date, we have lost more than 40% of the world's tropical

235

forests. Forests encompassing an area twice the size of Austria are destroyed each year. The rate of deforestation, now estimated conservatively at perhaps 50 million acres each year, is doubling rapidly. Brazil, home to one of the largest remaining stands, lost 12 million acres of forest in 1988; a year later, more than 22 million acres disappeared. More than half of Indonesia's forests are gone; more than 80% of Vietnam has been laid waste. More than half the jungles of Africa have been destroyed; 86% of its rich savannahs—the plains that witnessed humanity's birth—have been converted into barren deserts.[1]

Unlike our familiar temperate forests, once a tropical forest is cleared, it does not regenerate. Tropical soils contain little humus and few nutrients. Once the energy-rich forest is gone, the soils can support agriculture or grazing for only a few years. Rains strip the soils of nutrients and the sun bakes the earth into barren, compacted, unarable sands. A rich tropical forest gives way to uninhabitable badlands in a decade or less. The perennially shortsighted exploiters either die of famine and drought or move on to clear another forest. The tropical forest may return someday, millions of years hence, when continents collide and volcanoes spew forth nourishing soils. New forests may appear someday, but our species will be long extinct.

The Extinction of Knowledge

These rapidly vanishing tropical forests contain the knowledge base necessary to understand our own evolution. Tropical forests are home to our fellow primates. Most lemurs, monkeys, and apes will soon be extinct. Once lost, we will remain forever ignorant of their behavior, their genetics, their physiology, and their complicated interactions with their environment.

Anthropologist Russell Tuttle, in an article about apes, outlines the direct human loss that will be suffered by the extinction of any primate species:

> Without immediate moves to preserve the apes and their habitats, we will lose forever a wealth of information. This would be especially tragic now that we have many well-formulated hy-

potheses to test, incisive research tools and approaches, and the technology to process great quantities of data. We are on the threshold to move from viewing apes as amusements to considering them creatures which truly reveal things about ourselves.[2]

The accounts of human social evolution—presented in this or any other book—may have to stand largely unchallenged, for soon there will be no new data to gather, no troops of close relatives to observe. New questions will arise and new doubts about old ideas will surface, but, with no wild primates left to study, new hypotheses will be stillborn. Mounted museum pelts and drawers filled with fresh bones can tell us little or nothing about the evolution of our behavior. Word games, not science, will be all that remain. The subject matter of evolutionary psychology will be gone.

Zoos provide the last best hope for salvaging a little of the world's wildlife. The zookeeping profession, selflessly dedicated to saving as many species as possible, works with few resources to provide cages and suitable captive environments for endangered primates.[3] Zoo workers are literally plucking primates from the fire, in the hopes that, someday, they'll be able to reintroduce their captive descendants to the wild. Zoo workers concede that the wild will have to be managed like some mega-zoo if it is to survive.[4]

Our present joy at the survival of some captive primates must be tempered with the knowledge that most species cannot be saved, that zoos themselves are damaged by economic downturns and destroyed by war, that the wild may well be gone, and that, eventually, captive primates will become as domesticated—and as scientifically uninteresting—as cows. The crucial connection between the animals and their ecology will have vanished.

In the twenty-first century, a few primates will remain prisoners behind glass, feeding on monkey chow and behaving like inmates in a sanitized, plasticized world. As they stare back at our children from across a moat or from behind bars, a haunting look in their eyes will serve as a silent indictment of our generation—the last generation that could have saved nature, but didn't.

A lemur giving birth in a cage.

Priorities

Human priorities have always been measured monetarily. By that yard-stick, we place little value on the invaluable libraries of evolution. For example, in 1985, the International Union for the Conservation of Nature, one of the world's preeminent conservation groups, was able to fund only $8.5 million worth of projects. In that same year, Band Aid raised $90 million for sub-Saharan peoples who were suffering from the effects of human-created droughts, famines, and wars. In 1985, humanity spent $75 *billion* for the tools of war.[5]

Without drastic, unprecedented conservation action now, the future of evolutionary science is as doomed as its subjects. At present, all the conservation efforts on earth are easily outpaced by singular acts of violent destruction. For example, by willfully unleashing millions of gallons of crude oil into the Persian Gulf in 1991, the Iraqis destroyed more marine creatures than Greenpeace and the Cousteau Society have saved in three decades of hard work. A single lumber or mining company in Brazil destroys more forest habitats in a year than the Sierra Club can save in a decade.

The pressure on the last remaining wild lands increases with every development project, with every birth of every unwanted child. Regardless, many humans strive to abolish birth control efforts and to feed every abandoned human child. Well-intentioned humanitarian groups feed, clothe, and house surplus children.

In the 1970s, the prestigious Club of Rome conferences urged that family planning should be sent to Third World countries in lieu of food and economic assistance. Their suggestions were roundly criticized as a "Let 'em starve" approach to humanitarian aid. More recently, though, the Chairman of the American House Permanent Select Committee on Intelligence has suggested the same approach to foreign aid.[6]

The logic of these propositions is impeccable: why feed prolific human breeders when we know that soon we will not have enough food to feed all their children? Feeding millions of people now will, at best, doom remaining habitats to continued overexploitation and, at worst, doom billions of children to starvation in the future. Currently, food and economic assistance to people who have destroyed their agricultural base, however sporadic, continues unabated. Subsequently, the physical, political, and social needs of the saved adults—the grown children—are largely ignored. Saved children become breeding adults who repeat their parents' mistakes. The cycle of poverty and overpopulation continues to escalate.

Currently, the human population stands at more than five billion—a staggering number, exceeded by only a few other species such as microorganisms, some invertebrates, some fish, and some rats. Within eighty years, the human population is expected to triple. For comparison, a few species populations of lemurs number under 100; many species number fewer than 1,000 individuals. Almost no nonhuman primate species approaches the population numbers of humans in even a small city. Fewer gorillas are alive today worldwide than residents of a modest African village. Even so, we continue to slash and burn primate habitats. We continue to buy and sell souvenirs made from the body parts of murdered gorillas (and ivory art works made from the tusks of butchered elephants, knife handles and potency pills crafted from rhino horns, combs carved from the shells of slaughtered turtles, etc.).

In an ethical, logical, and economic sense, the human species devalues itself by its unwanted numbers. It seems reasonable, then, that we should value endangered species and our rare primate relatives as much or more than ourselves. Reason, logic, and common sense aside, we remain a human-centered animal. Single-minded, selfish devotion to our own needs, wants, and desires may be a characteristic we share with most perceptive species. Our evolutionary history has produced a species that values reproductive priorities far above even its own quality of life. As the human population grows, oceanographer Jacques Cousteau predicts that humans will live "like rats."[7]

Only our species can understand the long-term implications of its actions. Only our species can selfishly destroy the planet—or save it.[8] The exponential growth of the human population is the hallmark of our evolutionary success. It is *our* legacy. Humans, unlike any primate species that came before, are pushing their flesh into every nook and cranny of Earth's landscapes. Our evolutionary imperatives are a smashing success, even if we destroy forever the library of evolution that we need to fully understand them.

Notes

Preface

1. John Casti, *Paradigms Lost: Images of Man in the Mirror of Science,* William Morrow and Company, Inc., New York, NY, 1989, p. xi.

Acknowledgments

1. Those who know me and knew John Buettner-Janusch ("B-J") will be puzzled to see his name in this section of the book. A few words of explanation are in order. During the late 1960s and early '70s, B-J was arguably the most powerful and well-known physical anthropologist in the world. His introductory textbook, *Origins of Man* (John Wiley & Sons, Inc., New York, NY, 1966), pioneered a holistic approach (anatomy, taxonomy, paleontology, ethology, biochemistry) to understanding human evolution. It quickly became the global, professional standard.

   B-J was a wonderful intellectual synthesizer, a founder of the Duke University Primate Facility (devoted to breeding, studying, and conserving lemurs), and a maker and breaker of academic careers. In 1969, B-J sponsored my graduate career at Duke University and introduced me to the lemurs. He taught me much, but sadly, within a few years, he and I were unequal enemies. Always something of a flamboyant sociopath, B-J made more enemies than friends. I struggled beneath his long-reaching shadow for many years thereafter.

   Later, B-J became Chairman of New York University's Anthropology Department and there crossed a clearly marked line of uncivilized conduct following the sudden death of his beloved wife, Vina. Ostensibly to make up for a lost government research grant, B-J made street narcotics in his university laboratory.

241

He was caught and was sentenced to four years in a federal penitentiary. His fall from the pinnacle of scientific power was the greatest in modern times.

After his release, B-J failed to regain a respectable position and, for reasons never made clear, poisoned chocolates and sent them to the judge who sentenced him and to some of his old academic colleagues. Several innocent victims became ill, but no one died. Caught with a Willy Wonka–sized cache of chocolates and toxins in his apartment, B-J pled guilty to attempted murder charges and was sentenced to forty years in prison. Denied parole, he committed suicide in 1992.

B-J's life story is an enormous drama, a terrible, self-inflicted tragedy. I will remember him not only for the pain he inflicted on himself and others, but for the significant, albeit momentary, kindness he showed me so many years ago. B-J introduced me to lemurs and, most significantly, he introduced lemurs to American science. History, I suspect, will not deal kindly with the memory of Professor John Buettner-Janusch. He is fast becoming a non-person in the literature and in the halls of the academe. B-J was many people, some good, some bad: *Requiescant In Pace,* B-J.

Chapter 1

1.1 Mary Wollstonecraft is best known for *Vindication of the Rights of Woman* (1792), the first modern feminist manifesto. Her daughter, Mary Godwin Shelley, second wife of poet Percy Bysshe Shelley, wrote the Gothic novel *Frankenstein, Or the Modern Prometheus.*

1.2 The *Scala Naturae*—scale of nature—was a common concept in eighteenth-century biological thought. It was rejected formally by Cuvier in the early nineteenth century (Ernst Mayr, *One Long Argument: Charles Darwin and the Genesis of Modern Evolutionary Thought,* Harvard University Press, Cambridge, MA, 1991).

Chapter 2

2.1 Quoted in *ABC's of the Human Mind,* edited by Alma E. Guinness, The Reader's Digest Association, Inc., Pleasantville, NY, 1990, p. 63.

2.2 A second edition of this work is available with a 147-page author's postscript answering many criticisms (published by Routledge & Kegan Paul, London, 1981).

2.3 *King Solomon's Ring: New Light on Animal Ways* was published by Thomas W. Crowell Company, New York, NY, 1952.

2.4 Mark Ridley in *The Oxford Companion to Animal Behavior,* edited by David McFarland, Oxford University Press, New York, NY, 1987, p. 571.

2.5 Before becoming a popular science writer, Ardrey had gained a measure of professional fame in humanistic Group Theater. The Group Theater movement was organized by Lee Strasberg, Harold Clurman, and Cheryl Crawford in 1931 and lasted about a decade. Ardrey's most famous play, "Thunder Rock," was performed in 1939.

2.6 Both *The Social Contract* in 1970 and *The Hunting Hypothesis* in 1976 were published by Dell Publishing Company, New York, NY. Ardrey also promoted the work of another "outcast" researcher, Eugène Marais: *The Soul of the Ape,* Atheneum, New York, NY, 1969. Today, neither Ardrey nor Marais are discussed within academia.

2.7 In S. J. Gould's "The Nonscience of Human Nature" in *Ever Since Darwin: Reflections in Natural History,* W. W. Norton & Company, Inc., New York, NY, 1977, pp. 237–242.

2.8 Leakey was academically unorthodox in his time. Interestingly, the L. S. B. Leakey Foundation is today's orthodoxy—in large measure due to the highly visible support of America's National Geographic Society for Leakey's colorful, controversial work.

2.9 Jane Goodall's first, slim popular book was an instant success: *My Friends the Wild Chimpanzees* by Baroness Jane Van Lawick-Goodall, National Geographic Society, Washington, DC, 1967.

2.10 Dr. Goodall's book jacket (published by Houghton Mifflin, New York, NY, 1990) proclaims boldly: "Perhaps the best book ever written about animal behavior . . . In the mirror of chimpanzee life, we see ourselves reflected." Frans de Waal's books (published by Harper & Row Publishers, Inc., New York, NY, 1982, and Harvard University Press, Cambridge, MA, 1989, respectively) concur: chimpanzee and human social behavior is a difference in degree, not kind.

2.11 Quote from "Ethology" by P. P. G. Bateson in *The Oxford Companion to the Mind,* Oxford University Press, Oxford, p. 230.

2.12 P. B. Medawar and J. S. Medawar, *Aristotle to Zoos: A Philosophical Dictionary of Biology,* Weidenfeld and Nicolson, London, 1984, p. 256.

2.13 Published by Harvard University Press, Cambridge, MA.

2.14 Especially interesting are: *The Sociobiology Debate: Readings on the Ethical and Scientific Issues Concerning Sociobiology,* edited by Arthur L. Caplan, Harper and Row Publishers, New York, NY, 1978, and *Sociobiology: Beyond Nature/Nurture?: Reports, Definitions, and Debate,* edited by George W. Barlow and James Silverberg, AAAS Selected Symposium 35, published by the American Association for the Advancement of Science, Washington, DC, 1980.

2.15 From pages 21–22 of Edward O. Wilson's *Sociobiology: The New Synthesis,* Harvard University Press, Cambridge, MA, 1975.

2.16 Both books were published by Harvard University Press, Cambridge, MA.

2.17 Dawkins's book, an engagingly written "classic" of the genre, was published in 1976 by Oxford University Press.

2.18 For an example, Ashley Montagu chaired a debate, then edited *Sociobiology Examined,* Oxford University Press, Oxford, 1980. Leonard Lieberman provides an update regarding the acceptance of Sociobiological thought in anthropology in "A Discipline Divided: Acceptance of Human Sociobiology Concepts in Anthropology," *Current Anthropology 30* (1989): 676–682.

2.19 Kitcher's critique of Sociobiology and Sociobiologists remains one of the best available: *Vaulting Ambition: Sociobiology and the Quest for Human Nature,* The MIT Press, Cambridge, MA, 1985. Note that "fraudulent" is a severe criticism; "self-deceptive" may be closer to the truth, but equally severe.

2.20 For an example of the tortured turns of mathematical biology, see King's College Sociobiology Group's *Current Problems in Sociobiology,* Cambridge University Press, Cambridge, 1982. Biology has long been a science with a chip on its shoulder. A century ago, when biology fought for legitimacy among the hard sciences, biologists felt that they had to display complex formulae (like physicists or chemists) to be considered bona fide scientists. Many biologists still feel this way.

2.21 *The Origin of Species by Means of Natural Selection, Or the Preservation of Favored Races in the Struggle for Life,* first edition 1859, reprinted by Penguin Classics, London, England, 1985, p. 69.

2.22 "The Spandrels of San Marco and the Panglossian Paradigm: A Critique of the Adaptationist Programme," *Proceedings of the Royal Society of London 205,* 1978, pp. 581–598.

2.23 Quotes from Ernst Mayr's *One Long Argument: Charles Darwin and the Genesis of Modern Evolutionary Thought,* Harvard University Press, Cambridge, MA, 1991, p. 154.

2.24 Herbert Spencer was a nineteenth-century philosopher and popularizer of evolution. His most famous (or perhaps infamous) contribution to philosophy was an ethical justification for laissez-faire industrial capitalism. He equated poverty with "unfitness"—an absurdity which stuck in the public's mind for the past century and a quarter. [NB: Darwinian fitness refers only to reproductive advantage, not truth, beauty, or wealth] Marvin Harris chronicled the rise of Spencerism in *The Rise of Anthropological Theory: A History of Theories of Culture,* Thomas Y. Crowell Company, New York, NY, 1968, pp. 108–144. Richard Hofstadter followed the course of social Darwinism in America in a classic study: *Social Darwinism in American Thought,* University of Pennsylvania Press, Philadelphia, 1944; reprinted by The Beacon Press, Boston, 1955.

2.25 One of the best balanced, entitled "Darwin and the Double Standard," by journalist Scott Morris, appeared in the August, 1978, issue of *Playboy.*

2.26 I was a participating professor in one such year-long business school symposium at UCLA. Information flowed freely between business people and scientists. It was clear that Sociobiology and capitalist thinking have much in common.

2.27 From "Psychologists in a Fog," *American Mercury,* July, 1927, p. 383.

2.28 Howard Gardner's *The Mind's New Science: A History of the Cognitive Revolution,* Basic Books, New York, NY, 1985, remains one of the most accessible and interesting stories of the birth of this new academic coalition.

2.29 See Daniel C. Dennett, *Consciousness Explained,* Little, Brown, New York, NY, 1991.

2.30 Quote from Richard D. Alexander, John L. Hoagland, Richard D. Howard, Katharine M. Noonan, and Paul W. Sherman, "Sexual Dimorphisms and Breeding Systems in Pinnipeds, Ungulates, Primates, and Humans," in *Evolutionary Biology and Human Social Behavior: An Anthropological Perspective,* edited by Napoleon A. Chagnon and William Irons, Duxbury Press, North Scituate, MA, 1979, p. 415.

2.31 For example, see Leda Cosmides and John Tooby's essay "From Evolution to Behavior: Evolutionary Psychology as the Missing Link," in John Dupré's edited volume *The Latest on the Best: Essays on Evolution and Optimality,* A Bradford Book, The MIT Press, Cambridge, MA, 1987, pp. 277–307, or David M. Buss's "Toward an Evolutionary Psychology of Human Mating," *Behavior and Brain Sciences 12* (1989), pp. 39–49.

2.32 The second edition of this popular book was published by Willard Grant Press, Boston, MA, in 1983.

2.33 From Drs. Kalman Glantz and John K. Pearce's *Exiles from Eden: Psychotherapy from an Evolutionary Perspective,* Norton, New York, NY, 1989, p. 204.

2.34 There is a wonderful array of stimulating books about the evolution of human behavior. Many of these books are, in the tradition that I noted in the Preface, conversations. They are designed, at least in large measure, to stimulate thought, to engender debate. A few mentioned here are: Mariette Nowak's *Eve's Rib: A Revolutionary New View of the Female,* St. Martin's Press, New York, NY, 1980; Melvin Konner's *The Tangled Wing: Biological Constraints on the Human Spirit,* Holt, Rinehart and Winston, New York, NY, 1982; Helen Fisher's *The Sex Contract: The Evolution of Human Behavior,* Quill, New York, NY, 1983; John McCrone's *The Ape That Spoke: Language and the Evolution of the Human Mind,* William Morrow and Company, New York, NY, 1991, and Dean Falk's *Braindance: New Discoveries About Human Origins and Brain Evolution,* Henry Holt and Company, New York, NY, 1992. More such references may be found in other endnotes within this book.

2.35 Carl N. Degler's *In Search of Human Nature: The Decline and Revival of Darwinism in American Social Thought,* Oxford University Press, New York, NY, 1991.

2.36 Melvin Konner disputes this statement, writing in a politically correct fashion, ". . . anyone who investigates or writes about behavioral biology without recognizing the potential for grave misuse of it . . . is either a dangerous charlatan or a dangerous fool." Less than a sentence later, though, he concludes: ". . . [c]losing one's eyes to the truth cannot make it go away, or prevent other people from distorting it" (Konner, *Tangled Wing,* op. cit., p. 446).

So there you have it: knowledge can be a dangerous thing, sometimes subject to misuse. Properly, I think, the scientist tests hypotheses as best he or she can; the larger society must decide how best to use or misuse the information.

2.37 Quoted by Ralph Estling in the December, 1982, *newscientist* (reprinted in *World Press Review,* April, 1983, p. 36).

2.38 In any single book about the evolution of human behavior, it is impossible to convey the rich complexity of evolutionary theory. Its historical development has been well traced by Harvard evolutionist Ernst Mayr in *The Growth of Biological Thought: Diversity, Evolution, Inheritance* (1982) and a companion book, *Toward a New Philosophy of Biology: Observations of an Evolutionist* (1985), both published by the Harvard University Press, Cambridge, MA. Two other books that examine the philosophical conundrums (such as the thorny definitions of chance, fitness, selection, adaptation) and methodological concerns (such as tautology, reductionism, and causality) are worthwhile reads: Elliott Sober's *The Nature of Selection: Evolutionary Theory in Philosophical Focus,* A Bradford Book, The MIT Press, Cambridge, MA, 1984, and Alexander Rosenberg's *The Structure of Biological Science,* Cambridge University Press, Cambridge, 1985.

Chapter 3

3.1 The primacy of ideas is all-important in the academe. The idea of natural selection arose simultaneously in the minds and writings of Charles Darwin and Alfred Russel Wallace. However, Darwin was well-placed in the politics of nineteenth-century British science, Wallace was not. Further, Darwin capitalized on the theory by publishing a definitive account of how natural selection worked. Wallace, a field worker, stayed in the jungles. Hence, today, we think of evolution by means of natural selection as the hypothesis of Charles Darwin exclusively. In the vernacular, Wallace (himself never bitter) was robbed. A delightful book exploring the relationship between Darwin, Wallace and the theory of natural selection has been written by journalist Arnold C. Brackman, *A Delicate Arrangement: The Strange Case of Charles Darwin and Alfred Russel Wallace,* Times Books, New York, NY, 1980.

3.2 An interesting, accessible, and up-to-date account of sexual selection has been provided by James L. Gould and Carol Grant Gould, *Sexual Selection,* Scientific American Library, New York, NY, 1989.

3.3 In 1988 alone, 70,000 American women underwent breast augmentation surgery; reported by Paddy Calistro in *The Los Angeles Times Magazine,* April 8, 1990, p. 32.

3.4 Rose E. Frisch, "Fatness and Fertility," *Scientific American 258* (3): pp. 88–95, March, 1988.

3.5 See Martin Daly and Margo Wilson's review of this subject in *Sex, Evolution, and Behavior,* Willard Grant Press, PWS Publishers, Boston, MA, 1983, pp. and articles by Susan M. Essock-Vitale and Michael T. McGuire's "Woman's Lives Viewed From an Evolutionary Perspective. I. Sexual Histories, Reproductive Success, and Demographic Characteristics of a Random Sample of American Women," *Ethology and Sociobiology 6* (1985): 137–154, and David M. Buss's

"Sex Differences in Human Mate Preferences: Evolutionary Hypotheses Tested in 37 Cultures," *Behavior and Brain Sciences 12* (1989): pp. 1–14.

3.6 MTV television interview, June 9, 1990.

3.7 An excellent introduction to behavioral measurement and comparison can be found in Philip N. Lehner's *Handbook of Ethological Methods,* Garland STMP Press, New York, NY, 1979.

3.8 Drs. Robert J. Sternberg and Michael J. Barnes' work, *The Psychology of Romantic Love,* Yale University Press, New Haven, CT, 1988 (an edited collection of papers), signals a significant, welcome shift in scientific respectability for the subjects of love and romance.

3.9 E. B. Keverne, "Reproductive Behavior," in *Reproductive Fitness: Reproduction in Mammals: 4* edited by C. R. Austin and R. V. Short, Cambridge University Press, Cambridge, 1984, pp. 133–175.

3.10 Jean-Didier Vincent, a professor of neurophysiology at the University of Bordeaux, has written a delightful, almost poetic, account of feelings and physiology: *The Biology of Emotions,* well translated from French by John Hughes, published by Basil Blackwell, Cambridge, MA, 1990.

3.11 Many scholars now agree with the late Norman Cousins who believed strongly that the body's immune system often responds positively to positive thoughts. Cousins advocated sound spirits as a necessary adjunct to the physical treatment of disease. For an overview of the relationship between mental health and physical disease, see Blair Justice's *Who Gets Sick: How Beliefs, Moods, and Thoughts Can Affect Your Health,* Jeremy P. Tarcher, Inc., Los Angeles, 1989.

3.12 The newfound American interest in dynamics was shadowed by yet another new form of dynamic modeling called "Catastrophe Theory." Catastrophe Theory was pioneered by French mathematician Rene Thom in the 1970s. Both mathematical paradigms are extremely useful in finding order in seemingly unordered natural events and in describing the course of sudden, heretofore unpredictable changes (like speciation). Their models have been used successfully to, among other things, understand diseases, population changes, the shape of a leaf, the development of an embryo, canine aggression, human jokes, and the evolution of a language. It is likely that dynamics and Catastrophe Theory will lead much of science into the twenty-first century.

For a readable introduction, see "Evolution and Catastrophe Theory" by Christopher Zeeman in *Understanding Catastrophe,* edited by Janine Bourriau, Cambridge University Press, Cambridge, 1992, pp. 83–101. This new area of mathematical modeling has been simply and elegantly explained in James Gleick's widely acclaimed book *Chaos: Making of a New Science,* Viking Penguin Inc., New York, NY, 1987. For more details about the mathematics of Catastrophe Theory, see E. C. Zeeman's "Catastrophe Theory," *Scientific American 234* (4): pp. 65–83, April, 1976; for a more rigorous explanation of dynamics, see the series called *Dynamics: The Geometry of Behavior,* a colorful, four-volume set by

Ralph H. Abraham and Christopher D. Shaw, Aerial Press, Inc., P. O. Box 1360, Santa Cruz, California, 1984.

3.13 A thorough discussion of measuring evolution is properly the subject of taxonomy and beyond the scope (or the needs) of the present book. You can pursue this fascinating subject in Theodosius Dobzhansky, Francisco J. Ayala, G. Ledyard Stebbins, and James W. Valentine's *Evolution,* W. H. Freeman and Company, San Francisco, 1977, or E. O. Wiley's *Phylogenetics: The Theory and Practice of Phylogenetic Systematics,* John Wiley and Sons, New York, NY, 1981.

3.14 Rupert Sheldrake, *The Presence in the Past: Morphic Resonance and the Habits of Nature,* Vintage Books, New York, NY, 1989, pp. 157, 158.

3.15 See, for example, Chiye Aoki and Phillip Siekevitz's "Plasticity in Brain Development," *Scientific American 259* (6): pp. 56–64, December, 1988.

3.16 C. F. Hockett and R. Ascher, "The Human Revolution," *Current Anthropology 5:* pp. 135–168, 1964.

3.17 *The Cambridge Encyclopedia of Language* by David Crystal (Cambridge University Press, Cambridge, 1987) covers the A to Z of language in an accessible manner, while the entire issue of *Scientific American 267* (3), September, 1992, presents syntheses about the mind and brain including language, learning, and memory (all components of human communication). Both are worthwhile reads.

3.18 *Neural Darwinism: The Theory of Neuronal Group Selection,* published by Basic Books, New York, NY, 1987.

3.19 *The Society of the Mind,* published by Simon and Schuster, New York, NY, 1986.

3.20 Field researcher Robert M. Sapolsky has provided an exciting look at neurochemistry and behavior with his study of baboons, "Stress in the Wild," *Scientific American 262* (1): pp. 116–123, January, 1990.

3.21 From page 29 of "Eight (or Fewer) Little Piggies: Why do we and most other tetrapods have five digits on each limb?," *Natural History Magazine,* January, 1991, p. 22–29.

3.22 For an example biased unashamedly toward molecular evidence, see *The Search for Eve* by Michael H. Brown, Harper & Row, New York, NY, 1990.

3.23 My apologies here to Marvin Minsky, *The Society of the Mind,* op. cit. for appropriating an example.

3.24 Evolutionary contingency was discussed and championed well by Stephen Jay Gould in *Wonderful Life: The Burgess Shale and the Nature of History,* W. W. Norton & Company, New York, NY, 1989.

Chapter 4

4.1 Sexual reproduction may have appeared with the first eukaryotic cells (cells with nuclei), about 2.5 billion years B.P. We know that by about 600 million years B.P., multicelled ancestors of vertebrates reproduced sexually. If your interest is piqued, try Graham Bell's extraordinary *The Masterpiece of Nature: The Evolution of Genetics and Sexuality,* University of California Press, Berkeley, 1982. Other worthwhile (and easier) reads include Michael Ghiselin's *The Economy of Nature and the Evolution of Sex,* Yale University Press, New Haven, CT, 1974, or Lynne Margulis and son Dorian Sagan's *The Origins of Sex,* Yale University Press, New Haven, CT, 1986.

4.2 See J. William Schopf and Malcom R. Walter's chapter, "Archean Microfossils: New Evidence of Ancient Microbes" in *The Earth's Earliest Biosphere: Its Origin and Evolution,* edited by J. William Schopf, Princeton University Press, Princeton, NJ, 1983, pp. 214–239.

4.3 An excellent essay on the modular nature of chemical and genetic evolution has been written by William F. Loomis: *Four Billion Years: An Essay on the Evolution of Genes and Organisms,* Sinauer Associates, Inc., Sunderland, MA, 1988.

4.4 Presumably, the sex-determining genes are located on the "sex chromosomes." Mammalian males contain a mismatched pair of chromosomes called the "X" and the "Y" chromosomes. Females contain a matched set of the X sex chromosomes. Research by David Page, a molecular biologist at Boston's Whitehead Institute, suggests that the sex-determining switch is a very small gene located on the male Y chromosome (see a report by June Kinoshita in *Discover 12* (1), January, 1991, p. 47).

Genetic mistakes occur. Sometimes, an embryo will form from a fertilized egg that contains three X chromosomes, only one X chromosome or two X chromosomes and a Y. Usually, these unfortunate embryos abort. Sometimes, a few survive and often display developmental abnormalities. For example, one in every 600 male births has an XXY chromosome complement. XXY males may exhibit Klinefelter Syndrome after puberty. Klinefelter's males are sterile and may have underdeveloped genitalia and a striking long-legged, short-trunked body build. Most have learning disorders; ten percent of institutionalized, mentally retarded males have Klinefelter Syndrome (*Professional Guide to Diseases,* Stanley Loeb, executive editorial director; Third Edition published by the Springhouse Corporation, Springhouse, PA, 1986, p. 30).

4.5 P. W. Atkins, *Molecules,* Scientific American Library, New York, NY, 1987, p. 177.

4.6 For additional (technical) discussion, see Eric R. Kandel and James H. Schwartz's text *Principles of Neural Science,* Elsevier, New York, NY, 1985.

4.7 See, for example, J. Inglis and J. S. Lawson's "Sex differences in the effect of unilateral brain damage on intelligence," *Science 212:* 693–695, 1981.

4.8 For an excellent discussion of this issue, see Martin Daly and Margo Wilson's *Sex, Evolution, and Behavior,* Willard Grant Press, Boston, MA, 1983.

4.9 *The Psychology of Sex Differences,* Stanford University Press, Palo Alto, CA, 1974. A classic presentation of sex differences in the brain and behavior entitled "Sexual Dimorphism," may be found in the March 20, 1981, issue of the journal

Science 211, pp. 1263–1324; the issue, edited by Frederick Naftolin and Eleanore Butz, is devoted to the topic.

4.10 From "Sex Differences in the Brain" by Doreen Kimura, *Scientific American 267* (3), September, 1992, p. 119.

4.11 See, for example, anthropologist G. P. Murdock's career survey of more than two hundred cultures in *Culture and Society,* University of Pittsburgh Press, Pittsburgh, PA, 1965.

4.12 The world's first computer programmer was Lady Augusta Ada Lovelace (1816–1852), the daughter of poet Lord Byron. She was the mentor to Charles Babbage, who designed a cumbersome, early mechanical computer called the "Analytical Engine." A hundred years later, Grace Murray Hopper became the world's second computer programmer and designed a computer language that is today nearly universal in the business world: COBOL (Jack B. Rochester and John Gantz, *The Naked Computer,* William Morrow and Company, Inc., New York, NY, 1983).

4.13 These ethnographic data were reported during the 1991 Annual Meeting of the American Anthropological Association (B. Bower, "Females Show Strong Capacity for Aggression," *Science News 140* (22), p. 359, 11/30/91).

4.14 Quote of Ophelia to the King, William Shakespeare's *Hamlet,* IV, v, ll. 41–42.

4.15 Naturalist Jared Diamond explores the plight of human pseudohermaphrodites in "Turning a Man," *Discover 13* (6), June, 1992, pp. 71–77. These men suffer from androgen errors during their development.

4.16 The brain region is the INAH—the interstitial nuclei of the anterior hypothalamus. Reported by Thomas H. Maugh II and Nora Zamichow, "Study Ties Part of the Brain to Men's Sexual Orientation," *The Los Angeles Times,* 8/30/91.

4.17 Reported by science writer Bruce Bower in *Science News 142* (8), August 22, 1992, p. 117.

4.18 Michel Albeaux-Fernet, "Sex Hormones," in Albert Delaunay (chief scientific editor) et al., *Encyclopedia of the Life Sciences, Volume 5: The Human Machine: Mechanisms,* Doubleday & Company, New York, NY, 1965, pp. 58–60.

4.19 Don Monkerud, "Blurring the Lines: Androgyny on Trial," *Omni 13* (1), October, 1990, pp. 80–86, 111 (quote from pp. 84–85).

4.20 For a slightly different slant on gender differences, see Jared Diamond's "Sexual Deception: What's Evolutionarily Good for Males May Not Necessarily Be Good for Females. And Therein Lies the Cause of an Age-Old Struggle," *Discover 10* (8), August 1989, pp. 71–74.

Chapter 5

5.1 While our interpretation of the relationship between various and sundry living insectivore groups changes frequently, this represents a more or less accepted scheme*:

Class Mammalia (Mammals, in contrast to birds, insects, reptiles, etc.)
   Subclass Eutheria (placental mammals, in contrast to those who lay eggs or
      nurture their embryos in pouches like kangaroos)
     Order Insectivora
       Suborder Tenrecomorpha (the tenrecs)
         Family Tenrecidae (the tenrecs proper)
         Family Potomogalidae (otter tenrecs)
         Family Chrysochloridae (African golden moles; not directly related to
           moles per se, but they look like moles)
       Suborder Insectivora ("genuine" insectivores)
         Family Erinaceidae (the hedgehogs, common in Europe)
         Family Solenodontidae (the bizarre Solenodons of the Caribbean
           Islands)
         Family Talpidae (the familiar moles of garden and field)
         Family Soricidae (the "true" shrews)

[*]following a classification presented by mammalogist John F. Eisenberg in *Mammalian Radiations: An Analysis of Trends in Evolution, Adaptation, and Behavior,* University of Chicago Press, Chicago, IL, 1981.

5.2 One of the best introductory accounts of the tenrecs of Madagascar was provided by John F. Eisenberg and Edwin Gould: "The Tenrecs: A Study in Mammalian Behavior and Evolution," *Smithsonian Contributions to Zoology,* Number 27, 1970.

5.3 A colorful, easily-read account of the shrews by Christopher J. Barnard can be found in the superb *The Encyclopedia of Mammals,* edited by David Macdonald and published by Facts On File Publications, New York, NY, 1980, pp. 758–763.

5.4 For a readable, introductory account of the Order Primates, see J. R. and P. H. Napier's *The Natural History of Primates,* The MIT Press, Cambridge, MA, 1985. Primatologists cannot agree on the exact number of living primate species. Some primatologists are "lumpers." They prefer to define a species very broadly and place similar creatures together within a single species name. Other primatologists are "splitters" who prefer to name a new species for every minute difference they see in the physical appearance of similar animals. Both splitting and lumping have merit when applied to particular situations, so the ongoing debate about how many primates exist (or have existed) will probably continue long after most living primates are extinct.

5.5 *Shoshonius* resembled Malagasy mouse lemurs but was actually closely related to a modern, aberrant, Southeast Asian prosimian, the tarsier *(Tarsius).* Living tarsiers display a specialized form of leaping locomotion and have the largest eyes relative to the size of their body of any primate.

    Duke University paleontologist Elwyn Simons and others doubt that *Shoshonius* was on a direct ancestral line to monkeys, apes, or people. For a concise report, see B. Bower, "New Fossils Push Back Primate Origins," *Science News 139* (2), 1991, p. 20.

5.6 Ian Tattersall, a curator at the American Museum of Natural History in New York and a long-time student of Madagascar, has written a superb, technical review of the Malagasy prosimians: *The Primates of Madagascar,* Columbia University Press, New York, NY, 1982.

5.7 Paleoanthropologist John P. Alexander suggested recently that *Notharctus* did not move quadrupedally like modern members of the Genus *Lemur.* Instead, his anatomical reconstructions show that *Notharctus* leapt between trees like indriid lemurs, *Propithecus* or *Indri* ("Alas, Poor Notharctus," *Natural History,* August, 1992, pp. 54–59).

5.8 "New fossil apes from Egypt and the initial differentiation of the Hominoidea," *Nature* 205, 1965, pp. 135–139.

5.9 See Alan Walker and Mark Teaford's "The Hunt for Proconsul," *Scientific American* 260 (1), January 1989, pp. 76–82.

5.10 Vincent Sarich, "A Molecular Approach to the Question of Human Origins," in *Background for Man,* edited by V. Sarich and P. Dolhinow, Little Brown and Company, Boston, MA, 1971, pp. 60–81.

Chapter 6

6.1 In contrast to the glut of dinosaur books that grace the shelves at most bookstores, popular books about the many primitive mammals that scurried beneath the feet of the ruling reptiles are uncommon. Fortunately, at least three well-illustrated accounts of early mammals are available: R. J. G. Savage and M. R. Long's *Mammalian Evolution: An Illustrated Guide,* Facts On File Publications, New York, NY, 1986; Dougal Dixon, Barry Cox, R. J. G. Savage, and Brian Gardiner's *The Macmillan Illustrated Encyclopedia of Dinosaurs and Prehistoric Animals,* Macmillan, New York, NY, 1988, and Michael J. Benton's *The Rise of Mammals: The Story of the Mammalian Families, from Their Origins to the Dawn of the Age of Man,* Crescent Books, New York, NY, 1991.

John C. McLoughlin's iconoclastic and delightfully illustrated *Synapsida: A New Look into the Origin of Mammals* (The Viking Press, New York, NY, 1980) covers a fascinating period of life on earth not touched by our present survey: the reptile-mammal transition.

6.2 For a description of her sparse remains, consult Frederick S. Szalay and Eric Delson's *Evolutionary History of the Primates,* Academic Press, New York, NY, 1979.

6.3 Perhaps the best, most engaging book ever written about dinosaurs is Robert T. Bakker's *The Dinosaur Heresies: New Theories Unlocking the Mystery of the Dinosaurs and Their Extinction,* Zebra Books, New York, NY, 1988. Bakker carefully reconstructs the ecology of dinosaurs and notes that there were more dinosaur predators relative to their prey than mammalian predators in comparable, modern ecosystems. Our tiny ancestor's world was an order of magnitude more frightening in those days.

There are many other readable books about dinosaurs, but few capture their time or place particularly well. Richard Moody's *Prehistoric World: The 3400 Million Years Before Modern Man* (Chartwell Books, Inc., New York, NY, 1980) is a notable exception, as is David Lambert and the Diagram Group's *The Field Guide to Prehistoric Life* (Facts On File Publications, New York, NY, 1985).

6.4 Calculations made from data presented by Heinz Stephan, Roland Bauchot, and Orlando J. Andy, "Data on Size of Brain and of Various Brain Parts in Insectivores and Primates," in Charles R. Noback and William Montagna (editors), *The Primate Brain, Volume 1,* Appleton-Century-Crofts, New York, NY, 1970, pp. 289–297.

6.5 Adrian Forsyth, *Mammals of North America,* Camden House, Ontario, 1985, p. 313.

6.6 The relationship between the surface of a mammal and volume (mass) has been described approximately and well using a simple "Square-Cube Law." If we know the weight (mass) of a mammal, we can estimate its surface area as the two-third's power of its mass, *i.e.,* Surface Area = $\text{Mass}^{0.67}$. Note that the mammalian metabolic rate is estimated using a similar formula: metabolic rate increases as the three-quarter's power of mass, Metabolic Rate = $\text{Mass}^{0.75}$. This "close-but-no-cigar" similarity between mass and surface area and mass and metabolic rate has given generations of biologists fits: after many attempts, physiologists still cannot explain why the metabolic rate of mammals increases as the three-quarters, not two-thirds, power of mass.

6.7 Hugh Tyndale-Biscoe, *Life of Marsupials,* American Elsevier Publishing Company, Inc., New York, NY, 1973.

Chapter 7

7.1 In 1975, I reported that mouse lemurs and their close relatives, dwarf lemurs, hibernate briefly: Robert Jay Russell, "Body Temperatures and Behavior of Captive Cheirogaleids," in *Lemur Biology,* edited by Ian Tattersall and Robert W. Sussman, Plenum Publishers, New York, NY, 1975, pp. 193–206.

7.2 I have simplified the mouse lemur pattern of mating here. In fact, females who do not become pregnant during their estrus will recycle and ovulate again about two and one-half months later. Thus, males within this population will undergo their Jekyll and Hyde behavioral changes twice during five months (see Robert Jay Russell, "Body Temperatures and Behavior of Captive Cheirogaleids," 1975, op cit., p. 196 ff.).

7.3 From an interview in *Omni 13* (5), February, 1991, p. 76.

7.4 "Biochemical Defense Mechanisms in Herbivores Against Plant Allelochemicals," in *Herbivores: Their Interaction with Secondary Plant Metabolites,* edited by Gerald A. Rosenthal and Daniel H. Janzen, Academic Press, New York, NY, 1979, p. 199–270.

7.5 The figure was redrawn from a scientific paper I presented in Vienna, Austria: "Mother-Infant Bonding in Primates," presented at the symposium "The Child—a natural dissident," sponsored by Institut für Postuniversitäre Fortbildung und Forschung and the Internationale Mediziner Arbeitgemeinschaft, Vienna and Preß-baum, May 2–6, 1988, 26 pp.

7.6 From *The Little, Brown Book of Anecdotes,* edited by Clifton Fadiman, Little, Brown and Company, Boston, 1985, p. 141.

7.7 In *The Evolution of Human Sexuality,* Oxford University Press, New York, NY, 1979, pp. 212–213.

7.8 These mixed gender sleeping groups were noted by Robert D. Martin, now of Zürich, in his report: "A Preliminary Field Study of the Lesser Mouse Lemur (*Microcebus murinus* J. F. Miller 1777)," *Fortschritte der Verhaltensforschung 9,* 1972, pp. 43–90. Subsequently, I confirmed these observations with my own field study in 1973–1975.

7.9 Published by Weidenfeld & Nicolson, New York, NY, 1988.

7.10 From *Vienna Girl,* published by W. W. Norton & Company, New York, NY, 1986, p. 383. Lauterstein's novel shows the matriline in a much more optimistic light than Jelinek's.

7.11 Quote from Lynne Heffley's "A Less Than Perfect 'Daughter' Examines Child Abuse" (a review of the ABC Afterschool Special: "The Less Than Perfect Daughter"), *The Los Angeles Times,* January 24, 1991, p. F11.

The primacy of the mother-daughter nuclear family in primate society has been documented by Mariette Nowak in *Eve's Rib: a Revolutionary New View of the Female,* St. Martin's Press, New York, NY, 1980. Nancy Friday (*My Mother My Self: The Daughter's Search for Identity,* Delacorte Press, New York, NY, 1977) explores the sometimes stultifying effect of a daughter's relationship to her mother.

7.12 Susan Squire, in an insightful article about daughterly rebellion ("Are You Turning Out to Be Your Mother," *Cosmopolitan,* January, 1990, pp. 176–179), notes that "[s]ome daughters are so busy trying not to be mom . . . they don't notice they're making all the same mistakes" (p. 177). Paddy Calistro argues that daughters tend to look and feel like their mothers: "[h]ow a woman feels about the way she looks can be linked to maternal influence" ("My Mother, My Self-Image," *The Los Angeles Times Magazine,* 5/13/90, p. 32).

Chapter 8

8.1 The temperatures reported here are from my 1973–1975 study at Berenty, southern Madagascar. There are many different climate zones on Madagascar; temperatures here are merely for comparison.

8.2 Quote from p. 233 in *"Lemur catta:* Ecology and Behavior," in *Lemur Biology,* edited by Ian Tattersall and Robert W. Sussman, Plenum Press, New York, NY, 1975, pp. 219–235.

8.3 Syndicated columnist Ellen Goodman characterizes the ideal American male of the '90s as "introspective but decisive, caring yet competent, one of the guys and a leader." According to Goodman, the ideal, sensitive American male of the '90s is not Alan

Alda, but General Norman Schwarzkopf ("Meet the New Model Man: Tough and Tender," *The Los Angeles Times,* 3/15/91, p. B13).

8.4 From *The American Medical Association Home Medical Encyclopedia, Volume 2,* edited by Charles B. Clayman, Random House, New York, NY, 1989, p. 849.

8.5 From her acclaimed book *Females of the Species: Sex and Survival in the Animal Kingdom,* Harvard University Press, Cambridge, MA, 1986, p. 118.

8.6 From the FBI's Uniform Crime Reports, presented in *The 1991 World Almanac and Book of Facts,* edited by Mark S. Hoffman, World Almanac, New York, NY, 1990, p. 849.

8.7 "Sex in Relation to Society," in *Studies in the Psychology of Sex,* Random House, New York, NY, 1937, p. 80.

8.8 *Margaret Mead and Samoa: The Making and Unmaking of an Anthropological Myth,* Harvard University Press, Cambridge, MA, 1983, p. 249.

8.9 "Concealment of Ovulation, Paternal Care, and Human Social Evolution" in *Evolutionary Biology and Human Social Behavior: An Anthropological Perspective,* edited by Napoleon A. Chagnon and William Irons, Duxbury Press, North Scituate, MA, 1979.

8.10 From Johann Wolfgang von Goethe's essay "Die Natur" from *Werke IV,* 1885, quoted in *Readings in Early Anthropology,* edited by J. S. Slotkin, Aldine Publishing Company, Chicago, IL, 1965, p. 294.

8.11 "Factors affecting intergroup transfer by adult male *Papio anubis,*" in *Primate Ontogeny, Cognition and Social Behaviour,* edited by J. G. Else and P. C. Lee, Cambridge University Press, Cambridge, 1986, p. 371.

Chapter 9

9.1 Professor James Burke became an internationally-regarded media figure through his successful public television series about emergent properties in the history of technology and epistemology (the study of how we know what we think we know). His provocative and entertaining popular books that accompanied the programs have been widely read: *Connections,* Little, Brown and Company, Boston, MA, 1978, and *The Day the Universe Changed,* Little, Brown and Company, Boston, MA, 1985.

While Burke is always thought-provoking, he isn't always correct in his assertions. For example, he promulgated the view that Darwin was personally behind the concept of eugenics (breeding humans for racial purity) and Spencerian social agendas (let the poor suffer, after all, they're "unfit"). Darwin wasn't.

9.2 The Asiatic dryopithecines that may have been ancestral to the modern orangutan are sometimes called "sivapithecines," although they differ little from European dryopithecines. An accessible introduction to all the living apes, entitled "A Curious Kinship: Apes and Humans," by Eugene Linden, is available in the March 1992 issue of *National Geographic Magazine* 181 (3), pp. 2–46. In the same issue, an article by the same author, "Bonobos, Chimpanzees With a Difference," highlights the pygmy chimpanzee (pp. 46–53).

9.3 Anthropologist David Agee Horr has remarked on the similarities between the mouse lemur pattern of social organization [see Chapter 7] and the limited sociality of orangutans (personal communication, see also "Orang-utan Maturation: Growing Up in a Female World," in *Primate Bio-social Development: Biological, Social, and Ecological Determinants,* edited by Suzanne Chevalier-Skolnikoff and Frank E. Poirier, Garland Publishing Company, Inc., New York, NY, 1977, pp. 289–321).

9.4 New York Zoological Society's George B. Schaller pioneered modern field studies of great apes with his one-year field study of the mountain gorilla in 1961 (*The Mountain Gorilla: Ecology and Behavior,* The University of Chicago Press, Chicago, 1963; revised edition, 1976). Six years later, Leakey primatologist Dian Fossey began her observations of a gorilla population (*Gorillas in the Mist,* Houghton Mifflin Company, Boston, MA, 1983). Fossey's singular, unflinching devotion to preserving the last of these gentle giants led to her tragic, brutal, and lonely murder at her mountain field station on December 28th, 1985. The gorillas and humanity were the victims of her death as well.

9.5 The metaphorical linkage of tenured university faculty with gorillas is, I believe, apt. Years ago, Professor John Buettner-Janusch referred to some of his ever-posturing, career-driven colleagues as "silver-backs" or "alpha baboons."

9.6 One view of chimpanzee politics was presented by Frans de Waal in *Chimpanzee Politics: Power & Sex Among Apes,* Harper & Row, Publishers, New York, NY, 1982.

9.7 From Jane Goodall's *Through a Window: My Thirty Years with the Chimpanzees of Gombe,* Houghton Mifflin Company, New York, NY, 1990, p. 99. Chimpanzee warfare has been well reviewed by Michael Ghiglieri in "War Among Chimps," *Discover 8* (11), November, 1978, pp. 66–76.

9.8 Jane Goodall, "Life and Death at Gombe," *National Geographic Magazine 155* (5), May, 1979, pp. 592–621.

9.9 S. Karoda, "Interaction over Food Among Pygmy Chimpanzees," in *The Pygmy Chimpanzee,* edited by Randall L. Susman, Plenum Press, New York, NY, 1984, pp. 301–324.

9.10 Reported by John Taylor in *New York* magazine, "Are You Politically Correct?" (1/21/91, p. 38). Alison Jagger is a professor at the University of Cincinnati and the chairperson of the American Philosophical Association's Committee on the Status of Women in Philosophy.

Chapter 10

10.1 Brain sizes from Robert D. Martin's *Primate Origins and Evolution: A Phylogenetic Reconstruction,* Princeton University Press, Princeton, NJ, 1990.

10.2 C. Owen Lovejoy provides an excellent review of the evolutionary anatomy of bipedality in "Evolution of Human Walking," *Scientific American 259* (5), November, 1988, pp. 118–125.

10.3 Quoted in Meridith Small's report of pygmy chimpanzee sexuality, "What's Love Got to Do with It?," *Discover 13* (6), June, 1992, pp. 46–51.

10.4 Sue Savage Rumbaugh and Beverly Wilkerson, "Socio-sexual Behavior in *Pan paniscus* and *Pan troglodytes:* A Comparative Study," *Journal of Human Evolution 7:* 327–344, 1978; and *The Pygmy Chimpanzee: Evolutionary Biology and Behavior,* Randall Susman, editor, Plenum Press, New York, NY, 1984.

    Takayoshi Kano suggests that pygmy chimpanzees are both far more sexy and more pacific than the common chimpanzee ("The Bonobos' Peaceable Kingdom," *Natural History,* November, 1990, pp. 62–71).

10.5 From Jared Diamond's *The Third Chimpanzee: The Evolution and Future of the Human Animal,* HarperCollins Publishers, New York, NY, 1992, p. 79ff.

10.6 Marvin Harris, *Our Kind: Who We Are, Where We Came From, Where We Are Going,* Harper & Row Publishers, Inc., New York, NY, 1989, p. 180.

10.7 The phylogenetic diagram presented here is currently in vogue. It was proposed by D. C. Johnson and T. D. White in "A Systematic Assessment of Early East African Hominoids," *Science 202:* 321–330, 1979. For a popular translation, see Donald C. Johanson and Maitland Edey's *Lucy: The Beginnings of Humankind,* Simon and Schuster, New York, NY, 1981.

10.8 Brain sizes and body weights from Robert D. Martin, 1990, op. cit.

10.9 "The Great Leap Forward," *Discover 10* (5), May 1989, pp. 50–60.

10.10 For an excellent review of various interpretations of Habilis-to-Erectus-to-human evolution, see Bruce Bower's "Erectus Unhinged," *Science News 141* (25), June, 1992, pp. 408–409, 411.

10.11 Meridith F. Small, "Political Animal: Social Intelligence and the Growth of the Primate Brain," *The Sciences 30* (2), March/April, 1990, pp. 36–42.

10.12 Population figures from my own studies, from Jaclyn Wolfheim's *Primates of the World: Distribution, Abundance, and Conservation,* University of Washington Press, Seattle, WA, 1983, and *The World Almanac and Book of Facts, 1992,* Mark S. Hoffman, editor, Pharas Books, New York, NY, 1991.

Chapter 11

11.1 The near universality of polygyny in mammals was noted by Richard D. Alexander, John L. Hoagland, Richard D. Howard, Katharine M. Noonan, and Paul W. Sherman, "Sexual Dimorphism and Breeding Systems in Pinnipeds, Ungulates, Primates, and Humans," in *Evolutionary Biology and Human Social Behavior: An Anthropological Perspective,* edited by Napoleon A. Chagnon and William Irons, Duxbury Press, North Scituate, MA, 1979, pp. 403–435.

11.2 Alexander et al., 1979, op. cit, p. 433.

11.3 John C. Caldwell and Pat Caldwell, "High Fertility in Sub-Saharan Africa," *Scientific American 262* (5), May, 1990, pp. 118–125; quote from p. 122.

11.4 Danny DeVito as Gavin D'Amamto in "The War of the Roses," Twentieth Century Fox Pictures, 1989.

11.5 David Maybury-Lewis, *Millennium: Tribal Wisdom and the Modern World,* Viking, New York, NY, 1992, p. 103.

11.6 The role of tactile sensations in human life is examined in detail in Ashley Montagu's *Touching: The Human Significance of Skin,* Second Edition, Harper & Row Publishers, New York, NY, 1978. A broader review of the mechanics of intimacy is provided in Desmond Morris's *Intimate Behavior,* Random House, New York, NY, 1971.

11.7 Norman Cousins happily celebrated the life extension made possible within modern societies ("Don't Tuck Me In," *The Los Angeles Times,* 12/3/90).

11.8 U.S. Bureau of Labor Statistics, presented in "Speaking of the Changing Family," *The Los Angeles Times,* 7/3/90, p. H7.

11.9 William Rasberry, "When Manhood is Taught on the Streets: Young Black Males, the Worst Underachievers, Tend to Grow Up Without a Parent of Their Own Gender," *The Los Angeles Times,* 8/28/90.

11.10 For a readable report of the linguistic playing field, see Deborah Tannen's *You Just Don't Understand: Women and Men in Conversation,* William Morrow and Company, Inc., New York, NY, 1990.

11.11 Jared Diamond, "Sexual Deception," *Discover 10* (8), August, 1989, pp. 70–74.

11.12 Quoted by Thomas H. Maugh II, "The Lies That Bind: Nearly All Species Deceive," *The Los Angeles Times,* 4/1/91, p. B5.

11.13 From Ludwig Wittgenstein's *Philosophical Investigations,* Third Edition, Macmillan, New York, NY, translated by G. E. M. Anscombe, p. 47e. Philosopher Mary Midgley, no fan of Wittgenstein, notes disdainfully that "no philosophical article is complete without its quotation from Wittgenstein—('for what saith Wittgenstein?')" (in "Rival Fatalisms: The Hollowness of the Sociobiology Debate," in *Sociobiology Examined,* edited by Ashley Montagu, Oxford University Press, Oxford, 1980, pp. 15–38). I offer no apologies for the present quote.

Chapter 12

12.1 Bruce Bower reviews many of the more recent theories to explain war in "Gauging the Winds of War: Anthropologists Seek the Roots of Human Conflict," *Science News 139* (6), 2/9/91, pp. 88–89, 91.

12.2 Quoted in "Whys of War" by Bruce Bower, *The Los Angeles Times,* 2/18/91, p. B7.

12.3 Ali A. Mazuri, "Armed Kinsman and the Origins of State," quoted by Gwynne Dyer in *War,* Crown Publishers, Inc., New York, NY, 1985, pp. 8–9.

12.4 Statistics compiled by the Lentz Peace Research Laboratory and presented in "The Human Cost of War," *The Los Angeles Times,* 2/15/91, p. A5.

12.5 Stuart and Doris Flexner's *The Pessimist's Guide to History,* Avon Books, New York, NY, 1992.

12.6 Thomas T. Struhsaker and Lysa Leland, "Colobines: Infanticide by Adult Males," in

Primate Societies, edited by Barbara B. Smuts, Dorothy L. Cheney, Robert M. Seyfarth, Richard W. Wrangham, and Thomas T. Struhsaker, University of Chicago Press, Chicago, IL, 1986, pp. 83–97.

12.7 Glenn Hausfater and Sarah B. Hrdy, *Infanticide: Comparative and Evolutionary Perspectives,* Aldine, New York, NY, 1984.

12.8 Data from Marvin Harris's *Our Kind: Who We Are, Where We Came From, Where We Are Going,* Harper & Row Publishers, Inc., New York, NY, 1989, p. 210–214.

12.9 Freud also claimed that every boy pines sexually for his mother and considers his father a sexual rival (the Oedipus Complex). Undoubtedly, some boys experience feelings, fantasies, and desires that could be called Oedipal, but the same probably holds true for some girls. There is no evidence in either evolutionary biology or anthropology to support Freud's claim that the Oedipus Complex is a universal feature of the human psyche.

12.10 Excellent discussions of the dangers of inbreeding, such as Katherine Ralls and Jonathan Ballou's "Extinction: Lessons From Zoos," (pp. 164–184) appear in Christine M. Schonewald-Cox, Steven M. Chambers, Bruce MacBryde, and Larry Thomas's edited volume *Genetics and Conservation: A Reference for Managing Wild Animal and Plant Populations,* The Benjamin/Cummings Publishing Company, Inc., Menlo Park, CA, 1983.

The data here are from a study of beagles by C. E. Rehfeld, "Definitions of Relationships in a Closed Beagle Colony," *American Journal of Veterinary Research 31,* 1970, pp. 442–445. Note that the values for inbreeding are derived using a formula called "Wright's Coefficient of Inbreeding," a fairly useful but crude estimation of relatedness. For an understandable explanation of this formula, see Frederick B. Hutt's *Genetics for Dog Breeders,* W. H. Freeman and Company, San Francisco, CA, 1979.

12.11 *The History of Human Marriage,* Macmillan, New York, NY, 1891.

12.12 P. W. Shepher, "Mate Selection Among Second Generation Kibbutz Adolescents and Adults: Incest Avoidance and Negative Imprinting," *Archives of Sexual Behavior 1,* 1971, pp. 293–307, and J. Shepher, *Incest: A Biosocial View,* Academic Press, New York, NY, 1983.

12.13 Quote from p. 273, "Sexual Selection, Dimorphism, and Social Organization in the Primates" in *Sexual Selection and the Descent of Man 1871–1971,* edited by Bernard Campbell, Aldine Publishing Company, Chicago, IL, 1972, pp. 231–281.

12.14 Reay Tannahill, *Sex in History,* Stein and Day Publishers, New York, NY, 1980, p. 109.

12.15 Quoted in *A New Dictionary of Quotations on Historical Principles From Ancient and Modern Sources,* edited by H. L. Mencken, Alfred A. Knopf, New York, NY, 1942.

12.16 Paternal relationships in primates has been reviewed by Patricia L. Whitten ("Infants and Adult Males," pp. 343–357) and Anne Wilson Goldizen ("Tamarins and Marmosets," pp. 34–43) in *Primate Societies,* op. cit.

12.17 Reported by John Taylor in *New York* magazine, "Are You Politically Correct?," 1/21/91, p. 38.

12.18 Social data from *The 1991 World Almanac and Book of Facts,* edited by Mark S. Hoffman, World Almanac, New York, NY, 1990, pp. 838–842.

12.19 Robert Bly, *Iron John: A Book About Men,* Addison-Wesley Publishing Company, Inc., Reading, MA, 1990.

12.20 Robert Bly, "A Gathering of Men," a discussion with Bill Moyers, produced for PBS Television, 1990.

12.21 From "The Birds and the Bees," *The Nation,* 10/28/91, p. 509.

12.22 Reported by Thomas H. Maugh II in "AIDS is Creating 16 Million Orphans in Africa, Experts Say," *The Los Angeles Times,* 2/17/91.

12.23 Data from *The Washington Post,* reported in "8 Million Carrying AIDS Virus, Health Group Says," *The Los Angeles Times,* 8/1/90.

12.24 The estimate that eight to ten million humans are HIV positive was released by the World Health Organization, 11/12/91 (reported in *The Los Angeles Times*). At that time, the WHO estimated that 40 million humans would be infected by the year 2000. However, a more complete Harvard University study (6/4/92, "New Study Boosts Forecast of AIDS Infection," *The Los Angeles Times*) estimated that 13 million people are currently infected and that 100 million people would be infected by the turn of the century.

Significantly, most AIDS estimates are conservative because health agencies often bend to political pressures to underestimate the pandemic. Dr. Jonathan Mann, director of the Harvard study and former director of WHO's 1987–1990 studies, said: "We [at Harvard] are unburdened by any constraints in terms of pleasing people, satisfying people, or responding to people's assumptions."

Even without politicized reports, disparities in HIV estimates can be expected because it is difficult to predict the exact rate of what we know is the exponential growth of HIV. Clocking the spread of HIV is much like estimating the exponential growth of a nuclear explosion; both occur so quickly that estimates of their rate of growth are almost certain to be inaccurate.

12.25 WHO estimates, op. cit.

12.26 Estimates released by Fred Hellinger, the agency's director, in November, 1991 (*The Los Angeles Times,* 11/29/91). These estimates are conservative. New treatment regimes and additional testing could increase the figures markedly. Note also that these costs do not include estimates of lost economic productivity, nor do they include projected medical research costs.

12.27 Marlene Cimons, "Study Says More Young Women Have Sex," *The Los Angeles Times,* 1/5/91. Other surveys report even higher rates of teenage sex: Patricia Freeman, "Risky Business: One Day's Look at the Pleasures and Pressures of Sex at an Early Age," *People Weekly 34* (18), 11/5/90, pp. 50–60.

12.28 Reported in *The Los Angeles Times,* 11/28/91.

12.29 Sevgi O. Aral and King K. Holmes, "Sexually Transmitted Diseases in the AIDS Era," *Scientific American 264* (4), February, 1991, pp. 62–69.

Chapter 13

13.1 Robert J. Campbell's *Psychiatric Dictionary,* 6th Edition, Oxford University Press, New York, NY, 1989, details nearly three dozen forms of therapy presently in use. These include: psychoanalysis (Freudian, Jungian, Adlerian, Rogerian, existential, transactional, transpersonal, yoga, etc.), behavioral therapy, cognitive therapy, group therapy (recreational, didactic, class methods), hypnotherapy, play therapy, Gestalt therapy, etc.

13.2 "Demand for Psychiatrists Growing," *The Los Angeles Times,* 11/26/90. Data reported by the American Medical Association.

13.3 Novelist Vladimir Nabokov, in lectures for the Wisconsin Studies in Contemporary Literature program (1967), criticized psychoanalysis succinctly: "Let the credulous and vulgar continue to believe that all mental woes can be cured by a daily application of old Greek myths to their private parts" (quoted in *Whatever It Is, I'm Against It,* edited by Nat Shapiro, Simon and Schuster, New York, NY, 1984, p. 222).

13.4 From *The Psychiatric Dictionary,* op. cit., p. 389.

13.5 From Dr. Joyce Brothers's "Severe Depression After Childbirth," *The Los Angeles Times,* 6/22/90. Dr. Brothers concludes that:

"Men whose self-esteem is based primarily on what their partner thinks of them, and who are overly dependent on that partner, are more likely to explode with jealousy when there's no cause. Basically what happens to these males is that they realize because of their dependence on their partner for self-esteem, with no one else to turn to, they'll be up the creek when threatened by a rival."

While Dr. Brothers's analysis might apply to one particular situation, her premise—that jealousy springs from low self-esteem—is not generalizable.

13.6 H. J. Eysenck's much maligned 1952 study "The Effects of Psychotherapy: An Evaluation," appeared in the *Journal of Consulting Psychology 16:* 319–324. Ralph Estling, in an article in *newscientist,* relates Eysenck's data in an instructive and apropos tale in the sociology of science:

". . . no psychiatrist in his right mind would pay credence to the findings, uncovered by Hans Eysenck some years ago, that patients undergoing psychoanalysis have an improvement rate of 44%; those subject to other psychotherapy recover at the rate of 64%; and those who have no treatment at all are cured at a rate of 72%.

"Aghast when the news first struck, psychiatrists quickly rallied, closed ranks, and conducted their own surveys—which only confirmed Eysenck's mordant findings. At this point, and with a sigh of profound relief, there being nothing else a true scientist could do under the circumstances, psychiatrists the world over dismissed Eysenck and his findings on the grounds that Eysenck is a racist."

Estling's article appeared in the December, 1982, *newscientist* and was quoted in *World Press Review,* April, 1983, p. 36.

13.7 For example: D. Malin, E. S. Heath, H. A. Bacal, and F. H. G. Balfour, "Psychodynamic changes in untreated neurotic patients," *Archives of General Psychiatry 32:*

110–126, and A. C. P. Simm's 1978 report, "Prognosis in severe neurosis," *Current Themes in Psychiatry, 1.*

13.8 "Assessment of Psychotherapy," in *The Oxford Companion to the Mind,* edited by Richard L. Gregory, Oxford University Press, New York, NY, 1987, p. 663.

13.9 Alma E. Guinness, editor, *ABC's of the Human Mind,* The Reader's Digest Association, Inc., Pleasantville, NY, 1990, p. 43.

13.10 All science, not just psychoanalysis, tends toward what a literary critic would call "journalese . . . a manner of writing which employs ready-made phrases and formulas, and which breeds its own clichés in abundance" (definition from J. A. Cuddon's *A Dictionary of Literary Terms,* Doubleday & Company, Inc., Garden City, NY, 1976, p. 347). The best scientists, like the best journalists, recognize this and attempt never to take themselves too seriously.

13.11 Quoted by John Hunter Padel in *The Oxford Companion to the Mind,* op. cit., p. 270. Padel, like many true believers, castigates those who would claim that psychoanalysis is unscientific. "Only the naïve or obsessional," he writes, "will see it as a weakness rather than a strength of psychoanalysis that . . . its practice and theory operate with provisional concepts and with metaphors and sustained hypotheses rather than with the accepted laws of science."

13.12 Alexander et al., 1979, op. cit, p. 435.

13.13 Hobbes's view of free will was sharply opposed to that of his contemporary, René Decartes. Decartes championed the division of mind and body (a view antithetical to that of modern science). He believed that free will was manifest in human indecision—a rather silly notion that freedom was best exhibited by a confused person. For a concise review of free will and determinism see Richard Taylor's essay, "Determinism," in the four-volume set *The Encyclopedia of Philosophy,* edited by Paul Edwards, MacMillan Publishing Company & The Free Press, New York, NY, 1967, pp. 359–373.

13.14 The diagram here is modified after one drawn by Marvin Minsky in *The Society of the Mind,* Simon and Schuster, New York, NY, 1986, p. 307.

13.15 *Social Evolution,* Macmillan, New York, NY; quotes from Richard Milner's *The Encyclopedia of Evolution,* Facts on File, New York, NY, 1990, p. 251.

13.16 Quotes in Jon Winokur's *A Curmudgeon's Garden of Love,* New American Library, Ontario, Canada, 1989, pp. 94–95.

13.17 *Beyond Good and Evil,* Penguin Books, New York, NY, 1973, p. 29.

13.18 William James (1842–1910), American philosopher and psychologist, argued that a deterministic argument that admits to some small measure of free will is "soft" determinism, hence not really deterministic at all. I respectfully disagree. Our biology limits—canalizes—our behavioral choices. Biological determinism does not mean "one behavior for every stimulus," rather it means "a limited range of behavior for every stimulus." The range of our behavior appears to be limited, hence determined (although the intellectual jury is still out with regard to this verdict on the matter of free will and determinism).

13.19 From a television interview "Gender—An Enduring Paradox," Smithsonian World,

PBS Television, 1991. Ultimately, of course, Dr. Hrdy's statement reveals an untenable philosophical position: no biological entity can ever "overcome its biology." Everything a being does is, *sensu stricto,* biological.

13.20 The Politically Correct (PC) movement, now in vogue in many intellectual circles, claims that individuality is wrong and that people should define themselves in terms of racial (or ethnic) groups. This represents a choice of social engineering (called "multiculturalism") that they find satisfying. However, encouraging group identity over individuality merely repeats the design of the ancient ape power coalition. Ultimately, the PC movement fosters scapegoatism and the direction of in-group aggressions toward other social groups. There's nothing new or liberating in this approach.

There has been much pro and con written about the PC movement. I now have more than three feet of library shelf space devoted to the subject. For those who want a quick, enjoyable introduction to the goals, motivations, and logic of PC, I recommend a well-referenced, thin book of humor that captures the essential points remarkably well: Henry Beard and Christopher Cerf's *The Official Politically Correct Dictionary and Handbook,* Villard Books, New York, NY, 1992.

13.21 Supernormal stimuli were first named and investigated by ethologists during the 1950s. They found that many animals could be tricked into exaggerated behavioral acts by stimuli that were larger, brighter, or louder than naturally occurring stimuli. Herring gulls, for example, would abandon their natural eggs to incubate larger wooden models of eggs placed into their nests. The shape of an egg is a normal stimulus; the larger the egg, the more super the stimulus. Humans are known to respond preferentially to some supernormal stimuli. For example, we naturally prefer (are adapted to seek out) the sweet taste of honey and fruit and will readily consume powdered sugar (a recently manufactured product) to excess (David McFarland, *The Oxford Companion to Animal Behavior,* Oxford University Press, New York, NY, 1987, p. 537–538). Metaphors and images may also act as human supernormal stimuli; consider the riveting effect of onscreen violence and the exaggerated features and unnatural postures of a Hollywood centerfold.

13.22 From *Fates Worse Than Death,* G. P. Putnam's Sons, New York, NY, 1991, p. 185.

Epilogue

1. Data, much of it current to June, 1990, from Geoffrey Lean, Don Hinrichsen, and Adam Markham's *World Wildlife Fund Atlas of the Environment,* Prentice Hall Press, New York, NY, 1990.

2. Russell H. Tuttle, "Apes of the World," *American Scientist* 78 (2), March-April, 1990, p. 124.

3. The crucial new role of zoos as the saviors of species is outlined in Robert Bendiner's *The Fall of the Wild and the Rise of the Zoo,* Elsevier-Dutton Publishing Co., Inc., New York, NY, 1981.

4. Thomas J. Foose, "Riders of the Last Ark: The Role of Captive Breeding in Conservation Strategies," in *The Last Extinction,* edited by Les Kaufman and Kenneth Mallory, The MIT Press, Cambridge, MA, 1986, pp. 141–165.

5. Figures cited by Lee Durrell in *State of the Ark,* Doubleday, Garden City, NY, 1986. Such figures change, but their proportions remain about the same. Human priorities have only shifted slightly toward conservation since the ecology movements began following World War II.

6. Anthony C. Beilenson, "Population Growth is the Great Enemy," *The Los Angeles Times,* 7/23/90. Beilenson is a Democratic legislator from Los Angeles, California.

7. Cousteau was addressing the Rio de Janeiro Earth Summit, held in 1992. He, and many others who study the environment, point to the inevitable decline in life quality suffered by present-day human populations that exceed the carrying capacity of their local environments (reported in *The Los Angeles Times,* 6/6/92). It should be noted, however, that living like a population of rats would be far preferable to the fate of the humans living in a population of 16 billion. Rat populations, unlike human populations, live in an ecological balance.

8. Excellent expositions of the problems at hand may be found in the special issue of *Scientific American* 261 (3), September, 1989.

Index